W9-CMP-778

Television Series
of the 1990s

Television Series of the 1990s

Essential Facts and Quirky Details

VINCENT TERRACE

ROWMAN & LITTLEFIELD
Lanham • Boulder • New York • London

Published by Rowman & Littlefield
An imprint of The Rowman & Littlefield Publishing Group, Inc.
4501 Forbes Boulevard, Suite 200, Lanham, Maryland 20706
www.rowman.com

Unit A, Whitacre Mews, 26-34 Stannary Street, London SE11 4AB

Copyright © 2018 by The Rowman & Littlefield Publishing Group, Inc.

All rights reserved. No part of this book may be reproduced in any form or by any electronic or mechanical means, including information storage and retrieval systems, without written permission from the publisher, except by a reviewer who may quote passages in a review.

British Library Cataloguing in Publication Information Available

Library of Congress Cataloging-in-Publication Data Available

ISBN 9781538103784 (ebook) | ISBN 9781538103777 (cloth : alk. paper)

♾™ The paper used in this publication meets the minimum requirements of American National Standard for Information Sciences—Permanence of Paper for Printed Library Materials, ANSI/NISO Z39.48-1992.

Printed in the United States of America

Contents

Introduction

This is the fifth in a series of books that relate the quirky (trivia) facts associated with select television series that premiered between January 1, 1990, and December 31, 1999. Series prior to this era can be found in *Television Series of the 1950s*, *Television Series of the 1960s*, *Television Series of the 1970s*, and *Television Series of the 1980s*.

This is *not* a book of essays or opinions, and information is based on viewing the episodes of the series listed; it is a presentation of facts only, such as that "We Specialize in Strange" was the slogan of Angel Investigations on *Angel*, Caitlin (*Spin City*) sued the *New York Times* for publishing a picture of her in mid-blink, and Drew Carey (*The Drew Carey Show*) had his first kiss with a girl who preferred to kiss girls.

It will also reveal that Jack Malloy (*Unhappily Ever After*) considers his three children "the mistake, the girl, and the accident" and that Vallery Irons (*V.I.P.*) has the Social Security number 904-38-2832.

If these few facts capture your attention, then you will be amazed by the many thousands of facts that are contained within these pages.

Programs that premiered in the 1980s but continued first-run production into the 1990s are not included here. Information on these programs can be found in the volume *Television Series of the 1980s*:

Baywatch
Coach
The Cosby Show
Dear John
Designing Women
Empty Nest
Family Matters
Full House
The Golden Girls
Growing Pains

Hunter
Magnum, P.I.
Married . . . With Children
Matlock
Mr. Belvedere
Murder, She Wrote
Murphy Brown
Night Court
Perfect Strangers
Roseanne
Saved by the Bell
The Simpsons
Star Trek: The Next Generation
21 Jump Street
Who's the Boss?
The Wonder Years

Ally McBeal
(Fox, 1997–2002)

Cast: Calista Flockhart (Ally McBeal), Peter MacNichol (John Cage), Lucy Liu (Ling Woo), Jane Krakowski (Elaine Vassal), Greg Germann (Richard Fish), Portia de Rossi (Nelle Porter).

Basis: Ally McBeal, a young woman working for a prestigious law firm, struggles to deal with the numerous incidents that complicate her life.

ALLISON MARIE "ALLY" McBEAL

Parents: George (James Naughton) and Jeannie McBeal (Jill Clayburgh).

Siblings: Ally mentions two sisters (one died at the age of five) and a brother.

Place of Birth: Boston on November 11, 1964. When she was 10 years old, she dreamed of becoming an artist "and painting the world with beautiful pictures."

Address: 1412 Dalton Lane.

Education: Harvard Law School. At this time, Ally, in need of money, donated an egg for research. Years later, she discovers that the egg was adopted and that a girl (Madison) was born. In high school, she was a cheerleader and voted "Most Likely to Become Julie Andrews."

Measurements: 30-24-30. She has brown hair and eyes and stands 5 feet, 2 inches tall.

Occupation: Attorney with the law firm of Cage & Fish (Cage, Fish & McBeal when she becomes a partner, but it is also called Fish, Cage & Associates).

Law Firm Address: 415 8th Street in Boston.

Good-Luck Charms: "My lucky white bra" and "a pair of old shoes."

About Women: "Some women gross me out, but others I find attractive and don't gross me out." After experiencing erotic lesbian dreams, she does kiss a woman (Ling Woo; as she said, "I kissed a woman—and can she kiss!").

Regina Hall and Calista Flockhart. *Fox/Photofest © Fox*

Wardrobe: Addicted to micro miniskirts ("Because I like to wear them"). When she becomes nervous or upset, she raises her skirt hemlines to a point where "if things don't change, I'm bound to get arrested for indecent exposure."

Character: Ally is beautiful but also thin and appears to be anorexic (but isn't). She wishes she could be heavier ("just to show cleavage") and has a strange allergy ("I'm allergic to criminals" and "I get the sniffles if I'm put in jail for contempt of court"). If Ally has to make a tough decision, she stares into a mirror until she decides what to do. She feels that when she is happy, she needs mental help ("I'm not used to it").

The Dancing Baby: Ally's worries over her ticking biological clock led her to seeing (a computer-animated) dancing baby to remind her that her time to have children is running out. She also claims that at the age of eight, she saw a unicorn.

Favorite Eatery: Jasper's Restaurant.

Favorite Ice Cream: Ben and Jerry's (no specific flavor mentioned).

Final Episode: Ally leaves the law firm to be with her daughter, Madison (now 18; played by Hayden Panettiere) in New York City.

JOHN CAGE

Occupation: Senior partner in Cage & Fish (later Cage, Fish & McBeal).

Pet Frog: Stefan (competes in frog-jumping contests); Nelle, his colleague, later gives him one he names Millie (after his pet hamster as a kid).

Favorite Musical Instrument: The bagpipes (which relax him).

Childhood Fantasy: The song "Something Stupid" (by Frank and Nancy Sinatra) made him imagine that Nancy was performing just for him.

Character: Shy and reclusive at times, well versed in the law, and known to use disruptive courtroom tactics to win a case. He is brilliant at cross-examinations and addressing juries, but to feel secure, he must be the star of cases he handles.

Nickname: As a child, he was called "The Biscuit" (a bit overweight and named after Pillsbury Doughboy commercials); "Funny Little Man" (as called by Ling).

Catchphrases: "This jury pleases me"; "Say it with me" (asking the jury to repeat a word he said); and "Repugnant" (when something upsets him).

Speech Problem: Stuttering. He devised a solution by saying, "Poughkeepsie," then a word related to New York.

Courtroom Distractions: His nose (produces a whistle sound) and his squeaking shoes (make opposing lawyers nervous during a trial).

Idol: Musician-singer Barry White.

The Unisex Bathroom: John has a remote control that not only flushes the bowl but also lowers and raises the seat. It also controls a secret door in John's stall that leads to a room where he finds comfort away from the pressures of work.

Closing Case Arguments: Walking around his office barefoot gives him the inspiration to create the perfect defense.

LING WOO

Occupation: Businesswoman, then lawyer with the firm of Cage & Fish (she originally did not practice law "because practice causes wrinkles"). She will sue anybody who crosses her and found it more profitable to make money through her businesses (like an escort service that supplies beautiful girls as dates for high school boys) than being a lawyer. Ling doesn't care if she is a defendant or a plaintiff, "but being a plaintiff gives me a martyr glow." She later chooses to practice law and is offered a judgeship by the governor of Massachusetts.

Measurements: 34-23-34. She stands 5 feet, 3 inches tall and wears a size 6 shoe.

Talent: Designing her own clothes in her spare time.

Education: Cornell University (editor of the *Law Review*).

Character: A very self-centered Asian American woman who is easily annoyed by other people (her reactions are heard as animal snarls or growls). She claims to have a gift of "magnetism" (the ability to bring people to court who would otherwise go unnoticed) and uses her beauty to control a partner (sometimes making him or her sign a health waiver or a contract to protect her sexual secrets). She dates men but is also drawn to women, especially Ally (but after sharing two kisses, they remain friends, not lovers). She is cold and calculating, uses sex as a weapon to get what she wants, and presents herself as unapproachable. ("It must be hard being human. I wouldn't know; I never tried it.")

ELAINE VASSAL

Place of Birth: Boston in November 1968.

Occupation: Ally's secretary at Cage & Fish.

Measurements: 34-31-38. She has blonde hair and blue eyes and stands 5 feet, 4½ inches tall.

Talent: Ability to sing (she auditioned for a part in the musical *A Chorus Line* but was rejected); performs songs at her favorite bar, Jasper's Restaurant.

Character: Presents herself as a sexual person "even though most people see me as a slut." She has a genius for inventing things that seem impractical (like "The Pregnant Dress" to make women look pregnant, "so they will get special attention even though they are not pregnant," and "The Face Bra to strengthen facial muscles").

Favorite Activity: Being a snoop (she eavesdrops through wiretapping "to find out all the secret stuff that goes on").

RICHARD FISH

Richard, the senior partner in Cage & Fish (which he established with John Cage), is more of a figurehead, as he is not actively involved in defending clients (although when he tackles a case, he is successful due only to sheer luck). Richard's attraction to women is based mostly on "The Neck Wattle" (loose skin on the neck) and is perhaps best known for his affair with Judge Jennifer "Whipper" Cone (Dyan Cannon), an older woman during first- and third-season episodes. In the final episode, however, he marries Deborah "Liza" Bump (Christina Ricci), a firm associate called "Lolita."

NELLE PORTER

Nelle is a lawyer with Cage & Fish whose sole ambition is to become a partner. She originally began a romantic relationship with John Cage, but circumstances did not mean for them to be together (like Nelle's fear of frogs and her reluctance to give up her career to start a family, which John wanted). Nelle is, however, a very ambitious and confident woman. She measures 33-24-35 and stands 5 feet, 7 inches tall. She has blonde hair and wears a size 2 dress and a size 8 shoe. Although beautiful, she rarely uses her assets to achieve something; she prefers to use her intelligence and genius as a litigator to win cases. Nelle is sarcastic and known for her witty responses to questions; she is not the friendliest person and had the nickname "Sub Zero." She can be caring but refuses to expose that trait, as she fears it will make her vulnerable.

Angel
(WB, 1999–2004)

Cast: David Boreanaz (Angel), Charisma Carpenter (Cordelia Chase), Amy Acker (Fred Burkle), James Marsters (Spike).

Basis: A spin-off from *Buffy the Vampire Slayer* that chronicles events in the life of Angel, a vampire with a soul who helps humans. The characters of Angel, Cordelia, and Spike first appeared on *Buffy* in 1997. (For additional information, see *Buffy the Vampire Slayer*.)

ANGEL

Place of Birth: Galway, Ireland, in 1727 (also given as 1746) as Liam (his parents earned a living as silk and linen merchants).

Change: A failed relationship with a woman (Sarah) when he was 18 set Liam on a path of self-destruction (drinking). In 1753 (later said to be 1757), a vampire named Darla (Julie Benz) seduced him and turned him into a creature of the undead.

Name: Liam's transformation presents him as a young man with an angelic face. He takes the name Angelus and begins a reign of terror with Darla. After each killing, Angel (as he is called) would carve a cross on a victim's cheek to let people know he was there.

Second Change: It is the year 1898 when Angel kills a young Romanian Gypsy girl. In vengeance, her people (Clan Kalderash) curse him by restoring his human soul and with it his conscience. Overcome with guilt for what he has done, Angel leaves Europe and flees to America, vowing to never feed on humans again. Angel, distinguished by a long black trench coat that he wears, retains his vampire traits, lives off pig's blood, and can be killed by a stake through the heart. He becomes close to Buffy Summers, a Slayer who originally set out to destroy him.

Business: To atone for his sins, Angel begins Angel Investigations, a firm that helps humans threatened by the supernatural. It is first housed in a small downtown office in Los Angeles, then at the Hyperion Hotel. Angel later joins Wolfram and Hart (located at 1127 Spring Street in Los Angeles), a law firm he originally battled (for unleashing and protecting demons). He can now use his position to fight evil before it gets out of control.

Angel Investigations Phone Number: 555-0162.

Angel's Car License Plate: NKO 714.

Charisma Carpenter, David Boreanaz, and Glenn Quinn. *The WB/Photofest*
© The WB

CORDELIA CHASE

Relationship: Assisted Buffy, then Angel, in the fight against the supernatural.

Place of Birth: Sunnydale, California, in 1980.

Education: Sunnydale High School (a cheerleader and a member of the fashion clique the Cordettes). She was a Queen Bee and looked down on people like Buffy until Buffy saved her from an invisible female demon who sought to disfigure her (at which time she befriended Buffy, Willow, Xander, and Giles and became a part of their demon-fighting team, "The Scooby Gang").

Nickname: "Cordy."

Car License Plate: Queen C.

Career: After graduating in 1999, Cordelia traveled to Los Angeles to pursue an acting career. With no money (as her family had lost their wealth and she could not afford to attend Columbia University) and no job, she became a secretary to Angel (whom she had known from the series *Buffy the Vampire Slayer*) at Angel Investigations (it was Cordelia who designed the company's business card with a drawing of an angel and the slogan "We Specialize in Strange").

Change: Cordelia becomes Angel's contact with the Other World when The Powers That Be select her to become their eyes (or, as Cordelia says, "Vision Girl"). When Cordelia receives a vision of the future, she says, "It gives me mind-bending, bone-cracking vision headaches." To make the visions bearable for Cordelia, the Powers That Be change her being to incorporate the essence of a demon; without the change, she would not survive. Her demon implant, however, fought to control her human destiny and caused Cordelia to fall into a deep coma. After several months, she awoke to tell Angel of a vision in which he was threatened by a man with strange tattoos. Cordelia helps Angel defeat the tattooed man (a demon) but could no longer remain with him. As Cordelia seemed to vanish, Angel receives a phone call from the hospital informing him that Cordelia had died and never awoke from the coma. It can be assumed that the Powers That Be allowed Cordelia one last vision to save Angel and mystically appear to him.

Address: Apartment 212 at 118 Silver Lake Road. Prior to this, she lived above Angel's loft, then in an apartment with a ghost named Dennis. (Cordelia was fine with this as long as Dennis didn't invade her privacy. It appears that to prevent Dennis from marrying a prostitute, his mother bricked him up behind a wall in the apartment.)

Powers: Levitation, astral projection, empathy (can feel the pain of others), ability to purify the souls of demons, and telekinesis.

WINIFRED "FRED" BURKLE

Relationship: A member of Angel Investigations.

Parents: Roger and Trish Burkle.

History: Fred, as she is called, was born on a small farm in the Midwest (later said to be in Dallas, Texas). She has a plush rabbit named Figenbaum, showed an interest in science, and later attended the University of California (majoring in physics). Here, while working at the Stewart Brunell Library, Fred found a book on demonology, opened it, and recited a cryptic text out loud. She was propelled through a time warp and into a land called Pylea (at the same time, Lorne [see below] was transported from Pylea to Los Angeles). Here, humans were treated as slaves, and to survive, Fred became a fugitive. She stole food and lived in a cave for five years until she was rescued by Angel when he was transported to Pylea to liberate its citizens from control of the Covenant of Trombli. Fred found excitement with Angel and joined him (first at Angel Investigations, then at Wolfram and Hart as head of its Practical Science Division).

Fred's Transformation into Illyria: Illyria, also known as "Illyria the Merciless," is a purebred, powerful demon that commanded the Army of Doom and ruled the Earth prior to the rise of mankind. Illyria was eventually killed by her rivals and her body placed in a stone sarcophagus to prevent her from ever rising to power again. The sarcophagus was placed in a mystical graveyard (the Deeper Well) but was found in 2004 and transported to the Wolfram and Hart science lab, where Fred, touching one of the crystals embedded in the sarcophagus, released Illyria's essence (seen as a gust of air), and it entered her mouth, causing extreme agony. Illyria was actually an infection that seized control of Fred's body and absorbed her memories. When Illyria realizes where she is and her army no longer exists, she joins with Angel in his fight against demons. Illyria is sophisticated and regal but ruthless and vicious. She possesses superhuman strength, speed, and reflexes and is skilled in hand-to-hand combat. She can manipulate time, is capable of interdimensional travel, and has the power to shape-shift. Later, the restoration of magic saves Fred's life by allowing her to retain Illyra's essence and control her actions.

Fred's Abilities: Moderate fighting skills, expertise with a crossbow, and using her scientific knowledge to devise weapons for Angel.

SPIKE

Character: A vampire who fluctuates between good (helping Buffy and Angel) and evil (preying on the living).

History: William Pratt, better known as Spike, was born in London, England (sometime between 1850 and 1853). Anne is his mother, but his father is not named. He attempted a career as a poet, but his work was said to be "bloody awful" and he was nicknamed "William the Bloody." It is the 1890s when William meets Drusilla (Janet Landau), a woman turned into a vampire by Angel and driven insane when she witnessed his killing her family for fun. William had become Drusilla's choice for a mate, and her turning him into a vampire led him to become known as "Spike" (for impaling his victims on railroad track spikes). When Drusilla suffers a serious wound from an angry mob in Prague in 1997, she and Spike flee to America, where Spike believes Sunnydale's Hellmouth (a portal for demons) can cure her (his introduction on *Buffy the Vampire Slayer*). The Hellmouth does heal Drusilla's wound, but she remains insane and leaves Spike for other demons. Spike's life also changes: he is captured by the Initiative, a government organization that hunts vampires and demons. He is tagged "Hostile 17," and a computer chip that causes extreme pain is implanted in his brain to prevent him from harming humans. It is at this time that Spike becomes "good" to help Buffy battle demons "out of the evilness of my heart." He lives in a crypt in the Sunnydale Cemetery.

Trademark: A black coat he took from the body of Nikki Wood, a female slayer he killed in 1977 aboard a New York City subway train. The scar over Spike's left eye is a result of an encounter with a Slayer named Xin Rong, who, during the Boxer Rebellion in China (1900), slashed his head with her sword before he killed her.

Catchphrase: "Bloody Hell."

Favorite TV Show: The NBC soap opera *Passions*.

Favorite Music: Punk rock.

Final Buffy Episode (May 20, 2003): Buffy and Angel survive a battle in which vampires are seeking to take over the world, but Spike appears to have been killed. When *Angel* began its new season in the fall of 2003, Spike was reincarnated, first as a spirit, then as an actual being when a magic amulet releases him from the spirit world. He is now seen as a savior and an ally to Angel.

OTHER CHARACTERS

Wesley Wyndam Pryce (Alexis Denisof) is a rogue demon hunter and prior Watcher (cares for and guides Slayers) who joined with Angel after they crossed paths several times. He was originally a third-grade schoolteacher and volunteers at the Food Bank. He incorporates an array of demon-fighting weapons and is an expert on guns and crossbows but relies mostly on ancient prophecies to battle the unknown (he can also translate ancient languages). He is most often called "Wes," but Cordelia sometimes calls him "Mr. Grouchy Pants" for his somewhat smug attitude.

Charles Gunn (J. August Richards), called "G," heads an independent team of demon fighters that came into being when Gunn became aware of vampires in Los Angeles. He was born in Los Angeles and cared for his sister, Alonna, when his parents were killed in a car accident. He eventually joins with Angel to battle a common evil (first with Angel Investigations, then with Wolfram and Hart). He is knowledgeable in legal codes and has a keen interest in comic books.

The Host (Andy Hallett), a green, peace-loving demon with horns, is the owner of the Karaoke Spot (also called Caritas), a nightclub for demons. He is also known as Lorne and is actually Krevlornswath of the Deathwok Clan (from a dimension called Pylea). He accidentally found a dimensional portal (as did Fred) and was transported to Los Angeles when Fred was transported to Pylea. He found Los Angeles a better place and chose to stay when he became fascinated by music. He assists Angel as a snitch, and, with an ability to sing, Angel made him the head of the entertainment division of Wolfram and Hart when Angel was appointed its chief executive officer. Lorne's singing could shatter glass, harm human hearing, and destroy demons (for reasons that are unknown, Lorne can tolerate music while others of his species cannot and suffer pain when hearing it).

Allen Francis Doyle (Glenn Quinn) was sent by the Powers That Be to assist Angel (Doyle's father was a Brachen demon; his mother was a human). He was born in Ireland and was married to Harriet, but their relationship ended when she discovered what he had become. Doyle is a messenger who receives telepathic images of people in need and relates the information to Angel. In a fierce battle against demons, Doyle is mortally wounded. Before he dies, he kisses Cordelia and passes his "gift" to her, making her Angel's contact with the other world.

Connor (Vincent Kartheiser), the son of Angel and Darla, was born in Los Angeles in November 2001. He was considered a miracle child, as he was born of two vampires (Darla, unable to physically give birth, sacrifices herself by driving a stake through her heart to save her baby). The infant quickly advanced to an adult and became part of Angel's team (although he first hated and tried to kill his father; they eventually reconciled). When Angel brought the infant Connor to the hospital after his birth, he used the name "Geraldo Connor," and the baby was registered as "Connor Angel." Connor's powers include superhuman strength and agility, durability (since Connor did not inherit vampire traits from his parents, he can withstand damage to his body), and heightened senses.

Becker
(CBS, 1998–2004)

Cast: Ted Danson (John Becker), Terry Farrell (Reggie Kostas), Hattie Winston (Margaret Wyborn), Shawnee Smith (Linda), Nancy Travis (Chris Conner), Alex Desert (Jake Malinak).

Basis: Life with John Becker, a loud, gruff, and complaining neighborhood doctor (family practitioner) treating patients in the Bronx, New York.

JOHN BECKER

Father: Fred Becker (Dick Van Dyke).

Age: 50 when the series begins.

Address: Apartment 3B on Katon Avenue.

Rent: $450 a month (low because there was a murder in the residence "and nothing a chalk eraser, some bleach, and a few open windows couldn't cure," claims John).

Marital Status: Married and divorced twice (as he says, "My next wife gets half of nothing"). He mentions only his first wife, Sandra, and refers to her as "the castrating bitch from Hell." He has no children "because kids annoy me."

Education: Harding High School and Harvard Medical School (Class of 1972; he still wears his college jacket because "if you keep it long enough, everything comes back in style"). He turned down a position as a researcher at Johns Hopkins Medical Center in Boston, as he felt his services were better utilized in his old neighborhood. It was at this time that his wife left him "for the man who details her car."

Internship: Boston General Hospital.

Office Telephone Number: 555-0199.

Favorite Eatery: The Diner (owned first by Reggie, then Christine). He orders a muffin and a cup of coffee each morning. The King Food Chinese Restaurant is across the street (but John frequents Ming's Chinese Restaurant).

Favorite Newspaper: Said to be the *New York Post* (seen as the *New York News*).

Car: "A beat-up green Oldsmobile." It has Saran Wrap for a broken back window.

Fear: Spiders.

Banned: John can no longer shop at Thrifty Mart for pushing a handicapped person who tried to get ahead of him in a cash register line.

Bad Habits: Smoking, drinking, and eating mostly fatty foods. If he tries to quit smoking, he becomes edgy and irritable. He also needs to sleep with a TV set turned on.

Hates: Holidays, sentimentality, and people who squander money.

Expertise: Juggling with bowling pins.

Trait: Has an opinion about everything, hates to be wrong, and is cheap when it comes to spending money.

New York Medical Review *Article:* "A-Typical Micro Bacterial Phenomena."

Relatives: Cousin, Barry Becker (Richard Schiff); Barry's wife, Melissa (Melinda Gilb).

Flashbacks: John, at age 10 (Charles Roman).

OTHER CHARACTERS

Margaret Wyborn is John's nurse. She is a Baptist, quotes from the Bible, and had thoughts of becoming a singer. She is a graduate of New York University (NYU) Nursing School and did her internship at Mount Sinai. She is married to the never-seen Lewis (who despises Becker and vice versa) and worked previously as a private-duty nurse for five years before becoming Becker's nurse in 1991 (she acquired her job by not leaving John's office until he hired her). When money became tight (Lewis out of work), she took a second job as a health care provider (to an eccentric rich woman's dog, Wally).

Linda, the office assistant, is a pretty but slightly dense young woman who got the job because John owed her father a big favor. She is not given a last name and sells Lady Fair Cosmetics "to pay off my huge bills." John doesn't know what Linda does around the office, "but she looks good in a skirt" (on her résumé, Linda put "standing around and looking pretty" as her qualifications). She measures 36-27-36 and stands 5 feet, 3 inches tall and wears a size 8 dress and a size 10 shoe. Margaret describes her job as "reading magazines, talking on the phone, and screwing stuff up"; she calls her "a Hooter's graduate. Hooter's University is not turning out the graduates it used to." Linda does mention attending "manicure school" and lives in a luxury penthouse (given to her by her wealthy parents). While not a nurse, she does attend to kids when they need shots. She can speak Portuguese and Mandarin, refers to John as "Doctor," and fears being left alone in the office. Her hair changes from brunette to blonde as the series progresses.

Regina Kostas, called "Reggie," and Christine "Chris" Conner are Becker's love interests. Reggie is a college dropout who, after failing in an attempt to become a model, returned to her home in the Bronx to help her father when he became ill and could no longer run his diner. She appears to enjoy running the diner despite complaints about her cooking and the regrets she has over her decision to quit college (she later returns to NYU to take psychology courses). Reggie stands 6 feet tall, wears a size 8 dress and a size 10 shoe, and measures 37-25-37. After four years, her on-and-off relationship with Becker ended when Reggie moved to Europe to redirect her life. In high school, she was a member of the photography club and was voted "Most Likely to Succeed" by the Class of 1983 (who also voted her Homecoming Queen).

Chris is introduced at the end of season four as Becker's neighbor (Apartment 4B on Katon Avenue) and the new diner owner (which, in some prior episodes, was referred to as Reggie's Diner; it is now called simply the Diner). Although Chris is Becker's complete opposite (cheerful and always nice), it appeared that a marriage would have taken place, but the series ended before anything was finalized. Chris is 5 feet, 4 inches tall and measures 36-27-38 and wears a size 8 dress and a size 8½ shoe. She hates frizzy hair (uses Sculpted and Shine shampoo) and often uses flattery to get out of things (like parking tickets). She eats pizza with a knife and fork, and when the diner cash register is seen, the cash amount displayed is "$0.0"; there are two dents on the right side (facing screen) of the soda machine; a Bonn coffeemaker can be seen in the background. Jon Cryer plays Chris's ex-husband, Roger; Jaime Pressly is her sister, Gracie.

Jake Malinak, John's friend, runs the newspaper and magazine stand inside the diner (he also sells New York Lottery tickets, and the Lotto jackpot is always set at $500,000). M&M's candy can be seen, as can the magazines *Cosmopolitan*, *Home*, and *Redbook*, at Jake's stand. Jake lost his eyesight in a car accident and marries Amanda (Lindsay Price) 20 hours after they meet (it is annulled when Amanda cheats on Jake with a delivery man named Stan). Jake lives at 180 Montgomery Street, was a National Scrabble Champion, and left to pursue a college education in Chicago (where he takes up residence with a relative who is a schoolteacher).

Beverly Hills, 90210
(Fox, 1990–2000)

Cast: Shannen Doherty (Brenda Walsh), Jason Priestley (Brandon Walsh), Jennie Garth (Kelly Taylor), Tori Spelling (Donna Martin), Gabriella

Carteris (Andrea Zuckerman), Luke Perry (Dylan McKay), Ian Ziering (Steve Sanders).

Basis: Events in the lives of a group of teenagers living in Beverly Hills, California.

BRENDA WALSH

Place of Birth: Minneapolis, Minnesota, in 1974.

Parents: Jim (James Eckhouse) and Cindy Walsh (Carol Potter). Jim, an accountant for the firm of Powell, Gaines and Yellin, received a transfer to California in 1990, prompting their move to the West Coast. Jim and Cindy later move to Hong Kong when Jim is again promoted.

Fraternal Twin Brother: Brandon Walsh (Brenda is four minutes older).

Minneapolis Address: 1408 Walnut Avenue.

California Address: 933 Hillcrest Drive, Beverly Hills, California 90210.

Education: West Beverly Hills High School (at her prior, unnamed high school, she was a member of the drama club and the student council).

Dream: To become an actress.

Character: Brenda is beautiful but feels "I'm not California beautiful." She desperately wants to change her image and become popular. As for clothes, Brenda is not rich, and "I make for free what the trendy stores sell for $150."

Fear: Heights.

Trait: Totally honest; somewhat rebellious at times.

Childhood: When she was thrown from a horse named Sylvester and too frightened to ride again, her father bought her a plush horse she named "Mr. Pony." She had a plush lion ("Mr. Lion") and four dogs: Ruby (who was uncontrollable), Mr. Pepper (froze to death one winter; Brenda was nine years old and says, "How was I supposed to know about wind chill factors?"), Bruno (bit the mailman), and Wally (a stray she adopted). She played Juliet in her seventh-grade production of *Romeo and Juliet*.

Favorite TV Show: The mythical *Keep It Together*.

Hobby: Collecting porcelain dolls.

Toothpaste Brand: Colgate.

Job: Waitress (under the name "Laverne") at the hangout, the Peach Pit. She later attends a summer program at London's Royal Academy of Dramatic Arts, stars in a production of *Cat on a Hot Tin Roof*, and tours as an actress.

Nickname: Called "Beautiful" by her father.

BRANDON ANDREW WALSH

Place of Birth: Minneapolis, Minnesota, in 1974.

Parents: Jim and Cindy Walsh.

Fraternal Twin Sister: Brenda (he is four minutes younger).

Minneapolis Address: 1408 Walnut Avenue.

California Address: 933 Hillcrest Drive, Beverly Hills, California 90210.

Education: West Beverly Hills High School (sports editor of the school newspaper, the *Blaze*). At his prior high school, he was a member of the swim team; wrote for the school newspaper and was called "Mr. Popularity"); California University (coeditor of the newspaper, the *Condor*; news director for its TV station, CU-TV).

Alarm Clock: Shaped like Godzilla.

Car: A 1965 yellow Mustang he calls "Mondale."

License Plate: 2BR1 645.

Dream: To become a journalist.

Nickname: Called "Big Guy" by his father.

Jobs: Waiter at the Peach Pit (the after-school hangout); cabana boy at the Beverly Hills Beach Club; journalist for a small newspaper (the *Beverly Beat*); a reporter, based in Washington, D.C., for the New York *Chronicle*.

Addiction: Gambling (places sports bets that he can't cover).

As a Kid: Enjoyed hiking near Gull Lake in Minnesota.

KELLY MARLENE TAYLOR

Relationship: Friends with Brenda and Brandon.

Parents: Jackie (Anne Gillespie) is drug addicted; her absentee father, Bill (John Reilly), had been arrested for embezzlement.

Siblings: Erin (half sister), David (stepbrother).

Place of Birth: Beverly Hills in 1974.

Education: West Beverly Hills High School (voted "Spring Queen" at the 1991 Junior Prom Spring Dance).

Character: Beautiful, fashion conscious, worships the sun, but is rich and spoiled (called "The Rich Bitch" by boys who have dated her).

Pet Dog: Max.

Exercise Classes: Bob Silvers World.

Trait: A reputation as a slut, making it difficult for her to find a decent relationship. She is saddled with caring for her mother, whose questionable practices she sometimes finds herself copying.

Traumas: Lost her virginity to Steve Sanders; almost burned alive in a rave fire; became addicted to cocaine; raped (killed her attacker and was acquitted); suffered a miscarriage; wounded in a drive-by shooting at Los Angeles International Airport.

Career: After graduation, Kelly joins with Donna to open a fashion boutique called Now Wear This; Kelly later leaves to pursue her dream of a job in public relations (although she finally settles down as a guidance counselor at West Beverly Hills High School).

DONNA MARIE MARTIN

Mother: Felice Martin (Katherine Cannon).

Relationship: Friend to Brenda.

Place of Birth: Beverly Hills on December 25, 1974.

Education: West Beverly Hills High School (she has a learning disability that makes taking written exams very difficult).

Character: Lacks confidence and rarely makes a good first impression. Although pretty, she fantasizes about what it would be like to be beautiful and popular. She mentions being allergic to chocolate.

Favorite Movie: Pretty Woman (she fantasizes about "running away, becoming a hooker, and meeting Richard Gere on Hollywood Boulevard").

Hangouts: The Peach Pit; After Dark (a nightclub).

Account: The National Bank of the West.

Ability: To draw and illustrate. This leads to Donna taking designing classes and opening a boutique (Now Wear This) with Kelly (who eventually leaves to begin a career in public relations); Donna later strikes out on her own as a fashion designer.

ANDREA ZUCKERMAN

Andrea, born in California in 1974, is a friend of Brenda and Brandon (on whom she had a crush, but they retained only a platonic relationship). She is attending West Beverly Hills High School illegally (she lives outside the school's district and lies about where she lives to take advantage of its programs). She was editor of the school newspaper, the *Blaze*, and valedictorian of her graduating class, and she rejected an acceptance to Yale University to attend California University to remain close to her family and friends. She volunteered (with Brenda) at the Rap Line (a hotline for troubled teens), and life changed for her when she met a man (Jessie), became pregnant, and gave birth prematurely to a daughter she and Jessie name Hannah. They later move to Connecticut, where Andrea enrolls in Yale University.

DYLAN McKAY

Dylan is the son of Jack (Josh Taylor) and Iris McKay (Stephanie Beacham). He was originally depicted as a loner until he befriended Brenda and Brandon and became a part of their world. He first attends West Beverly Hills High School, then California University. He has a half sister named Erica (Noely Thornton), and his father, Jack, was apparently associated with the Mafia and killed (in a car bombing) by a Mafia hit man.

Dylan was also involved with drugs and alcohol, and although he dated Brenda, he married Toni Marchette (Rebecca Gayheart), the daughter of Anthony Marchette (Stanley Kamel), the man who killed his father (in an ironic twist of fate, Toni is mistakenly killed by Anthony when he becomes aware of who Dylan is and plots to kill him). It is later revealed that Dylan's father is alive and under FBI protective custody.

STEVEN "STEVE" SANDERS

Steve is the adoptive son of Samantha (Christine Belford) and Rush (Jed Allan). His upbringing was quite diverse, as Rush was often abusive but also is said to be a caring father. Samantha, an actress (and star of the TV series *Hartley House*), had doubts about her sexuality and later reveals that she is a lesbian. Steve was born in 1974 and attended West Beverly Hills High School, where, being the son of rich parents, he was somewhat brash and prided himself on driving a Corvette. He was popular, partied, and seemed a bit out of control until his friendship with Brandon Walsh began to mature him. Rush felt that Steve had no direction in life, and through his help, Steve purchased his own newspaper, the *Beverly Beat*, running it first with Brandon, then with Janet Sosna (Lindsay Price), a woman whom he eventually married and with whom he had a child. Steve was also a key figure in establishing the college hangout, the After Dark club.

Blossom
(NBC, 1991–1995)

Cast: Mayim Bialik (Blossom Russo), Ted Wass (Nick Russo), Joey Lawrence (Joey Russo), Michael Stoyanov (Anthony Russo), Jenna Von Oy (Six LeMeure).

Basis: Events in the life of Blossom Russo, an effervescent 13-year-old girl, as she experiences life growing up in Southern California.

BLOSSOM RUSSO

Father: Nick Russo. He and Blossom's mother, Madelyn (Melissa Manchester), divorced after 20 years of marriage; Nick later marries (1994) Carol (Finola Hughes), a widow with a young daughter, Kennedy (Doren Finn).

Brothers: Anthony and Joey Russo.

Place of Birth: Southern California in 1978.

Address: 465 Hampton Drive in Southern California.

Education: The Crestridge School for Girls, Tyler High School, and the University of California, Los Angeles (which she chose over Harvard, the University of California, Berkeley, and Northwestern).

Character: Described as "the perfect combination of a little sugar and a little spice." Blossom "became a woman in the first episode"; as Six, her friend, said, "Blossom blossomed."

Musical Ability: Plays the trumpet ("A little bit classical; a little bit jazz"; she hopes to become a musician like her father).

Favorite Soda: Bailey's Diet Cola.

Favorite Food: Pizza topped with green peppers and artichoke hearts. When she gets upset, only eating ice cream with pound cake will cure her.

Favorite Plush Toy: Her ALF (TV series) doll; a teddy bear (Dwight).

Award: National Spelling Bee champion (won in the seventh grade).

Imperfection: Blossom has a scar on her chin as a result of playing on (and falling off) the monkey bars (wherein she split open her chin).

Joey's Thoughts about Blossom: At age 13, he called her "A Borderline Babe" ("You're in the Honors Society, you play the trumpet but you haven't been visited by the Hooter Fairy yet").

Pet Cat: Scruffy (which she had as a child).

Relatives: Blossom's grandfather, Buzz Richman (Barnard Hughes).

Flashbacks: Young Blossom (Autumn Winters); Madelyn in 1986 (Margaret Reed, then Paige Pengras).

JOSEPH "JOEY" RUSSO

Relationship: Blossom's older brother (the second-born child).

Age: 16 when the series begins.

Character: Not too bright, lazy, girl crazy, and obsessed with breasts (which, in front of Blossom, he calls "Hooters," "Boobs," and "Gozangas").

Talent: According to Blossom, "Drinking Pepsi through his nose."

Education: Tyler High School (although in one episode he calls it Grant High).

Blossom's View of Joey: A dork ("If the dorks had a navy, he'd be their admiral").

Occupation: Student. He is also a delivery boy for Mario's Pizza.

Dream: To become a professional baseball player. He is a member of the Tyler High baseball team, the Bulldogs. This led him to being accepted to Arizona State College, but his decision to remain at home or attend college was left unanswered when the series ended. He did receive a chance to play second base with the Philadelphia Phillies.

Catchphrase: "Whoa."

Flashbacks: Young Joey (Andrew Lawrence).

ANTHONY "TONY" RUSSO

Relationship: The eldest child.

Character: Sober but was a drug addict for four years. It is suggested that he became addicted to pot (at age 12) while attending a summer camp called Camp Mountain High.

Education: Tyler High School.

Occupation: Delivery boy for Fatty's Pizza; counter waiter at Dante's Donut Shop; an EMT (emergency medical technician) ambulance driver (actress Justine Bateman [*Family Ties*] was the first celebrity he helped when she fell and injured her elbow).

Moneymaking Venture: Writing a play called *Naked Chick Academy*.

Marriage: During a trip to Las Vegas, Anthony met Shelly Lewis (Samaria Graham). They had drinks that night, got drunk, and later married; they had a child (in 1994) they named Nash Metropolitan.

Flashbacks: Young Anthony (Aaron Gelt).

SIX DOROTHY LEMEURE

Relationship: Blossom's best friend (also 13 years old). Six received her name from her father (who had six beers on the night Six was conceived).

Mother: Sharon LeMeure (Gail Edwards).

Education: Tyler High School (Six says, "That if detention were frequent flyer miles, I'd have enough miles for a free trip to Hawaii").

First Thing Learned about Six: "I wonder what my husband will look like naked or if I'll laugh the first time I see him. I wonder what it will be like to have a mortgage, a baby, and breasts."

Biggest Worry: "That my father will go into my bedroom and read the lyrics on my album covers if I stay away from home too long."

Character: Very pretty but also a bit unruly, as she has a smart mouth that often gets her in trouble. Because "Blossom is a real decent person with moral values," her parents like her having Blossom as a friend; Six, however, worries that Blossom's niceness is going to rub off on her.

Favorite Activity: Shopping at the mall with Blossom and dancing ("To get all sweaty and dizzy and see stars").

Volunteer Work: The Beacon Light Mission.

Final Episode: Six is accepted into San Diego State College, Northwestern, and West Orlando State but had not made a decision on which one to attend.

Flashbacks: Young Six (Marisa Rosen).

NICHOLAS "NICK" RUSSO

Relationship: Father to Anthony, Joey, and Blossom.

Occupation: Musician. Performs at clubs and was a backup for stars like Chuck Berry, Anita Baker, and B. B. King. He also played music for such movies as *Ghost*, *Fame*, and *Dirty Dancing*.

Education: The Juilliard School of Music.

Band: In his younger years, he was a member of Neon Wilderness.

Car: Mentioned only as a yellow car painted "Sunrise Surprise."

Divorce Attorney: The law firm of O'Hara, Schmitt and Bailey. Nick and Madelyn divorced when Madelyn wanted to pursue a singing career in Europe.

Buffy the Vampire Slayer
(WB, 1997–2001; UPN, 2001–2003)

Cast: Sarah Michelle Gellar (Buffy Summers), Alyson Hannigan (Willow Rosenberg), Anthony Stewart Head (Rupert Giles), Nicholas Brendon (Xander Harris), Michelle Trachtenberg (Dawn Summers), Charisma Carpenter (Cordelia Chase), Amber Benson (Tara Maclay), Jason Marsden (Spike), Eliza Dushku (Faith Lehane).

Basis: A teenage girl (Buffy) endowed with special abilities and called "The Slayer" battles the supernatural evils that threaten the people of her generation. Based on the 1992 feature film wherein Kristy Swanson played Buffy. (See also the spin-off series *Angel.*)

BUFFY ANNE SUMMERS

Parents: Joyce (Kristine Sutherland) and Hank Summers (Dean Butler). Joyce, the owner of an art gallery, has two sisters, Arlene and Lolly, and met Hank Summers at her freshman-year college prom. Their marriage ended when Hank cheated on Joyce, having an affair with his secretary.

Sister: Dawn Summers.

Birthday: May 6, 1979 (later said to be October 24, 1980), in Los Angeles.

Address: 1630 Revello Drive in Sunnydale, California.

History: Buffy was born of a legend that is countless centuries old. It was a time when evil ruled the world and Shadow Men, mysterious and powerful forces for good, gathered to endow one girl with the necessary power to battle the evil that surrounded them. From that moment on and for each generation that passed, one girl has been chosen to become the Slayer. Buffy is the 1990s Slayer. Rupert Giles, the Sunnydale school librarian, becomes her Watcher, a man with special abilities to help her defeat the evil that a Hellmouth dispenses (a Hellmouth is a mysterious portal that attracts evil, and Sunnydale High School is the center of one such portal). As Giles trains Buffy to fulfill her destiny, three schoolmates, Willow, Xander, and Cordelia, join with Buffy in an effort to destroy evil.

Childhood: Buffy imagined herself as a super crime fighter she called Power Woman. She was fascinated with ice-skater Dorothy Hamill and dreamed of becoming an Olympic ice-skater. She had a plush pig (Mr. Gordo) and a security blanket (Mr. Pointy).

Alyson Hannigan, Nicholas Brendon, Sarah Michelle Gellar, and Charisma Carpenter. *The WB/Photofest © The WB*

Teenage Years: At the age of 15, Buffy (still in Los Angeles) began experiencing unsettling dreams about women of past historical periods battling demons. She learns her dreams were of Slayers and that she too is a Slayer. Her first battle against a vampire cult at Hemery High School resulted in her destroying the school gym; it was then that she and her mother (now divorced) moved to Sunnydale.

Favorite Breakfast Cereal: Sunshine Crisp Flakes.

First Demon Encounter: The Master (Mark Metcalf), an ancient vampire seeking rebirth to rule the world. He is trapped in a Sunnydale underground cavern and attempting to complete a ritual known as the Harvest to regain his position as the leader of a vampire cult called the Order of Aurelis. It is at this time that Willow and Xander (and later Cordelia) join Buffy and Giles (forming what they call "the Scooby Gang") to defeat the Master.

Weakness: Her inability to leave anyone behind even if it means risking her own life. When a new group of vampires appears, Buffy calls it "a fang club."

Regret: Buffy feels that she is no longer a normal teenage girl and that her strange behavior alienates her from the "in crowd" at school.

Character: Before her life as a Slayer, Buffy was a superficial blonde Valley Girl type who looked down on people of a lower social class standing. She became rebellious and did not conform to the standard conventions of a Slayer (always overconfident and breaking Slayer tradition). Buffy was, in essence, a reluctant hero, doing what she did only because she had to. She has little patience when dealing with demons and enjoys taunting them (even making jokes in the midst of a battle).

Education: Hemery High School (in Los Angeles; she was a cheerleader, Prom Princess, and Fiesta Queen); Sunnydale High School (where she has a 2.8 grade-point average). After graduating and before becoming a freshman at the University of Sunnydale (where she resides in room 214 of Stevenson Hall), Buffy worked as a waitress at a diner called Helen's Kitchen.

Romantic Encounters: Angel, the vampire who helped her defeat evil (for information, see *Angel*). Riley Finn (Marc Blucas), a member of the Initiative, a secret government organization that hunts demons. She lost Riley when he was recalled by the military. Spike (see below), the vampire first seeking to kill Buffy rather than love her.

Buffy's Fate: When Joyce dies from an aneurysm following surgery to remove a brain tumor, Buffy is forced to leave college to support herself and Dawn. She held a number of odd jobs, including slinging hash at the Double Meat Palace before she found a permanent position as the guidance counselor at Sunnydale High School (helping students overcome problems while still battling demons: "I'm the thing monsters have nightmares about"). In the January 27, 2004, episode of *Angel,* it is learned that Buffy had quit her job at Sunnydale High to live in Europe and become part of a team that trains new Slayers.

Relatives: Buffy's cousin, Celia (not seen), who was killed by a demon who preyed on sick children (Celia being in the hospital at the time).

DAWN SUMMERS

Relationship: Buffy's 14-year-old unnatural sister (she did not exist in human form until the year 2000). Dawn is, in reality, the Key, an unknown power source that operates beyond our normal reality. The Key is countless centuries old, and its origins are unknown. The monks of the Byzantine Order discovered the Key and sought to control its powers. It is a concentration of living energy that can be used to shatter the veil that separates dimensions. The monks sought to use this power for good until they were attacked by the hell goddess Glorificus, who is seeking the Key to return to her dimension. In the year 2000, the monks invoked a powerful spell that, with Buffy's essence, transformed the Key into a human girl (Dawn) and a sister for Buffy to protect. To make it always appear that Dawn was a part of the human world, the monks altered reality (including Buffy's and Joyce's memories) to accept the fact that Dawn was always a part of the Summers family.

Nicknames: "Dawnie" (by Buffy); "My Little Pumpkin Belly" (by Joyce); "Dawn Patrol" (by Xander); and "Bitty Buffy," "Little Bit," and "Niblet" (by Spike).

Abilities: To open the portals to other dimensions and destroy dimensional barriers. She also has minor witchcraft abilities and is learning to hunt vampires through Buffy (she later becomes a member of the Scooby Gang [also called "The Scoobies," based on the TV series *Scooby-Doo, Where Are You?*]).

Education: Sunnydale High School (beginning in 2002).

Favorite Breakfast Cereal: Sugar Bombs.

Favorite Sandwich: Peanut butter and salami on white bread.

Food Creation: Peanut butter and banana waffles.

Character: Strong willed, caring, and confident (much like Buffy). Dawn, however, felt overshadowed by Buffy and often wonders "who or what I am." She believes Buffy thinks of her as "a dumb little sister" and "Little Miss Nobody." Buffy's reassurance that she does care for Dawn bonds their sisterhood: "It doesn't matter where you came from . . . you're my sister, and I love you."

The Change: Dawn learns she is the key when Glorificus, called Glory (Clare Kramer), finds her and tells her. Glory, a beast banished from hell, is seeking the Key to return to her dimension. To achieve the power of the Key, Glory must bleed it. Once Dawn's blood is spilled, the portal to her world will open, and all dimensions will collide and unleash havoc on earth. The monks made Dawn out of Buffy. With that knowledge, a finale was filmed for the WB that changed for UPN. In an attempt to save Dawn, who has been captured and about to be bled by Glory, Buffy engages Glory in a fierce battle. With the help of Willow's supernatural powers, Buffy defeats Glory—but not before Dawn is slashed across the stomach. As blood drips from her body, an energy portal is opened, and evil is unleashed on the earth. Dawn is about to sacrifice her life to save the world when Buffy stops her—"I'm part of you. My blood is your blood." Buffy leaps into the portal and reverses the ritual. Buffy is next seen lying on the ground, apparently dead.

At this point, the WB had been expected to renew the series. Two final scenes are shown: a gravestone with Buffy's name on it and Willow in Los Angeles to tell Angel that Buffy has been killed. When Angel sees Willow with tears in her eyes, the scene fades to black. That was on May 22, 2001. When the episode was repeated (July 26, 2001), the scene with Willow and Angel had been deleted, as UPN had acquired the series and a cross-over of *Buffy* and *Angel* was not possible. Dawn is no longer the Key. Buffy's sacrifice has given her human life. Buffy, however, died not of natural causes but by mystical energy. In a midnight ceremony, Willow performs a ritual before Buffy's grave and restores her to life to continue her fight against the supernatural.

WILLOW DANIELLE ROSENBERG

Relationship: Buffy's best friend and a member of the Scooby Gang. It was by Buffy's rescuing her from vampires that she (and Xander who helped) learned that Buffy is a Slayer.

Parents: Sheila and Ira Rosenberg.

Place of Birth: Sunnydale, California, in 1980.

Ancestry: Witch (she later develops an interest in magic). Performing a transformation spell causes her headaches and nosebleeds.

Fears: Spiders and frogs.

Character: Pretty, shy, a bit naive, and considered a wallflower. She delights in helping Buffy's Watcher, Giles, conduct research on the supernatural. Although she accepts the term "witch," Willow calls herself "a powerful she-witch."

Education: Sunnydale High School (straight "A" student and a member of the computer, science, and math clubs); University of Sunnydale (shares room 214 in Stevenson Hall with Buffy). Willow was accepted into Oxford, Yale, and Harvard but chose to remain in Sunnydale to continue her battle against demons.

Principal Romances: Willow was first in love with Xander (her childhood friend) but realized they could never be more than just friends. Three years later, when Willow begins classes at the University of Sunnydale, she reveals that she is a lesbian and bonds with Tara, a lesbian who is also a witch (Willow moves into room 217 with Tara after Buffy leaves; she and Tara now combine their powers to help Buffy defeat evil).

ALEXANDER "XANDER" HARRIS
Relationship: Buffy's friend and a member of the Scooby Gang.
Parents: Anthony and Jessica Harris (Anthony was addicted to alcohol; Jessica was a negligent mother).
Place of Birth: Sunnydale, California, in 1981.
Character: Charming and outgoing; does not possess any special powers.
Education: Sunnydale High School. Before Willow and Xander became friends with Cordelia in high school, they formed the We Hate Cordelia Chase Hate Club in grammar school because they felt Cordelia believed she was superior to them.
Occupation: First worked as a kitchen helper at the Fabulous Ladies nightclub, then as a carpenter when he chose not to attend college. Prior to this, he worked as a phone sex operator, a deliveryman, and a bartender at the University of Sunnydale campus bar (serving a brand of beer called Black Frost that, unknown to him, was cursed [turned drinkers into cavemen]). He then worked at a construction site building the town's new cultural center.
Fear: Clowns. (When he was six, his mother hired a clown for his birthday party. The clown chased and scared him, and as a result he suffered nightmares about clowns.)
Principal Romance: Anya (Emma Caulfield), 1,100-year-old former demon trying to adjust to a mortal life. Anya's real name is Audi. When she matured, she developed the powers of a vengeance demon to protect wronged women and punish evil men. She became known as Anyanka (although called Anya). She can teleport herself from one place to another and was stripped of her powers when she began using them for evil. She now helps Buffy battle demons and works with Giles as his assistant at the Magic Box.

RUPERT EDMUND GILES
Position: Watcher. He was first seen as the librarian at Sunnydale High School (where he met Buffy) and is the occult expert of the Scooby Gang.
Nicknames: "G-Man" (by Xander); "Rupy" (by Anya).
Character: A bit rebellious but devoted to his loved ones. He was looked on by Buffy as a father figure and often defied the Watchers Council by fighting side by side with Buffy (which eventually caused his dismissal from the Council).
Powers: Psychic link with unearthly beings carrying the Mark of Eyghon (through a tattoo he wears); demonic and black arts knowledge; able to

speak ancient Greek, German, Latin, English, and Sumerian; expert in hand-to-hand combat, magic, and ancient weapons.

Education: Oxford University.

Background: Rupert's father and grandfather were Watchers, members of a secret society that is based in England. The society trains men and women to protect Chosen Ones (Slayers) through their knowledge of demons and proficiency with weapons. After graduating from college, Giles refused to become a Watcher and struck out on his own as a rogue magician. After the death of a close friend, Giles gave up magic and became a member of the Council. He was working at the British Museum when he was chosen to protect Buffy and guide her as she takes on the abilities of a Slayer.

Greatest Asset: The *Pregamum Codex,* an ancient book of prophecies and writings concerning Slayers.

Business: The Magic Box (at 1524 Maple Court), which sold items dealing with the occult; it also provides a meeting place for the Scooby Gang.

Relatives: Father (unnamed); grandmother, Edna Giles; great aunts, Livinia and Sofia Fairweather.

CORDELIA CHASE

A friend to Buffy, Giles, Willow, and Xander and a member of the Scooby Gang. Her character was spun off into the series *Angel* to become a member of The Powers That Be and use her special abilities to help Angel battle demons. (For details, see "Cordelia Chase" under *Angel.*)

SPIKE

William Pratt, better known as Spike, is a vicious vampire who first sought to kill Buffy (making her his third Slayer trophy) before he was killed, returned as a spirit, and had his essence restored to help Buffy and Angel battle demons. (For details, see "Spike" under *Angel.*)

TARA MACLAY

Tara, Willow's girlfriend and a member of the Scooby Gang, was born on October 16, 1980. Her mother and grandmother were witches and helped her develop her powers. Tara has telekinesis and can manipulate magical forces, perform spells and rituals, and levitate. She is a student at the University of Sunnydale and a member of the campus WICCA group (pagan witchcraft). It is revealed in her freshman year that she is a lesbian and met Willow when they joined forces to battle "the Gentlemen" (demons who stole human voices to obtain hearts). As Tara and Willow became close, they practiced witchcraft together and became surrogate parental figures to Dawn following Joyce's death.

Tara was killed when a bullet meant for Buffy struck her instead. They had a pet cat they called "Miss Kitty Fantastico."

FAITH LEHANE

Faith, a Slayer and member of the Scooby Gang, was born in Boston, Massachusetts. She had a difficult upbringing, made even more tragic when her parents (both alcoholics) were killed by a vampire named Kakistos. A teenager at the time, Faith moved to Sunnydale, were she met and befriended Buffy (a senior in high school) and her circle of friends. Kakistos also killed Faith's Watcher, and she revealed to Buffy that she came to Sunnydale to escape her fears of facing Kakistos (who is later killed by Faith with Buffy's help). She later travels to Los Angeles, where she becomes a part of Angel's efforts to destroy demons. Faith is also known as Hope Lyonne, the Rogue Slayer, and has the typical Slayer abilities of strength and agility.

Caroline in the City
(NBC, 1995–1999)

Cast: Lea Thompson (Caroline Duffy), Amy Pietz (Annie Spadaro), Malcolm Gets (Richard Karinsky).

Basis: Events in the life of Caroline Duffy, a single woman living in New York City and earning a living as a cartoonist.

CAROLINE DUFFY

Place of Birth: Wisconsin in 1961.

Education: Webster Grammar School; Matheson High School; Wisconsin State College.

Address: 54 Gramercy Place, Apartment 2A, in Manhattan.

Occupation: Creator and artist of the daily newspaper comic strip "Caroline in the City" (about a girl's experiences in the big city); it is syndicated to 565 newspapers.

Cartoon Creation: When she was 10 years old, Caroline developed a sudden interest in art but also in her developing figure. "I wanted breasts, and I drew boobs on everything." Shortly after entering college, she became bored and dropped out. She acquired a job as a copywriter but was fired for doodling instead of working. She realized those drawings were her way of expressing herself and chose to become a cartoonist.

Second Job: Designer for the Cassidy Greeting Card Company. Del Cassidy (Eric Lutes) runs the company for his father but quits to begin his own business (the Eagle Greeting Card Company, where Caroline is his only client).

Pet Cat: Salty (as a kid, Caroline had a dog named Sparky).

Favorite Eatery: Remo's Restaurante.

Favorite Drink: Ginger ale.

Measurements: 34-26-34. She has red hair and light brown eyes. She stands 5 feet, 4 inches tall and wears a size 7½ shoe.

Breakfast Cereal: The Dartland Food Company marketed a puffed wheat cereal called Sweet Carolines.

Dates: Caroline is very selective about whom she dates. She cooks chicken to impress a man, but when she breaks up with someone she liked, she goes to the Museum of Natural History to talk to the exhibits.

Dislikes: The comic strip "Cathy" because if she misses a deadline, papers run two "Cathy" strips ("and I hate that girl").

ANNE "ANNIE" SPADARO

Relationship: Caroline's best friend.

Place of Birth: Passaic, New Jersey, in 1969.

Education: Paramus High School.

Measurements: 36-23-36. She stands 5 feet, 5 inches tall and wears a size 10 shoe.

Occupation: Professional dancer. She is a regular cast member of the play *Cats* (at the Winter Garden Theater). She left *Cats* to become Princess Neptuna, the live-action model for a cartoon character. She was then the understudy for Julie Andrews in the Broadway production of *Victor/Victoria*, the star of an unnamed TV pilot film, and the inspiration for "the slutty neighbor next door" for Caroline's strip (although Annie insists, "My breasts are bigger than Caroline draws them").

TV Commercial: "Dr. Furman's Foot Powder."

Address: Apartment 4D at 166 Amsterdam Avenue in Manhattan.

Family-Owned Business: The Spadaro Funeral Parlor.

Childhood Idol: Carol Brady (Florence Henderson) from *The Brady Bunch* TV series.

RICHARD KARINSKY

Relationship: Caroline's colorist (works with Caroline out of her apartment). He is a struggling artist who feels unappreciated.

Place of Birth: Manhattan.

Address: 424 East 6th Street in Greenwich Village.

Childhood: Richard showed interest in being an artist at a young age. When he drew an object, it looked like what it was supposed to be. He excelled in art throughout his school years but has yet to be recognized as a true artist. He took the job with Caroline "because I won't be able to make money for my art until after I'm dead."

Character: Although Richard's art reflects courage and originality, he is boring and lacks a sense of humor ("I'm working on my people skills"). He is very high strung, and when something upsets him, he stands in the corner of Caroline's kitchen and sulks.

Quirks: Richard will not come to work before 10:00 in the morning; doesn't work on weekends and requires 90 minutes for lunch.

First Art Showing: The Arabia Gallery on Spring Street.

First Public Painting: Commissioned to paint a mural on the wall of the Reisman Building in Manhattan.

Charmed
(WB, 1998–2006)

Cast: Shannen Doherty (Prue Halliwell), Holly Marie Combs (Piper Halliwell), Alyssa Milano (Phoebe Halliwell), Rose McGowan (Paige Matthews), Brian Krause (Leo Wyatt).

Basis: Three beautiful witch sisters (Prue, Piper, and Phoebe), called "the Charmed Ones," use their powers to protect people threatened by evil.

OVERALL SERIES INFORMATION

Sisters' Parents: Victor Bennett (James Read), a mortal; Patty Halliwell (Finola Hughes), a witch.

Grandmother: Penny "Grams" Halliwell (Jennifer Rhodes); seen as a ghost.

Halliwell Address: 1329 Prescott Street in San Francisco (also given as 7511 and 1829 Prescott).

Telephone Number: 555-0198.

Education: The sisters attended Baker High School; played at Kenwood Park and attended Camp Skylark.

Sisters' Imaginary Fairy Friend: Lily.

Sisters' Guardian: Leo, a White Lighter (see below).

"The Girl Who Started It All": Melinda Warren, a seventeenth-century witch who possessed three powers: future sight, moving objects, and freezing time. When Melinda was discovered to be a witch, she was burned at the stake. Before she died, she willed her spirit to carry the Power of Three over time until it found three sisters (Prue, Piper, and Phoebe) to become the present-day world's most powerful good witches. It is when the sisters inherit their late mother's San Francisco home that their lives change. The sisters grew up in the home but had since gone their separate ways (Prue and Piper living in Los Angeles, Phoebe in New York). When they unite at the home, Phoebe finds the spirit board she played with as a child and sees it spell out the word "attic." There, the sisters find *The Book of Shadows.* Phoebe reads the incantation from the open page ("bring your powers to

we sisters three"), and she, Piper, and Prue are endowed with Melinda's powers. At this same time, a white cat they call Kit magically appears. The cat wears a collar with the symbol of the Triquetra—which also appears on the cover of the *Book of Shadows* and supposedly transferred Melinda's powers to the sisters.

The House: It was built on a spiritual nexus and a pentagram as a battleground between good and evil (it serves as an instrument to reclaim good). Because Phoebe was born in the house, she is most connected to it and is more susceptible to possible evil.

When the *Book of Shadows* is seen, the pages appear to be turning by themselves. It is revealed that the spirit of the sisters' grandmother, whom they call "Grams" (and whom she called "My Darlings"), is responsible for the page turning and her way of looking after them.

PRUDENCE "PRUE" HALLIWELL

Birthday: October 28, 1970, in San Francisco (she was killed by a demon on May 17, 2001).

Relationship: The eldest sister (28 years old). She is considered the most powerful of the sisters and called "the Power of One."

Ability: Move objects by thought. She channeled her powers through her eyes and three years later developed the power of astro-projection (being in two places at once).

Nicknames: Phoebe calls her "Honey," "Sweetie," or "Darling."

Occupation: Curator at the American Museum of Natural History; appraiser for the Buckland Auction House; photographer for *4-One-5*, a trendy magazine.

Measurements: 37-26-36. She is 5 feet, 4 inches tall; has brunette hair and green eyes; and wears a size 6 shoe and a size 8 dress. Because she loves to wear low-cut, cleavage-revealing blouses, Piper calls her "an Einstein with cleavage."

Car License Plate: 2WAC 231.

High School: Popular; head of the student council and head cheerleader.

Romantic Interest: Andy Trudeau (W. T. King), a homicide inspector with the San Francisco Police Department. He learned that the sisters were witches shortly before he was killed while helping Prue fight the demons of the Triad (an organization behind demon attacks in San Francisco).

Flashbacks: Young Prue (Emmalee Thompson).

PIPER HALLIWELL

Date of Birth: August 7, 1973, in San Francisco.

Relationship: The middle sister (age 26). She most resembles their mother, Patty, who was killed in 1978 by a water demon at Camp Skylark shortly after Phoebe was born.

Shannen Doherty, Alyssa Milano, and Holly Marie Combs. *The WB/Photofest*
© *The WB*

Power: The ability to freeze time and cast spells (she buys the herbs needed in
   Chinatown) and to see and communicate with spirits of the dead.
Occupation: Chef at the Restaurante (later changed to Quake). She next pur-
   chases a failed nightclub from S.W.A. Properties that she converts into her
   own eatery, the Industrial Zone (later becoming a fashionable nightclub she
   calls P-3, for herself and partners Prue and Phoebe).
Blood Type: AB-negative.
Measurements: 36-26-36. She has brunette hair and brown eyes; is 5 feet, 2 inches
   tall; and wears a size 6 shoe and a size 4 dress.
Car License Plate: 26A3 123.
Trait: When Piper becomes nervous, she babbles and waters flowers.
Transformation: Unnatural forces have turned Piper into a Windago ("a were-
   wolf but only worse") and a Furrie (a demon that kills anyone she fears
   is evil).
Flashbacks: Young Piper (Hunter Ansley Wryn, Alexis Raich, Megan Corletto).
Flash-Forwards: Elder Piper (Ellen Geer).

PHOEBE HALLIWELL
Birthday: November 2, 1975, in San Francisco.
Relationship: The youngest sister (20 years old).
Alias: Phoebe, Queen of the Underworld.

Powers: Passive. She later develops the power to see the future (premonitions), the ability to levitate, and empathy (sensing and experiencing the emotions of others). Phoebe also composes the spells they need to vanquish demons.

Greatest Fear: The basement (as a child, she saw "the Woogie Man," an evil force that thrives in the dark).

Occupation: In New York, she worked as a hostess at the Rainbow Room and later the Chelsea Bar. In San Francisco, she attends the College of the Humanities, hosts a call-in radio program (*Hotline*), and writes the advice column "Ask Phoebe" for the *Bay Mirror*.

Measurements: 37-25-26. She has brunette hair and brown eyes; is 5 feet, 2 inches tall; and wears a size 6 shoe and a size 4 dress.

Car License Plate: 3B58 348.

Transformation: Through evil, Phoebe has become a banshee and a mermaid. She was later possessed by the Woogie Man she feared.

Romantic Interest: Cole Turner (Julian McMahon), a powerful demon, posing as the assistant district attorney and known as Belthazor. He is a member of the Brotherhood and has been a demon for 1,000 years; he is later transformed into a human when Phoebe creates a power-stripping spell that kills the evil within Cole.

Flashbacks: Young Phoebe (Samantha Goldstein).

Flash-Forwards: Elder Phoebe (Frances Bay).

PAIGE MATTHEWS

Birthday: August 2, 1977, in San Francisco.

Relationship: Half sister to Prue, Piper, and Phoebe. In a cliffhanging third-season finale, the sisters battle a fierce demon named Shax. Phoebe and Piper survive, but Prue is killed (Shannen Doherty's exit from the series). Rather than continue the role of Prue, a long-lost half sister named Paige was added.

History: Paige is the result of an affair that Patty had with her White Lighter (Sam Wilder) after her divorce from the girls' father, Victor. At this time, it was unnatural and forbidden for a witch and her White Lighter to be together. Patty and Sam kept the affair a secret because Patty feared repercussions (her daughters would be denied Melinda's legacy). Prue, Piper, and Phoebe were toddlers at the time "and thought Mommy was just getting fat." Patty wanted to keep the baby but couldn't. She took her to a church and gave her to a nun (Sister Agnes). Patty said, "Let her name begin with a 'P'" and orbed out (vanished in a sprinkling of white lights). The nun, who believed she received a heavenly visit, named the baby Paige and found her a good home (with the Matthews family), knowing that one day she would fulfill a preordained destiny.

Adulthood: Paige is actually the youngest of the sisters. She is working at South Bay Social Services and experiencing visions of a girl being attacked by a demon (Shax). Phoebe's visions bring her to Paige to save her, but Paige is astonished to see the girl "orb out" to safety. It has to be assumed that Paige is drawn to Piper and Phoebe as she finds their home but has been unknowingly followed by Shax. Phoebe instructs Paige to follow her and Piper upstairs to the attic. There, at the *Book of Shadows*, Paige is told by Piper and Phoebe to chant a spell with them. The spell vanquishes the demon but leaves a bewildered Paige remarking, "What are you guys, witches?" "So are you," responds Phoebe. At that moment, the Power of Three is reborn. (When Phoebe learned that their unknown sister's name was Paige, she remarked, "Imagine that, another 'P.'")

Being: Paige is actually half witch and half White Lighter. She has Prue's power to move objects through concentration or by "orbing the object" (making it appear from one place to another). She can also heal wounds and sense evil.

Fear: Claustrophobia.

Home: Lives with Piper and Phoebe (Piper convinced her that they need to be together to evoke the Power of Three [strongest when together]). After Prue's death, Piper changed the name of her club to the Spot. It became hipper and more active, but she now had another sister and changed it back to P-3.

Measurements: 35-24-35. She has brunette hair and brown eyes; is 5 feet, 4 inches tall; and wears a size 6 shoe and a size 2 dress.

Transformation: Paige had a prior life wherein she was an evil enchantress.

Occupation: Teaches young witches as headmistress of the Magic School.

Flash-Forwards: Elderly Paige (Donna Hardy).

LEONARDO "LEO" WYATT

Year of Birth: May 6, 1924, in San Francisco (to Christopher Wyatt and an unnamed mother).

Background: While studying to be a doctor, Leo met and later married a woman named Lillian. In 1942, he became a doctor and volunteered for medical duty in Europe during World War II. He was killed on November 14 of that year and reborn as a White Lighter the same day (through the power of the Council of Elders).

Association: Member of the Council of Elders; head of the Magic School.

Relationship: A White Lighter (a guardian angel for good witches and the Halliwell sisters' protector). He works for the Founders (later called the Elders), who watch over witches. He disguises himself as the sisters' handyman; refers to his superiors as "the Others" and later becomes an avatar.

Power: The ability to heal—but not himself or animals.

Enemy: Dark Lighters, who seek to destroy witches and create evil.

Romantic Interest: Piper (they married on February 22, 2001, and became the parents of Wyatt [Jason and Kristopher Simmons, then Wes Ramsey] and Chris [Drew Fuller]) and infant Melinda.

Clueless
(ABC, 1996–1997; UPN, 1997–1998)

Cast: Rachel Blanchard (Cher Horowitz), Stacey Dash (Dee Davenport), Elisa Donovan (Amber Mariens).

Basis: Life with three wealthy teenage girls (Cher, Dee, and Amber) attending a posh high school in Beverly Hills, California.

CHER HOROWITZ

Father: Melvin "Mel" Horowitz (Michael Lerner, then Doug Sheehan), a lawyer and owner of Mel Horowitz and Associates; her mother is deceased. Mel enjoys meals at a restaurant called Wheat Sprouts, and he is writing a novel called *Hung Jury.*

Brother: Josh (David Lascher).

Religion: Jewish.

Address: 2232 Karma Vista Drive.

Phone Number: 555-5149.

Education: Rodeo Drive Preschool; Rodeo Drive Elementary School (played Glenda, the Good Witch in a production of *The Wizard of Oz*); Bronson Alcott High School (starred in a production of *Grease*).

Future Plans: Attend Stanhope College; become a fashion designer.

Character: Very pretty, very friendly (always willing to help others), and endowed with "a passion for fashion." She is a bit self-conscious over the fact that she has small breasts. She claims "to get depressed when I'm boyfriend challenged" and believes in "the three C's when approaching a boy—casual, cool, and collective."

Bra: The "Bust Builder '98" (which was designed especially for her to give her a fuller look).

Curfew: 10 p.m. on weeknights; midnight on Saturday.

Writer: Pens the column "Buzzline" for the school's newspaper, *The Alcott Buzz.*

Hangout: The Koffee House.

DIONNE "DEE" DAVENPORT

Relationship: Cher's best friend.

Address: 607 Chantilly Lane.

Education: Rodeo Drive Preschool; Rodeo Drive Elementary School; Bronson Alcott High School (where she is a member of the Honors Society).

Future Plans: Attend Stanhope College with Cher, then marry into wealth.

After-School Hangout: The Koffee House.

Character: Dee believes that she is not only gorgeous but also physically perfect. She dresses in the latest (and most expensive) outfits and, for a 16-year-old girl, loves to show cleavage.

Typical Day: Relaxes by "shopping the retail experience."

Trait: Although Dee will not admit it, she does have a problem: rambling on about something that bothers her. Cher calls it "Bimbo Babble." She also becomes very upset "if I hear the 'A' word" ("almost"), and "I sink into a bottomless pit of bumming" if she breaks up with a boyfriend.

Favorite Movie: Wayne's World.

Business: On Valentine's Day, Dee teams with Cher to sell "Pops for Pups" (lollipops to raise money for the animal shelter). When Dee and Cher became obsessed with muffs, they combined a muff with a purse and created Brad-Keanu Muff Purse International, Inc. (after their favorite actors, Brad Pitt and Keanu Reeves).

Boyfriend: Murray Lawrence DuVal (Donald Faison). While Murray in no way appears to be in the same league with Dee, they do like each other and date. They had their first date at To Kill a Shrimp. Murray cries at movies, loves chili fries and animals, and "worships the dirt Dee grinds me into." He considers himself a ladies' man and calls himself "the Rodeo Romeo" and "the Bronson Bad Boy."

AMBER PRINCESS MARIENS

Parents: Dr. Tripp Mariens (Dwayne Hickman), Ginger Mariens (Linda Carlson).

Relationship: Cher and Dee's best friend.

Address: 111 Jeannie Court.

Education: Rodeo Drive Elementary and Grammar Schools; Bronson Alcott High School.

Future Plans: Attending Stanhope College with Cher and Dee, then becoming a fashion model or marry rich ("If you date me," she says, "never buy me a gift from a store with 'barn' in the name").

Character: Beautiful and fashion conscious but believes "people see me as a self-centered wacko." She flirts with male teachers to get better grades and flaunts $20 bills to female teachers for a passing grade (she is normally an average student). Cher claims, "She has supermodel delusions and is in love with herself."

Nicknames: Her father calls her "Rose Petal," "Buttercup," and "Candy Cane," but because of her red hair ("Smoldering Cherry, please, not red"), she is called "Big Red."

Pet Dog: Tippy.

Proudest Moment: Her father donating money to the local zoo and officials naming an animal after her (unaware that it was an orangutan).

Volunteer Work: The Retired Actors Home in Hollywood.

School Note: Named after its multibillionaire founder, Bronson Alcott (Bert Remsen). It is part of the Westside Unified School District. It has a tanning salon (donated by actor George Hamilton, its most prestigious graduate) and has a basketball team, the Tortoises, represented by Snappy, the Fighting Tortoise.

Cybill
(CBS, 1995–1998)

Cast: Cybill Shepherd (Cybill Sheridan), Christine Baranski (Maryann Thorpe), Alicia Witt (Zoe Woodbine), Alan Rosenberg (Ira Woodbine), Tom Wopat (Jeff Robbins), Deedee Pfeiffer (Rachel Blanders).

Basis: An aging actress (Cybill Sheridan) struggles to cope with two ex-husbands (Ira and Jeff), her daughters (Zoe and Rachel), and a snooty best friend (Maryann) while attempting to find acting roles in an industry where "I lose jobs to younger girls."

CYBILL SHERIDAN

Parents: A. J. (Charles Durning), the owner of a car lot called Sheridan Motors, and Virginia Sheridan (Audra Lindley).

Place of Birth: Memphis, Tennessee, in 1951 (she is 44 when the series begins).

Religion: Baptist.

Oddity: Cybill has two webbed toes.

Teen Years: In high school, Cybill was pranked at a slumber party when rubber cement was put in her sleeping bag. She got out of the bag, lint-like particles adhered to her body, and she was called "Beach Booger Barbie." In the Girl Scouts, Cybill made a bust of her mother out of macaroni and gumdrops, and when she first arrived in California, she went surfing and lost her bikini top.

Address: 11291 Moss Canyon in Los Angeles.

Representative: The William Morris Agency.

Car: A red 1964 Dodge Dart convertible (plate UPU 878).

Measurements: 36-34-38. She has blonde hair and blue eyes; stands 5 feet, 8 inches tall; and wears a size 8 shoe.

Ex-Husbands: Ira Woodbine and Jeff Robbins.

Daughters: Zoe (by Ira), Rachel (by Jeff).

Career: Cybill entered a beauty contest in her hometown and was crowned "Miss Pickled Pigs Feet." In 1968, at the age of 18, she went to New York City, where she became a top model before venturing into show business. To sustain herself, she also dressed as a monkey to deliver singing telegrams for Monkey Gram.

Nightmare: Being naked at an awards ceremony but not receiving an award.

Stage Plays: The all-nude version of *Death of a Salesman* (for experimental theater in Manhattan); Mary Todd Lincoln in *What Now, Mr. Lincoln?*; *A Doll's House* (at the Main Stage Theater, where she played Nora "in a bubble wrap dress").

Television: Family House, a sitcom where "I played the husband's secretary"; *Life Forms* (playing Sara McCullum, a sexy woman who battles aliens; because of the camera shots used for Sara, Cybill says, "The actual stars of the show are my breasts and legs, which receive more airtime than the rest of me"); *Julie in the Morning* (a talk show she cohosted; it was later titled *Julie and Cybill*); *Major Milo*, a kids' show where she played "Booty the Clown" (a clown with a big butt) to spaceship commander Major Milo (Tim Conway); *Invincible Girl* (a superhero series playing Galaxy Gal); and *Island Cop* (played a police officer), which was so bad that the six produced episodes never aired in the United States; it did, however, become the number one TV series in Russia for seven years. She was also the vocalist on an updated version of the game show *Name That Tune* and the mother on *Steffi's World* (about a teenage girl named Steffi [played by Maggie Lawson]), appeared in *Why Is It Always Me?* (a woman plagued by bad luck) and *Hello Dickie* (a sitcom), and was the voice of "Polly the Potty Mouth Parrot" in an unnamed cartoon series.

TV Guest Roles: The Partridge Family, Stories of the Highway Patrol ("I was hit by a bus"), *Joanie Loves Chachi, Matlock* (as a bulimic attorney), *Hart to Hart* (a murder victim), *Barnaby Jones* (a college sorority sister), and *Richie Brockelman, Private Eye* (all real series). She was also offered the role of Jill Monroe on *Charlie's Angels* but turned it down (Farrah Fawcett became Jill). She is barred from the set of *The Muppet Show* for setting Grover on fire (although claiming Grover set himself on fire). She also hosted a cooking segment on *Wake Up, L.A.*

Movie Roles: Monday's Child, What She Did for Love (contains Cybill's first nude scene), *Oliver the Twisted* (won the Golden Stinky Award for "Worst Horror Film Ever Made"), *A Star Is Gorged, Punchout* (where she costarred with ex-husband Jeff); *Zombie Vacation, Romeo and Goulette, Shut Up Little Suzie*, and *Debutants from Hell*. Her first film audition was for the movie *Rocky* (which she didn't get), and her audition for the vampire movie *The Hooker with a Heart of Gold* made her realize she was aging when she lost the role to a younger actress. She also appeared with Kenny Rogers in his movie *The*

Gambler as a prostitute (she kept the "bordello outfit" she wore). Although she did not appear in the adult film *The Last Picture Ho*, her face (placed on another girl's body) appears on the VHS release box cover.

TV Commercials: "The Psychic Pals Network," "Granny's Snack Cakes," "Can Do Supermarkets," "Fraumeister Beer," "Art's Classic Chips," "Femgel" (a feminine product), "The Thorpe Veterinary Clinic," "United Florists," "Viking Mist" (a spray breath freshener), "Beef Baby" (a snack), and an unnamed fish stick product. For Japanese TV, she was spokesgirl for the "Yirko Automobile" (Cybill mentioned that she always wanted to go to Japan "because all my toys [as a kid] were from Japan").

Songstress: In her youth, Cybill attempted a singing career (that failed) in a New York club called Lunchie at 44th Street and Ninth Avenue.

Billboard Ad: "Foot First Shoes."

Hollywood Walk of Fame: In the opening theme, when the walk is seen, the following names appear: Carole Lombard, Lana Turner, Kim Novak, Lassie, Jean Harlow, and "Cybill" (a star drawn in chalk). A wax figure of Cybill appears in Madame Tuso's Wax Museum in Hollywood.

Favorite Restaurant: Firenze Trattoria (where she also worked as a waitress).

Allergy: Chocolate (her favorite candies were Almond Joy, Baby Ruth, Mounds, and Butterfinger). Before this was revealed, Cybill ate Oreo cookies by splitting the cookie in half and eating the noncreamy filling side first; if the filling should also become a part of each cookie half, she became upset, as that cookie was ruined.

Dislike: Eating fish two days in a row.

Quirk: While known around the world, Cybill is idolized by the people of Siberia.

Award: Her only "recognition," declared by the Golden Stinky Awards: "Stupidest Death Scene" (from *Oliver the Twisted*).

Fan Club: The International Cybill Sheridan Fan Club.

Relatives: Niece, Claire Martin (Paula Cale), the daughter of her brother, Martin; cousin, Mae (lives in San Francisco); aunt, Laura (lives in Memphis).

THERESA MARYANN THORPE

Parents: Roy (Dick O'Neill) and Marge Yulevitch (Eileen Heckart).

Place of Birth: Buffalo, New York, in 1953 (she is 41 when the series begins).

Education: St. Dominic's High School (Class of 1971).

Maiden Name: Theresa Yulevitch. She uses her middle name as her first name and her ex-husband's last name.

Ex-Husband: Dr. Richard Thorpe (Ray Baker), an apparently wealthy plastic surgeon (however, in one episode, when his practice is seen, it is a veterinary clinic). Maryann calls him "Dr. Dick" and has vowed to spend every cent he has (as she is bitter for his divorcing her). Dr. Dick later marries Andrea (Morgan Fairchild).

Son: Justin Thorpe (Danny Masterson).

Addiction: Alcohol (she has been at the Betty Ford Clinic twice to help her control her problem). When the series begins, she appears to have her drinking under control but is constantly seen (no matter where she is) sipping a martini (her favorite drink) or some other alcoholic beverage.

Measurements: 34-24-35. She stands 5 feet, 9½ inches tall and wears a size 10 shoe.

Quirk: Loves posing nude for paintings and shopping when she is sad, panics if she cannot find the right earrings for an outfit, and never wears the same, expensive clothes twice (she discards them rather than give them to charity).

First Meeting: Before marrying "the fabulously wealthy Dr. Dick," Maryann worked as a temp office secretary at a casting company where Cybill auditioned for (and lost) a role in the movie *Rocky*.

Award: The United Hospital's Humanitarian Award (not for the work she does but for the money she donates).

ZOE WOODBINE

Relationship: Cybill's daughter by Ira Woodbine.

Place of Birth: Los Angeles in 1979 (she is 16 when the series begins). She weighed 11 pounds, 6 ounces at birth and was born at 5:10 a.m.

Dream: To attend the Los Angeles Conservatory of Music (she is a talented pianist).

Address: Same as Cybill, but she temporarily moves to her own apartment (2R) in Venice Beach, California.

Measurements (from 1998): 34-24-35. She stands 5 feet, 9 inches tall and wears a size 7 shoe and a size 2 dress.

Occupation: Student (an unnamed high school). She gives piano lessons from home and worked at a movie theater concession stand (selling snacks), as a mascot (as a bumblebee) for the Busy Bee Burger Barn, as an unnamed museum tour guide, and as an office assistant at the Los Angeles Philharmonic.

Favorite Pie: Coconut Cream.

Favorite Cereal: Count Chocula.

Quirk: Enjoys making fun of her older sister (Rachel) and her husband (Kevin) with snide remarks; threatens to become a lesbian if Cybill doesn't learn to accept her boyfriends.

OTHER CHARACTERS

Jeff Robbins is Cybill's first husband, a movie stuntman. He has been in the business for 26 years, and his mentor was a stuntman named Stitch Sullivan. He has a pet dog (Duke) and has recently remarried (Marilu Henner plays his second wife, Terry Belmont). He and Cybill met for the first time when she was a struggling actress. Jeff also sings and plays the guitar. He calls Cybill "Pumpkin" and her breasts "The Pointer Sisters" and before remarrying lived in an apartment over Cybill's garage.

Ira Woodbine is Cybill's second husband, a lawyer turned novelist (penned *Lowenstein's Lament*). They divorced after 14 years of marriage (another episode states 15 years, and they lived in New York when they first married). Ira mentioned that his first job (at age 15) was as a cabana boy in the Hamptons. Ira is a basketball fan and a bit neurotic at supper (he hates it when his vegetables touch his meat). Cybill's mother called him "Isaac" for 20 years; Florence Stanley played his mother, Ruth.

Rachel, Cybill's daughter by Jeff, is 24 years old when the series begins. She is married to Kevin, and they are later the parents of William. As a child, Rachel loved the game of "Operation" and dreamed of becoming a doctor. Kevin is an untenured college professor and unemployed (Rachel's efforts to get him to find a job are a focal point of early stories, as is her pregnancy while they live with Cybill). He and Rachel move to Boston when Kevin acquires a job as a third-grade schoolteacher. Kevin calls Cybill "Mother Sheridan."

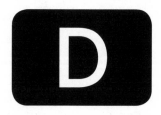

Dharma and Greg

(ABC, 1997–2002)

Cast: Jenna Elfman (Dharma Montgomery), Thomas Gibson (Greg Montgomery), Alan Rachins (Larry Finkelstein), Mimi Kennedy (Abby O'Neill), Mitchell Ryan (Edward Montgomery), Susan Sullivan (Kitty Montgomery).

Basis: A very conservative attorney (Greg) and a rather kooky woman (Dharma) marry, set up housekeeping in San Francisco, and encounter a life that is anything but normal.

DHARMA MONTGOMERY

Parents: Larry Finkelstein and Abby O'Neill. They are liberals and lived together for 30 years before marrying in 1999.

Place of Birth: A hippie commune in an old stand-alone bathtub; Larry and Abby called her "Our Flower Child."

Childhood: Dharma's baby bed was a rope tied to a hammock with a banana leaf as a blanket (Abby felt that "cribs were little jails for babies"). When she began to crawl, she would find her way under the house and play with Fluffy (Dharma mentions she is not sure what kind of animal it was, "but it sure was fluffy"). As she grew, she was not allowed to play with dolls (Abby believed that it fostered unnecessary motherly instincts). She was given "alternative dolls" (a dump truck that she would dress up and call Barbie, and her Ken "doll" was a plastic ant farm), and she never had a jack-in-the-box ("I had a mouse under a Dixie cup"). She played with a "shoe boat" (an old sneaker), and her baby stroller was a homemade blanket tied to the back of her father's bicycle. When Dharma turned 12, she learned that people eat meat. Curious to try it, she bought a hamburger at Tasty Freeze but was caught and scolded by her mother. The following day, she had her first period and now associates meat with her time of the month. At the age of

13, Dharma began to develop and wanted a bra like her girlfriends. When Abby refused to buy her one ("too constricting"), Dharma stole one from the Sears lingerie department. A year later, Dharma shaved her head, hoping her straight hair would grow back curly; it didn't. She says she wore a wig, and because of it she can now wiggle her ears. Dharma took ballet lessons as a child and was called "The Graceful Little Bastard" by other students (as Larry and Abby were not married).

Education: Home taught by Abby (early years); Berkeley College (where she had a number of lesbian girlfriends); the University of Central California.

Occupation: Housewife. She worked as a blackjack dealer in Las Vegas, a NASCAR pit crew girl, a mermaid in a Florida theme park, and a waitress at Jerry's Rice Bowl. She now walks dogs and teaches yoga classes at night.

Address: A renovated former battery factory building in Los Angeles (a beaded Mona Lisa curtain can be seen as a room divider; she also has a toaster she calls "Willie").

Quirks: Every spring, Dharma dances nude on the roof of her building to celebrate the annual rebirth of the earth. When something in her life goes wrong, she believes "the universe is trying to tell me something." She can speak in three languages (English, French, and Spanish) and can swear in Mandarin. She has a hand-painted, watercolor birth certificate (made by her father).

Bra Size: 38C (although, because of her past experience with bras, she rarely wears one). She calls her breasts "Lyle" and "Eric."

Musical Ability: Plays drums and was in two bands: the Jamaican Steel Band (played on Fisherman's Wharf) and the garage band Snot's Army.

Pets: As a child, Dharma had a dog named Doobie; she now has one named Stinky. Stinky also has his own pet dog, Nunzio (whom Dharma gave to Stinky on his bar mitzvah); she takes them to You Wash Doggie Place for their baths.

Favorite Meal: Tofu barley soup.

Superhero: Dharma appears in a comic book as "The Blonde Tornado" (a beautiful girl who can turn herself into a tornado to battle crime; she also attends comic book conventions as the character).

Religion: Jewish.

Laundry: Has her clothes cleaned at the Fluff and Fold Laundromat.

Radio Station: Operated an illegal two-watt station (capable of broadcasting only in her neighborhood) she called "Radio Dharma."

Politics: Ran for a seat on the San Francisco Board of Supervisors under the slogan "Improve Your Karma, Vote for Dharma"; she lost.

TV: Appeared in a commercial for Anaconda Beer.

Sports: Wears jersey 13 as a member of the Sheeps, an all-girl softball team.

Thomas Gibson and Jenna Elfman. *ABC/Photofest © ABC*

GREG CLIFFORD MONTGOMERY

Parents: Edward and Kitty Montgomery.

Place of Birth: San Francisco.

Wife: Dharma Finkelstein (they met on a blind date, fell in love, and married that same day).

Occupation: U.S. attorney for the Department of Justice. He quit when he felt the job was not fulfilling and became a private-practice attorney; he next gave up his practice to embark on a journey of self-discovery (where he worked in a cannery as a "squid skinner," then in a diner as a cook). When his journey ended, he joined his father's company as a member of the Montgomery Industries legal team.

Education: Brookside Academy; Harvard University (majored in law); Stanford University (acquired his law degree). At some point, he served in the military, as he possesses captain's bars and serves two weeks a year in the Army Reserve.

Hobby: Cooking (he is a gourmet cook).

Quirks: Very conservative next to the unpredictable Dharma. He organizes his credit cards by expiration date ("If the top card isn't expired, you're in good shape with the rest of them").

Sports: Captain of Dharma's softball team, the Sheeps.

Recognition: At the age of 18, Greg was the youngest delegate to ever attend the Republican National Convention. When Dharma ran for political office, she placed all available positions in a hat; Greg picked "stamp licker."

Hobby: Collecting stamps.

Religion: Episcopalian.

Favorite Ice Cream Flavor: Vanilla.

LARRY FINKELSTEIN AND ABBY O'NEILL

Myron Lawrence Finkelstein, called Larry, and Abigail O'Neill, called Abby, reside at 1421 Bank Lane in Mill Valley, California. Larry is Jewish; Abby is Catholic. They raised Dharma in the Jewish religion.

In 1968, Larry protested the Vietnam War, and in an attempt "to cripple the Vietnam War machine," he broke into the draft board office and set the building on fire. He fled before he knew the building's sprinkler system put out the fire and believes the government is looking for him (he has been in hiding ever since; as Abby says, "Every day that he is free is a gift"). He also has no Social Security number because "I don't want to be a part of the grid, and I don't want to be found."

Larry worked in Canada as a janitor before meeting Abby. He composed a song called "One Thing about Angels" and contemplated a music career, but no one would publish his song. He next attempted to start his own church ("the Church of Larry") but abandoned it when the IRS began investigating. He found he had a talent for handcrafting furniture, and "with handcrafting tools I handcrafted," he sells his furniture at the East Bay Swap Meet in San Francisco.

Larry has to finish what he starts no matter how long it takes "because if I don't, I forget." Larry also mentions working as a rodeo clown and that he invented "Spray on Gravy," but no one would market it. He is afflicted by a constant metal hum that he hears ("like a factory making metal shoes") but can't figure out why. He composed a five-hour rock opera play based on Watergate and has a pet goat named Goat.

Larry drives an old ice cream truck and mentioned *Lawrence of Arabia* and the X-rated cartoon *Fritz the Cat* as his favorite movies. "Hey Jude" is his favorite song, and he is famous for his vegetable chili (which has chopped meat as the secret ingredient).

Abby was born in Wisconsin and is a graduate of Berkeley College in California. She has a degree in feminine issues from the Goddess Institute. She runs a charity thrift shop, and when she moved in with Larry, Abby's mother put a curse on him.

Abby enjoys painting in the nude, depends on the zodiac to guide her life, and believes that the life she is now living is the first time in 600 years that she has been reincarnated as a woman. She is a licensed aroma healer and prescribes eucalyptus butter tea as a cure for the common cold. Tofu cannoli is her favorite dessert, and in 2001 she and Larry became the parents of Harold Christian Finkelstein.

EDWARD AND KITTY MONTGOMERY

Edward, the owner of the San Francisco–based Montgomery Enterprises, and Kathryn, called Kitty, is heir to the Standard Oil Company. They are also Greg's very conservative parents and sharply contrast with Dharma's parents.

Edward was a Green Beret during the Korean War. Before electing to join his father's company, he worked as a barber, fry cook, and shoe salesman (at Coach's Corner). The Tijuana Brass is his favorite musical group, and "Tijuana Taxi" is his favorite song. Strangely, he collects calypso records, enjoys the movie *The Piano*, and mentions his favorite color as being sky blue. Edward appears to have a gift for hairstyling, while Kitty is an expert at pool.

Kitty grew up in a world where looks and courtesy meant everything (she had the looks but was not a people person). She graduated from Vassar and dreamed of winning a beauty pageant (as a young woman, she entered contests like "Miss Congeniality of Santa Barbara" and "Young Miss Newport Beach" but always came in second). Kitty mentions she wears a size 36C bra (when she notices that Dharma needs to wear a bra) and stopped having children after Greg "because it hurt too bad. Smart women never forget that pain." Kitty is a member of the Women's Charity Committee (where she won the Evelyn Hofstadter Humanitarian Award). Aside from the fact that Dharma refuses to wear a bra but later does so to please Kitty, Kitty calls her "a nutty diamond in the rough" and "a big blob of clay that needs molding" and is determined "to make a Montgomery out of her."

Dinosaurs
(ABC, 1991–1994)

Voice Cast: Stuart Pankin (Earl Sinclair), Jessica Walter (Fran Sinclair), Sally Struthers (Charlene Sinclair), Jason Willinger (Robbie Sinclair), Kevin Clash (Baby Sinclair).

Basis: It is the year 60,000,003 B.C., and dinosaurs have come out of the forests and established a world where they marry and raise families. A look at the incidents that befall one such family living in the city of Pangaea is depicted: parents Earl and Fran Sinclair and their children, Charlene, Robbie, and Baby. Characters are named after oil companies, and costumed characters perform the action.

EARL SNEED SINCLAIR

Dinosaur Type: Megalasaurus.

Age: 43.

Occupation: Tree pusher (knocks down trees by pushing them).

Employer: The Wesayso Development Corporation (which has little respect for the environment; Earl's current assignment is to destroy a redwood forest for condos).

Boss: B. P. Richfield (Sherman Hemsley), a vicious three-horned triceratops.

Coworker: Roy Hess (Sam McMurray), a T-Rex "who eats like a pig and dresses like a slob."

Salary: $4 an hour (he has been working for Wesayso for 20 years).

Character: A chronic complainer who dreams of reverting back to the wilderness life of his barbaric grandfather.

Affiliation: Member of the YMCA (Young Men's Carnivore Association). Here, male dinosaurs are placed at the top of the food cycle as meat eaters (a code by which they live; the biggest eat the smallest, as "it gives order to the world").

Favorite Bar: The Meteor Tiki Lounge.

Favorite Newspaper: The Pangaea *Tribune.*

Social Security Number: 000-00-0018.

Telephone Number: 555–3000.

Favorite Breakfast Cereal: Boo Boo Bears.

Pet Cave Girl: Sparky (a human Earl later sets free; played by Hanna Cutrona).

Clock: Earl has a caveman alarm clock in his bedroom.

Superhero: After falling into a toxic dump at the Silver Springs Recreational Area, Earl acquired powers and called himself "Captain Impressive."

FRANCES "FRAN" SINCLAIR

Dinosaur Type: Allosaurus.

Mother: Fran (Florence Stanley). She is 72 years old and wheelchair bound and lives with the family. She calls Earl "Fat Boy," and her late husband was named Louie (voice of Buddy Hackett in a vision sequence).

Maiden Name: Fran Hinkleman.

Age: 38. She and Earl have been married for 19 years when the series begins (Earl keeps the marriage license under the TV to balance it).

Occupation: Typical housewife (cooks, cleans, and cares for the kids). She also held a job as host of the TV show *Just Advice with Fran* and worked at the Turf and Surf Center for Amphibians (a halfway house for amphibians seeking to make it on land).

Favorite TV Channel: The Dinosaur Shopping Network.

Food Shopping: The Swamp Basket (later called The Food Chain). The Kave Mart is her favorite department store.

Favorite Breakfast to Prepare: Waffle meat pancakes. As a special treat for the family, she makes Refrigerator Mold Pie.

Favorite Flower: Roses.

Birth Sign: Pisces.

ROBERT "ROBBIE" MARK SINCLAIR

Age: 14 when the series begins. He is an herbivore.

Character: A precocious visionary (believes that the primitive caveman will have a bright future).

Education: Bob LaBrea High School (he has locker 38). He is a "B-plus" student and studying "prehistory"; "Rampaging Trilobites" is seen on the back of his school jacket.

Favorite Movie: Teenage Mutant Ninja Cavemen.

Manhood: When Robbie turned 15, he had to observe "The Ceremony of the Howling." *The Book of Dinosaurs* rules how they live. It states that when a male dinosaur comes of age, he must go to the top of a mountain and howl at the moon. "Only by howling do we defeat the dark spirit which turns dinosaur against dinosaur and brings an end to our days on earth."

Gang: A member of the Scavengers for a short time.

CHARLENE SINCLAIR

Age: 12 when the series begins.

Education: Bob LaBrea High School. She is a "C" student and strives to remain so—"so I can be average." She is also not very bright (as her grandmother says, "The only way Charlene will get into college is in a cake in a frat house").

Trait: A material girl and totally into fashion, herself, and makeup.

Cosmetics Shopping: Fifth Avenue Scales in the mall.

BABY SINCLAIR

Dinosaur Type: Megalasaurus.

Official Name: After birth, dinosaurs must be brought to the chief elder for a name. As Baby was about to be named, the elder had a heart attack and said to his assistant, "Aaah, aah, I'm dying you idiot." The assistant recorded the quote as Baby's name. A newly elected elder renamed him "Baby Sinclair."

Quirk: Baby, who was hatched in the first episode, seems to know who everyone is except Earl (whom he often calls "Not the Mama"). He also has a habit of hitting Earl over the head with a Myman Frying Pan when saying it. When Fran complained to the company that the pan breaks when Baby hits Earl, they created the unbreakable "P-2000" and featured Baby and Earl (as "Sir Pan") in TV commercials.

Favorite TV Shows: Mr. Ugh (about a talking caveman), *Raptile* (a talk show), and *Ask Mr. Lizard* (a science program).

Catchphrase: "I'm the baby, gotta love me" (which he says after doing something wrong).

Note: Cave people are considered the lower form of life. In a home, possession of the TV remote is a symbol of authority. Calendars begin with the last day of the month and end on the first day; the elders rule from the Cave of Destiny, and "The Job Wizard" decrees what jobs dinosaurs will have. Dinosaur Christmas is called "Refrigerator Day" (a celebration of cold storage that allowed dinosaurs to stop searching for food and enabled them to remain in one place). Pistachios are said to be a dinosaur's favorite snack.

Dr. Quinn, Medicine Woman
(CBS, 1993–1998)

Cast: Jane Seymour (Dr. Michaela Quinn), Joe Lando (Byron Sully).

Basis: A young female physician (Michaela Quinn) attempts to establish a practice in a Colorado town in 1865 that is reluctant to accept women as doctors.

DR. MICHAELA QUINN

Parents: Michael and Elizabeth Quinn.

Year of Birth: February 15, 1833, in Boston.

History: Michaela has four sisters (not named). Michael, a doctor, had hoped for a son and, being a man of science, believed the odds favored that his next child would be a boy. When that didn't happen, he named the baby Michaela. Michaela grew up admiring her father's work as a doctor and set her goal to follow in his footsteps (something that greatly pleased him). Michaela, however, encountered great difficulty, as no medical school seemed willing to accept women until she found acceptance at the Women's Medical College in Pennsylvania. Michaela joined her father in his medical practice after graduation, and they worked side by side for seven years. "When he died, I lost my mentor, my advocate, my best friend. He spoiled me but gave me the freedom to discover myself. With my father gone, our practice virtually disappeared. I was afraid my life as a doctor was over. But I promised him to carry on."

Life Changer: Michaela found work at the Holy Mission Orphanage. It is now 1865, and while reading the *Boston Globe*, Michaela sees an ad for a doctor in Colorado Springs. She applies and is accepted. Michaela's arrival is met with mostly disenchantment, as she was thought to be a man and people are distrustful of doctors from the East, especially women doctors. "It was the frontier, a place where people make new beginnings; a place where my services would be needed; my skills appreciated; where I would finally be accepted as a doctor."

Lodgings: Mrs. Cooper's Rooms. She later rents a cabin (from Byron Sully; see below) for $1 a month.

Acceptance: Charlotte Cooper (Diane Ladd), a widow with three children; Colleen (Jessica Bowman, then Erika Flores); Matthew (Chad Allen); and Brian (Shawn Toovey), are the first to befriend her. Charlotte is called "Widow Cooper" out of respect (Charlotte and her husband had a farm in Topeka, Kansas; he deserted them when he went to mine for gold at Pikes Peak and the mine went bust).

Tragedy: A rattlesnake bite takes the life of Charlotte. Michaela, too far away at the time and unable to save Charlotte (as the poison had spread), honors her last request to take care of her children. Colleen and Matthew call her "Dr. Mike"; Brian calls her "Maw." Colleen's experiences with Dr. Mike make her proclaim that "Dr. Mike, I wanna be a doctor like you when I grow up."

Indian Belief: The local Cheyenne believe Michaela "is a crazy white woman" because "only white man make medicine."

Indian Name: When the tribal chief is injured (bullet wound), he trusts Michaela to help him when the tribal medicine man cannot. He then grants her the name "Medicine Woman" (which is then reflected on her shingle carved by Sully: "Dr. Michaela Quinn—Medicine Woman"). In a strange twist of fate, when Dr. Mike becomes ill with a fever and there is no medicine (quinine) for her (as she used her share to help other townspeople), Sully takes her to the Cheyenne, where she is saved by the medicine man.

Horse: Flash in the Sky (a present from an Indian woman when she saved the life of her child); she later has a horse named Belle.

BYRON SULLY

Relationship: Friend to Michaela (later her husband in 1867 and the father of their child, Katie).

Year of Birth: The Colorado Territory in 1829.

Occupation: Miner.

Pet Wolf: Boy.

Trait: A rugged mountain man and compassionate to the Cheyenne Indians. He is learned in the ways of both the Indian and the white man.

First Marriage: Sully, as he is called, was married to Abigail. They lived in a cabin that Sully built on the outskirts of town (the one Michaela rents), but lack of medical care (a doctor) costs Abigail and their unborn son their lives during childbirth. Abigail was said to have been born in 1839, and she and Sully

Joe Lando and Jane Seymour. *CBS/Photofest © CBS*

married in 1857 when she was 18. A camera shot of Abigail's gravestone reveals that she died in 1865, which would make him a recent widower when he first meets Michaela; dialogue, however, contradicts this by stating that Sully was a widower for several years before meeting Michaela.

Life Changer: Abigail's passing found Sully abandoning his cabin and retreating to life as a mountain man, earning a living by selling skins and doing odd jobs.

Weapon: A tomahawk.

Fear: Horses (until Michaela persuaded him to ride one).

Later Life: Sully works as the personal Indian agent in Colorado to President Grant, then for the Bureau of Land Management (which sets aside land for national parks; his first assignment is to survey Yellowstone National Park).

The Drew Carey Show
(ABC, 1995–2004)

Cast: Drew Carey (himself), Ryan Stiles (Lewis Kiniski), Diedrich Bader (Oswald Harvey), Kathy Kinney (Mimi Bobeck), Christa Miller (Kate O'Brien), Cynthia Watros (Kellie Newmark), Craig Ferguson (Nigel Wick).

Basis: Events in the lives of three friends (Drew, Lewis, and Oswald) living in Cleveland, Ohio.

DREW ALLISON CAREY

Parents: Beulah (Marion Ross) and George Carey (Stanley Anderson).

Address: 720 Sedgwick Road (distinguished by a pool table in the backyard).

Pet Dog: Speedy.

Education: Rhodes High School.

Occupation: Employed at the Winfred-Louder Department Store (1987–1995 as assistant personnel director, 1995–2000 as personnel director, 2000–2001, as head of personnel; and 2001–2002 as store manager). Drew was also the Internet expediency analyst (when Winfred-Louder went bankrupt and became the Internet company Never Ending Store Dot Com from 2002 to 2004). Nigel Wick, always called "Mr. Wick," is Drew's boss (he replaced the former personnel director, Mr. Bell [Kevin Pollack]). Wick is English and acquired the job without a green card; in order to secure one, he and Drew agreed to a same-sex marriage.

Computer Screen Name: Beer Stud 2.

Salary: $26,000 a year. He previously worked as a waiter at Antonio's Restaurant.

Workspace: Cubicle 17 (which he calls "the Drewbicle").

Host: "The House of Easy Living" on the store's website, www.winloud.com.

Jobs When Laid Off: Hash slinger at his former high school cafeteria; security guard at the Rock and Roll Hall of Fame.

Dream Job: Director of the Six Flags Amusement Park.

Childhood: Had a dog named Nibbles; had a crush on Oswald's sexy mother, Kim (Adrienne Barbeau), and had his first kiss when he was 14 years old (with a girl who preferred to kiss girls).

Favorite TV Series: Xena: Warrior Princess (he writes to star Lucy Lawless under the name "Junior Warrior Drew Carey").

Belief: Cher is the most beautiful woman in the world.

Religion: Protestant.

Car License Plate: DLW GA3.

Favorite Hangout: The Warsaw Tavern.

Invention: With Lewis and Oswald, he created a beer-and-coffee mix called "Buzz Beer, the Working Man's Beer."

High School Band: The Horndogs (with Lewis and Oswald).

Diedrich Bader, Drew Carey, Christa Miller, and Ryan Stiles. *ABC/Photofest © ABC*

Marriages: Drew was single when the series began. It ended with him marrying Kellie Newmark on the day their son (Drew Carey Jr.) was born (Kellie, a former high school friend of Drew's, became a bartender at the Warsaw Tavern in 2002; she was born in Bay Village, Ohio, and is the daughter of Don [Michael Gross] and Annette Newmark [Susan Sullivan]). Drew first married Diana Pulaski (Nicole Sullivan), whom he met on a business trip to Las Vegas (they divorced a week later); then Nicki Fifer (Kate Walsh), a real estate agent (divorced Drew when she discovered he and Mr. Wick were married); and then Lily (Tammy Lauren), a southern girl who suffered from night terrors (she deserted Drew on their wedding day).

LEWIS KINISKI

Mother: Misty Kiniski (June Lockhart).
Relationship: Drew's friend and partner in "Buzz Beer" (which they make in Drew's garage and sell at the Warsaw Tavern).
Address: An apartment over the Warsaw Tavern (which he shares with Oswald).
Education: Rhodes High School.
Occupation: Maintenance man, then janitorial manager at the DrugCo Chemical Company (which experiments with strange and dangerous drugs and which affect Oswald with strange behavior at times).
Dream Job: "Stud monkey at DrugCo."
Allergies: Strawberries and fish.
Sock Puppet: Professor Von Sock (helps him overcome his problems).
Wednesday Night Tradition: Conducts "Beer Robics" at the Warsaw Tavern.
Belief: He is a ladies' man (when he goes too long without a date, he sets up a candlelight dinner at home and listens to a Pat Benatar album).
Quirk: To discourage telemarketers from constantly calling him, he screams words in Chinese into the phone.
Favorite TV Series: Star Trek, Babylon 5, and *Buffy the Vampire Slayer.*
Favorite Activity: Drinking beer.
High School Band: The Horndogs (with Drew and Oswald).
IQ: 162.
Expertise: Considers himself an expert on serial killers.

OSWALD LEE HARVEY

Mother: Kim Harvey (Adrienne Barbeau).
Education: Rhodes High School. His name is a take on "Lee Harvey Oswald."
Address: Shares an apartment with Lewis over the Warsaw Tavern. Because they live together, they are often mistaken for being gay.
Occupation: Rodeo clown; driver for Global Deliveries (also called Global Parcel); male nurse; salesman for Never Ending Store Dot Com.

Owner: The Warsaw Tavern. When Oswald's untied shoelace became entangled in an escalator and he lost part of his pinkie toe, he used the $50,000 settlement money to buy his favorite hangout.

Creator: With Drew and Lewis, they mixed beer and coffee to create "Buzz Beer."

Character: A man of few words, a bit naive, and easily taken advantage of.

MIMI BOBECK

Relationship: Drew's coworker at the Winfred-Louder Department Store (personal assistant and secretary to Nigel Wick). She is, as Drew says, "800 pounds of trouble," and each despises the other. Her desk, which is opposite Drew's, is cluttered with troll dolls. She wears outlandish makeup and is angry at Drew for getting the job she wanted (personnel director) and has made it her goal to make his life miserable.

Computer Screen Name: Honeybee 28.

Prior Jobs: Phone salesgirl; photographer's darkroom assistant; office manager. She sells Sally Mae Cosmetics on the side and has a yearly business called Mimi's Door-to-Door Christmas Tree Service. Her father owns a trucking company, and Mimi later becomes the landlord for the Winfred-Louder real estate holdings.

True or Not?: Mimi claims to have been a roadie for the group Foghat; married for two weeks to singer Eddie Rabbitt; sleeping with singers Peter Frampton and Joe Walsh (she even claims that Frampton still carries a torch for her).

Ancestry: Polish and the Duchess of Krakow after her aunt's passing.

Term of "Endearment" for Drew: "Pig" and "Bite me Dough Boy" (as Drew is overweight).

Place of Birth: Ohio.

Religion: Catholic.

Education: Sacred Heart High School.

Address: Apartment 24 in a neighborhood where the kids think she is a circus clown ("Do you have numbers on your skin so you know what colors go where?").

Marriage: Mimi fell in love with Drew's brother Steve Carey (John Carroll Lynch), a cross-dresser who worked in the cosmetics department of Winfred-Louder and thought Mimi was "the most beautiful girl in the world." He abandoned his feminine side and married Mimi, and they became the parents of a boy they name Gus (Matthew Josten).

KATHRYN "KATE" O'BRIEN

Relationship: Friends with Drew, Lewis, and Oswald.

Place of Birth: Ohio.

Education: Rhodes High School.

Address: A home "near a naked guy with binoculars who lives in the house across the alley."

Religion: Catholic.

Nickname for Her Breasts: "The Kids."

Favorite Hangout: The Warsaw Tavern (where she enjoys drinking beer; as she says, "I save my sick days for hangovers and soap opera weddings"). She also helped develop Buzz Beer.

Jobs: Waitress at Sizzler; receptionist at a car body shop; cosmetics salesgirl at Winfred-Louder (later personal director to the store owner); waitress at Soup on a Stick; house sitter; "Massage on the Job" therapist; catering company employee; waitress at the Warsaw Tavern; security guard at the Rock and Roll Hall of Fame.

Problem: Making a commitment. Men she dated and dumped have formed the website Cold Hearted Bitch Dot Com. She and Drew had a romance, but in 2002 Kate married a navy fighter pilot (Kirk) and left the series when he was transferred to Germany.

Relatives: Grandmother (Patricia Cleveland).

ER
(NBC, 1994–2009)

Cast: Noah Wyle (John Carter III), Anthony Edwards (Mark Greene), George Clooney (Douglas Ross), Maura Tierney (Abby Lockhart), Juliana Margulies (Carol Hathaway), Goran Visnjic (Luka Kovac), Alex Kingston (Elizabeth Corday), Laura Innes (Kerry Weaver), Sherry Stringfield (Susan Lewis), Eriq La Salle (Peter Benton).

Basis: The professional and personal lives of the doctors and nurses attached to County General Hospital in Chicago.

DR. JOHN TRUMAN CARTER III

Parents: John (Michael Gross) and Eleanor Carter (Mary McDonnell). John, first called Roland, is caring but strict; Eleanor, after losing her older son, Robert, to leukemia, has become distant and cold.

Position: Third-year medical student (later specializes in emergency medicine).

Blood Type: O-negative.

Life Changer: Sustained serious back injuries when he and medical student Lucy Knight (Kellie Martin) were attacked by schizophrenic patient Paul Sobricki (David Krumholtz); he is now dependent on chronic painkillers.

Foundation: While working for Doctors Without Borders in Africa, Carter had an affair with Makemba "Kem" Likasu (Thandie Newton), a French-Congolese AIDS worker. Kem became pregnant but after eight months lost the baby (whom they had named Makalo). On his return to the United States, Carter established the Joshua Makalo Carter Center, an HIV/AIDS clinic adjacent to County General.

Relatives: Grandmother Millicent Carter (Frances Sternhagen), a hospital benefactor; first cousin, Case Carter (Jonathan Scarfe), a heroin addict.

DR. MARK GREENE

Parents: Ruth and David Greene. David served with the U.S. Navy as a pilot.

Wife: Jennifer (they met in high school and married after college when Mark entered medical school). Jen (Christine Harnos), as she is called, later becomes a lawyer and acquires a clerking position for a Milwaukee judge. Commuting from Chicago to Wisconsin (to accommodate Mark's job) ends their marriage.

Daughter: Rachel Greene (Hallee Hirsh, then Yvonne Zima). After Mark and Jen divorce, Rachel and Jen move to Milwaukee, then St. Louis.

Second Wife: Elizabeth Corday, a British surgeon whom Mark meets as part of a hospital exchange program. The two date and later marry, becoming the parents of Ella (Caroline Todd, then Brittany Baird).

Position: Emergency Department chief resident.

Mark's Fate: While attending a patient, Mark suddenly loses control of his faculties and is unable to speak. Mark, diagnosed with brain cancer, undergoes chemotherapy but the condition worsens, and he eventually succumbs to the disease at the age of 38.

DR. DOUGLAS "DOUG" ROSS

Parents: Ray and Sarah Ross (Ray deserted the family, and Doug was raised by his mother; Ray is later the owner of a hotel in Chicago).

Position: Emergency room pediatrician; attending physician at the University of Washington Medical Center.

Character: Compassionate, loves children, and does not always display the best judgment. He is a womanizer and drinks and is unable to handle authority well.

Doug's Fate: Resigns in the aftermath of a scandal in which he shows a mother how to bypass the lockouts on a hydromorphine medication dispenser, enabling her to give a lethal dose of medication to her terminally ill son (to stop his heart).

Note: George Clooney played a doctor (called Ace) on the 1984–1985 CBS series *E/R*, which was set at the Clark Street Hospital in Chicago.

DR. ABIGAIL "ABBY" LOCKHART

Maiden Name: Abigail Marjorie Wyczenski.

Position: Originally an obstetric nurse (labor and delivery nurse to Carol Hathaway); later a third-year medical student just beginning her ER rotation at County General (as mentioned in 2000, but in 1999 she is said to be a first-year resident), then a doctor. She was the only character to be both a nurse and a doctor.

Birthday: Born at 8:03 p.m. on January 10, 1969.

Parents: Maggie (Sally Field) and Eddie (Fred Ward). Maggie is suffering from bipolar disorder; Eddie abandoned the family due to Maggie's erratic behavior.

Brother: Eric (Tom Everett Scott), a U.S. Air Force pilot.

Ex-Husband: Dr. Richard Lockhart (Mark Valley). Shortly after their marriage, Abby became pregnant but chose to have an abortion (without telling Richard), fearing the child would inherit bipolar issues. Richard's discovery of Abby's action caused their breakup. As part of the divorce settlement, Richard was ordered to pay for her medical school tuition.

Second Husband: Dr. Luka Kovac (see below); they have a son named Josip (after Luka's father but called Joe because Abby's father was a fan of boxer Joe Louis).

Character: Abby becomes a doctor (2003) but is sarcastic toward patients who annoy her. When Joe turns three, Abby establishes a day care center and mentions hating cats; she is also seen as a recovering alcoholic and attending AA meetings.

Abby's Fate: Abby resigns from County General (fifteenth season) and moves to Boston with Luka and Josip to begin a new life.

NURSE CAROL HATHAWAY

Position: Registered nurse (head of the ER nursing staff).

Character: Carol has a master's degree in nursing and thought of becoming a doctor but felt her abilities were best served in the ER. She is aggressive toward doctor's assistants (who think they know more than her) and is often dismayed by the lack of recognition given to her nurses. After 20 years of service, Carol teams with Carter's grandmother, Millicent, to open an ER clinic to help the poor.

Romance: Dr. Doug Ross. Although Doug is a ladies' man, Carol becomes attracted to him, and, although not married, they decide to have a child (twins are born to them) and later move to Seattle.

Carol's Fate: An accidental overdose of medication causes the death of a child, in turn forcing Carol to resign from the clinic and also step down from her position as the nurse's manager at County General.

DR. LUKA KOVAC

Position: Attending ER physician.

Background: Born in Croatia and a family man (his wife Danijela, son Marko, and daughter Jasna were killed in the Croatian War of Independence [1991–1995] in a bombing that destroyed the apartment house in which they were living). Luka, a physician at the time, was away from his home when it was struck by a mortar shell; Marko was killed instantly, and Luka is now riddled with guilt over what happened next. Danijela and Jasna were alive but severely injured. He was torn between carrying his wife to the hospital or saving his daughter. He chose to perform CPR on Jasna (which failed) while Danijela bled to death. He later says that his family was killed not in a bombing but by soldiers who took them away. On his first day at County General, an oxygen tank exploded, flew past him, and almost killed him.

Family: Mentions having a brother and keeps in contact with his father, an engineer for Croatian Railways.

Second Wife: Dr. Abby Lockhart (see above).

Character: A dedicated doctor and one of the more approachable attending physicians for interns at County General. He has worked with Doctors Without Borders and is a supporter of world health. His faith has been shattered by what happened to his family, and he now questions religion.

Luka's Fate: In the final episode, it is revealed that Luka, Abby, and Joe have moved to Boston to begin a new life.

DR. ELIZABETH CORDAY

Position: A British physician who has moved from London to Chicago to acquire experience in trauma surgery at County General.

Background: Being the only girl in the family, she followed in the footsteps of her father, Charles (a consultant surgeon at St. Thomas' Hospital), and grandfather, also a physician. Her mother (Judy Pratt) is an astrophysicist with whom she shares a rocky relationship (Elizabeth feels her mother did not properly raise her, relying on boarding schools and nannies).

Character: A totally independent woman who relies on her European upbringing and apparently refuses to adjust to American ways. She is quite proper and prefers to be addressed as "Miss Corday" and not "Dr. Corday" (she explains this is a custom for members of the Royal College of Surgeons of England). She is a skilled surgeon, not impressed by hospital staff status, and cares about her fellow doctors and nurses as well as the patients she treats. Elizabeth becomes so impressed by County General that she elects to stay in Chicago after her fellowship ends (although she has to repeat her internship to acquire her U.S. medical license; she then acquires the position of associate chief of surgery).

Husband: Dr. Mark Greene. After a brief affair, Elizabeth becomes pregnant with his child, and they marry, naming their child Ella (see Dr. Mark Greene, above).

Elizabeth's Fate: Following Mark's passing from a brain tumor, Elizabeth is appointed chief of surgery. However, when Elizabeth performs an illegal donor procedure between two AIDS patients (believing it is the right thing to do), she is dismissed from County General. She is offered a job with no tenure or future at County General (clinical instructor) but turns it down to become the chief of trauma surgery at Duke University in Durham, North Carolina (where she lives with Ella, now nine years old). It is also revealed at this time that Mark's daughter, Rachel Greene, is living in Durham and attending Duke University to become a doctor.

DR. KERRY WEAVER

Position: Chief resident, then attending physician, chief of emergency medicine, and hospital chief of staff.

Character: Kerry has a hip birth defect (congenital hip dysphasia) that causes her to walk with a limp and use a forearm crutch. She strongly believes in administrative policies and involves herself in staff disagreements over patient care procedures. She is a lesbian and morally committed to civil and gay rights.

Kerry's Past: In 1995, it is revealed that Kerry was adopted and believes that her real mother (still unknown) could not raise a disabled child. In the episode "Just As I Am," Kerry meets her biological mother, Helen Kingsley (Frances Fisher), a Christian living in Terre Haute, Indiana (her biological father, Cody Boone, had died). Kerry learns that Helen, a teenager when she became pregnant, had limited options when the baby was born and believed that giving Kerry up for adoption (after 14 days) was the best thing to do for her, as it would give her a better chance at life. It is also revealed, after Helen asks about Kerry's limp, that Helen had no knowledge of it when she was born, thus relieving Kerry of the thoughts that her mother abandoned her because of her birth defect. In the episode "Out on a Limb," Kerry elects to have surgery to repair her hip; the episode "No Place to Hide" sees Kerry walking for the first time without the aid of a crutch. It is mentioned only once that Kerry had been previously married to a surgical resident.

Mentor: Dr. Gabe Lawrence (Alan Alda).

Romance: Kim Legaspi (Elizabeth Mitchell), the staff psychiatrist (they broke up when Kim, unable to deal with Kerry's internalized homophobia about her sexuality [unable to reveal she was a lesbian] left her and moved to San Francisco for a better job). Sandy Lopez (Lisa Vidal), a firefighter she met in a rainstorm while trying to extract a pregnant woman from a crashed ambulance, became Kerry's next girlfriend. Sandy initially refused to date Kerry (as she was still in the closet) until Sandy kissed Kerry in front of her coworkers in the ER, and her secret was revealed. Kerry loses Sandy when she is killed fighting a fire.

Kerry's Fate: During a news segment being filmed at the hospital by WTVJ-TV in Miami, Kerry is interviewed for a segment and impresses Courtney

(Michelle Hurd), the producer, who offers her a reporter's job at the station. When Kerry learns that the ER budget is going to be cut, she leaves County General to accept Courtney's offer. It is also seen that Kerry develops a romantic interest in Courtney, as she has the same feelings for Courtney as she did for Sandy.

DR. SUSAN LEWIS

Position: Second-year resident, then attending physician.
Parents: Henry and Cookie Lewis.
Sister: Chloe (Kathleen Wilhoite).
Husband: Chuck Martin (Donal Logue), a flight nurse she first met on a plane to Las Vegas. Susan becomes pregnant at the same time she is promoted to the position of chief of emergency medicine. A son (Cosmo) is born to them, and Chuck becomes a househusband while Susan retains her position at County General.
Character: A good doctor but somewhat incapable of asserting herself (thus finding herself being taken advantage of by senior physicians).
Susan's Fate: Susan leaves County General for a tenured position at an unnamed Iowa hospital. It is revealed in the final episode that she is caring for Cosmo after she and Chuck broke up.

DR. PETER BENTON

Position: Surgical resident, then surgical fellow and attending surgeon.
Mother: Mae Benton (Beah Richards).
Sister: Jackie Robbins (Khandi Alexander).
Character: Not the friendliest of people and quite arrogant but a gifted surgeon with a true passion for medicine. His romantic encounters define his role on the series (although he is seen attending patients). It begins with Jeanie Boulet (Gloria Reuben), a married physician's assistant at the hospital whom he hires as a physical therapist for Mae after she has a heart attack. The affair ends a year later. Peter next hooks up with Carla Reese (Lisa Nicole Carson), a former girlfriend who presents him with a son they name Reese Benton (Reese [Matthew Watkins], however, was born prematurely and deaf). Carla's disenchantment with Peter leads her to having an affair with Roger McGrath (Vondie Curtis Hall), the man she later marries, leaving Reese's fate uncertain (resolved when Carla is killed in a car accident and Peter petitions the court for full custody; he is granted it with Roger receiving visitation rights). Peter was also involved in a rocky relationship with Dr. Elizabeth Corday (Alex Kingston) and Dr. Cleo Finch (Michael Michele), a pediatrician he eventually marries.

Evening Shade
(CBS, 1990–1994)

Cast: Burt Reynolds (Wood Newton); Marilu Henner (Ava Newton); Charles Durning (Harlan Eldridge); Ann Wedgeworth (Merlene Eldridge); Melissa Martin, then Candace Huston (Molly Newton); Jay R. Ferguson (Taylor Newton).

Basis: Life in the small town of Evening Shade as seen through the experiences of the Newton family: parents Wood and Ava and their children, Molly, Taylor, and Will.

WOODROW "WOOD" NEWTON

Mother: Pauline Newton (Florence Schauffer).

Place of Birth: Evening Shade, Arkansas.

Address: 2102 Willow Lane.

Education: Evening Shade High School (called "Thumper" as a member of the school football team; wore jersey 37); the University of Arkansas.

Occupation: Physical education teacher and coach of the Mules (a losing football team) at Evening Shade High School.

Football Career: Quarterback for the Pittsburgh Steelers (wore jersey 22 and was called "Clutch").

Awards: Most Valuable Player (Southwest Conference); Honorable Mention, All-American; Heisman Trophy (runner-up); NFL Rookie Quarterback of the Year. He also holds the record for the most fumbles and yardage lost.

Greatest Moment: Single-handedly won the Eastern Division playoff game by completing six passes in the final minute and 53 seconds. And with 10 seconds left and no time-outs, he scored the winning touchdown with a broken collarbone.

Pet Dog: Brownie.

Favorite Song: "Blueberry Hill" (selection B-5 on the jukebox at Blue's Barbecue Villa, the local diner, owned by Ponder Blue [Ossie Davis]).

Good-Luck Charm: A towel he dyed black when he was with the Steelers.

TV Appearance: Colonel Rodney Stone on the CBS-TV miniseries *The Blue and the Gray.*

First Sexual Experience: "Big" Ruthie Ralston at the Purple Dawn Whorehouse in Hot Springs, Arkansas.

Relatives: Con-artist cousin, Alvin Newton (Billy Bob Thornton).

AVA NEWTON

Parents: Frieda (Elizabeth Ashley) and Evan Evans (Hal Holbrook), the publisher of the town's newspaper, *The Argus.*

Place of Birth: Evening Shade. She is 33 and married Wood when she was 18.

Maiden Name: Ava Evans.

Education: Evening Shade High School; the University of Arkansas.

Occupation: Prosecuting attorney (the town's first female attorney; she graduated second in her law school class).

Measurements: 37-26-36. She stands 5 feet, 7 inches tall and wears a size 8 dress and a size 8½ shoe.

Childhood: Very difficult, as she was overweight and called "Chubby Evans."

Prized Possession: An antique bathroom window.

Honeymoon: The Peach Blossom Suite of the Harrison Hotel in Harrison Point, Arkansas.

Thirteenth-Anniversary Gift: Ava gave Wood a jukebox that plays "Blueberry Hill," and she announced she was pregnant (a girl named Emily Frieda was born to them on May 6, 1991). As a surprise for Wood, his friends arranged for stripper Fontana Beausoleil (Linda Gehringer) to run naked across the football field during a Mules game.

MOLLY AND TAYLOR NEWTON

Molly is 11 years old when the series begins, but her parents treat her like she is nine ("So she can always be our little girl"; Molly wishes that "they would stop treating me like a baby"). She attends Evening Shade Grammar School, is starting to develop (she wears a Littlest Angel Bra), and wears a size 5½ shoe. She is also showing an interest in fashion and makeup but offers a sigh of relief to Wood, as she hasn't developed an interest in boys "and still likes to pal around with her girlfriends." Molly entered the Little Miss Evening Shade Beauty Pageant but lost when she attempted to walk in high heels and fell. *The Wizard of Oz* is her favorite movie, and her and Taylor's favorite hangout is Doug and Herman's Ice Cream Parlor.

Taylor is 15 years old when the series begins and attends Evening Shade High School. He is a member of the Mules football team but, believing he is a ladies' man, fears playing in any games, as he could injure his best feature—his face—and shatter his dreams of becoming an actor.

HARLAN AND MERLENE ELDRIDGE

Harlan and Merlene, friends of Wood and Ava, were born in Evening Shade and attended Evening Shade High School. Although Harlan is older than Merlene, they are happily married. Harlan is the town's only physician and is associated with City Hospital (also called Evening Shade Hospital). They have been influenced by the movie *Gone with the Wind* and call their plush estate Tara. Harlan, a member of the Civil War Society, is most proud of his trophy room (where he displays the various fish he has caught; his fishing boat is called *Tara of the Sea*).

Merlene is a sexy woman who believes "I am a magnet to perverts." She measures 34-24-33 and stands 5 feet, 5 inches tall. She has red hair and hazel eyes. As a child, she and her sisters, Jolene and Lerlene, performed as the Frazier Sisters (Frazier being her maiden name). Merlene is quite frugal and has a knack for taking inexpensive items and making them into something elegant. Her favorite magazine is *Southern Comfort*, and she is most proud of three pictures that hang on her walls: an American Indian, actor Tom Selleck, and evangelist Billy Graham.

When Merlene was a teenager, she became pregnant and, unable to care for the baby, put her up for adoption and never saw her again. Not wanting to see the same thing happen to other girls, Merleen places an ad in the *National Enquirer* for pregnant women who are alone and have no place to go (they will find a home and medical care at Tara). At first, Harlan objects but allows Merlene to proceed with her cause (which led to a 1993 unsold series first called *It's Never Too Late*, then *The Second Time Around*, and finally *Harlan and Merlene*). Three young women answer the ad: Frankie, Carmen, and Sherilee. Frankie (Leah Remini) was a former magician's assistant (for the Great Calzoni) who was fired when she became too big to fit in her costume, Carmen (Maria Canals) ran away from home when she became pregnant, and Sherilee (Rose Kristin), already the mother of April (Janna Michaels), deserted her husband when he began mistreating her.

Everybody Loves Raymond
(CBS, 1996–2006)

Cast: Ray Romano (Raymond Barone), Patricia Heaton (Debra Barone), Brad Garrett (Robert Barone), Peter Boyle (Frank Barone), Doris Roberts (Marie Barone), Monica Horan (Amy Louise MacDougall), Madylin Sweeten (Ally Barone).

Basis: Raymond Barone, a sportswriter married to Debra and the father of Ally, Geoffrey, and Michael, attempts to cope with a life that is complicated by his parents Frank and Marie and brother Robert.

RAYMOND "RAY" ALBERT BARONE
Address: 320 Fowler Street in Lynbrook (on Long Island in New York). The address is said to be 320, although 135 can be seen on the front door.

Place of Birth: Long Island in 1959 (1961 is also mentioned).

Childhood: Had a teddy bear (Hector Von Fuzzy), a pet bird (Tweedy), a dog (Shamsky; named after baseball player Art Shamsky), and a cat (Whiskers). He also took piano lessons from his mother (a piano teacher) and as a teenager had a CB radio with the handle "Straight Shooter." His hero at the time was baseball player Mickey Mantle.

Education: Hillcrest High School (Class of 1977); St. John's University (Class of 1981).

Occupation: Sportswriter for New York *Newsday* (of the column "More Than a Game"). Ray first claims that Mickey Mantle inspired him to become a sportswriter; he later says that Robert's inability to throw a spiral started him on the road to critiquing sports. Before *Newsday*, Ray worked as bed installer for Claude's Futons.

Religion: Irish Catholic (he doesn't attend mass on Sunday "because the football game is on at the same time").

Dream: To have an article published in *Sports Illustrated.*

Shoe Size: 11.

Favorite Breakfast Cereal: Alpha Bits.

Favorite Snack: Twix candy bars.

Favorite Eatery: Nemo's Pizzeria.

Favorite Magazine: Golf Digest (plays golf at the Brookside Country Club).

Awards: The 1996 Sportswriter of the Year Award; the Association of Sports-writers Award (in 2002; it earned him a promotion to the head of sports features at *Newsday*).

TV Appearance: Sports Talk (discussing steroid use in sports).

Biggest Regret: Erasing his and Debra's wedding video to tape a football game.

Archenemy: Peggy Ardolino (Amy Aquino), whom he calls "the Cookie Lady."

Flashbacks: Young Raymond (Daniel Hansen).

DEBRA LOUISE BARONE

Parents: Warren (Robert Culp) and Lois Whelan (Cathryn Damon).

Place of Birth: Connecticut in 1960.

Maiden Name: Debra Whelan.

Sister: Jennifer Whelan (Ashley Crow), a nun.

Childhood: As a teenager, she and her mother would go to Manhattan for a mother-and-daughter day of shopping. She spent her summers as a kid at Lake Sagatuck.

Education: Fairfield Grammar School; St. John's University (studied behavioral psychology and wrote a thesis on her favorite book, *To Kill a Mockingbird*).

First Meeting: Debra met Raymond while in college (she ordered a bed from Claude's Futons, and Raymond was sent to install it). They married after graduating and set up housekeeping in a small apartment in Lynbrook. Raymond became a sportswriter at *Newsday*, while Debra found work in a Manhattan public relations firm. It was at this time that she became pregnant and quit her job when her daughter Ally was born (1991). Twins

Doris Roberts, Peter Boyle, Sawyer Sweeten, Ray Romano, Sullivan Sweeten, Brad Garrett, Patricia Heaton, and Madylin Sweeten. *Tony Esparza/CBS/ Photofest © Tony Esparza/CBS*

Jeffrey (Sawyer Sweeten) and Michael (Sullivan Sweeten) were born several years later. When the house next to Raymond's parents became available, she and Raymond purchased it. He proposed to Debra on Valentine's Day and believes "I inherited a freak show next door" (referring to his parents).

Trait: Moody and critical; has a knack for being late for any occasion (which makes Raymond uneasy, as he needs to be on time).

Favorite Flower: Lilies of the valley.

Famous For: Her lemon chicken (although Marie thinks Debra is incapable of cooking a decent meal or even caring for her children).

Volunteer Work: St. Theresa's Hospital. She also held a temporary job as a copywriter at the Charlotte Sterling public relations firm in Manhattan.

Hobby: Enjoys Craftsman furniture.

ROBERT CHARLES BARONE

Birthday: April 6, 1957 (four years older than Raymond).

Marital Status: Divorced from Joanna Glotz, a stripper in an Atlantic City nightclub who left him for a man he arrested.

Occupation: A sergeant (then lieutenant) with the New York Police Department. He became a police officer in 1977. When he teaches traffic school, he does so with the help of a dummy he calls Traffic Cop Timmy. Robert now stands 6 feet, 8½ inches tall. At age 11, he was teased as the tallest kid in his grammar school class. One rainy day, Raymond stole Robert's rubber boots, and Robert had to walk to school without them. His shoes became rain soaked and his classmates called him "Sashquash" when he walked. From that moment on, he vowed to fight crime. To make extra money, Robert sold Castle Door alarm systems.

Belief: Everything good happens to Raymond, and everything bad happens to him.

Habit: Touching his food to his chin before eating it.

Education: Hillcrest High School; St. John's University.

Childhood: Played drums but had to give them up because of nosebleeds. He took opera lessons for a year and suffered his most embarrassing moment as an infant: his mother had wanted a daughter and dressed him in a pink dress and pretended he was her little girl. In grammar school, Robert wrote "The View from Up Here" for the school newspaper.

Secret Ambition: To become a dancer (his father wanted him to get a job at Carvel so he could get free Fudgie the Whale ice cream cakes).

Favorite Foods: Spareribs and key lime pie. He is afraid to eat out because he fears busboys.

Favorite Barber Shop: The Hair Barn.

Quirk: Separates his Good & Plenty candy into "the pink good ones" and "the white ones, the plenty."

Injury: Gored in the butt by "Nestor the Happy Bull" when he broke up an illegal rodeo.

Awards: Police accommodation recipient for perfect attendance three years in a row (1994–1996).

Police Car Code: Two-Three Sergeant. He usually rides with Sergeant Judy Potter (Sherri Shepherd).

Home: Robert first lived with his parents, then in his own apartment (F).

Girlfriend: Amy MacDougall. Amy was born in Pennsylvania and is the daughter of Hank (Fred Willard) and Pat (Georgia Engel) MacDougall. She has a brother, Peter (Chris Elliott), who owns a comic book store, lives at home, and has a pet cat (Miss Puss). Amy was raised by strict religious parents and, like Raymond, was preferred by her parents. She is sensitive, cries over minor incidents, and often apologizes for things she has not done. Amy and Robert marry during the seventh season and move into an apartment identified only by its door number (6).

Flashbacks: Young Robert (Ethan Glazer).

MARIE BARONE

Year of Birth: 1934.

Position: Matriarch of the Barone family (sort of self-appointed).

Personality: Passive and aggressive, making others feel uncomfortable and guilty until she gets what she wants (Debra calls her "the Guilt Bomb").

Occupation: Housewife. She previously gave piano lessons before retiring. She takes folk dancing lessons on Thursday nights.

Pride and Joy: Her cooking (she claims she cooks not from recipes "but from the heart").

Enjoyment: Looking at other people's mail and intruding in their lives; correcting Debra on everything she does.

Fear: Goes into a panic mode if someone doesn't ask for one of her recipes.

Quirk: Her living room furniture must have plastic covering the fabric.

Favorite Holidays: Thanksgiving and Christmas. She used to love Valentine's Day until she married the unromantic Frank.

Catchphrase: "I don't like that, Raymond"; "May I say something as an impartial observer?"

Relatives: Sister, Alda; niece, Stacy.

FRANCIS OSCAR "FRANK" BARONE

Year of Birth: 1932.

Parents: Joseph and Nonny Barone (who strictly disciplined him). Frank originally calls his father Alberto.

Brother: Mel Barone (Phil Leeds).

Military Service: The U.S. Army (1950–1953) during the Korean War. He often
   refers to his time in the service and how it made him a man.

Meeting: Frank met Marie in 1955, and he immediately fell in love with her cooking (seemingly the only reason why he married her). She prepared braciole
   (an Italian meat dish), and he has been in love with her ever since. They
   married in 1957.

Favorite Holiday: Thanksgiving (his favorite part of the turkey is "the part that
   goes over the fence last—the caboose").

Belief: The only way to do things is to do it his way.

Occupation: Bookkeeper with Pelk Accounting (although when Frank mentions
   the company name, it sounds like Polk Accounting), then real estate agent
   (sold Raymond their house across the street from him and Marie).

Religion: Italian Catholic (like the rest of the family). He is an usher at Our Lady
   of Faith Church.

Car: A 1972 Plymouth Valiant (plate W7F 540).

Catchphrases: "Jeez Alou" (refers to 1960s baseball player Jesus Alou); "Holy
   crap!" (said when something goes wrong).

Favorite Movie: Patton.

Published Story: His war experiences appeared in the "Humor in Uniform" section of *Reader's Digest* magazine.

Trait: Stubborn and lazy (enjoys being in the kitchen, reading a newspaper, and
   being close to the refrigerator); doesn't like to show people he has a soft side
   (as he always appears gruff).

Fantasy Woman: Harriet Lichman (Marie's bridge partner).

ALLISON "ALLY" BARONE

Relationship: Raymond and Debra's eldest child (born in 1991 in Lynbrook,
   New York).

Education: Our Lady of Faith Elementary School (where she played a yam in the
   school's Thanksgiving Day play).

Favorite Doll: Savannah.

Favorite Breakfast Cereal: Flutie Flakes (later Post Alpha Bits).

Membership: The Frontier Scouts; the Lynbrook T-ball team (Nemo's Pizza
   Parlor sponsors it).

Favorite Movie: Beauty and the Beast (Disney cartoon version).

Note: Each episode ends with a plate of food being offered to the viewer. Ray
Romano's real-life daughter (Alexandra Romano) plays the role of Molly, Ally's
friend. In the pilot episode, twins Geoffrey and Michael are called Matthew and
Gregory (played by Drew and Justin Ferreira). The large wooden spoon and fork
on the wall of Marie's kitchen often switch places.

Frasier
(NBC, 1993–2004)

Cast: Kelsey Grammer (Frasier Crane), David Hyde Pierce (Niles Crane), John Mahoney (Martin Crane), Jan Leeves (Daphne Moon), Peri Gilpin (Roz Doyle), Bebe Neuwirth (Lilith Sternin).

Basis: A psychiatrist's (Frasier Crane's) efforts to deal with all the situations that surround him, especially those of his brother, Niles, and father, Martin. The program is a spin-off from *Cheers*.

FRASIER WINSLOW CRANE

Prior History from Cheers: After acquiring his degree, Frasier moved from Seattle to Boston to begin his practice. He found relief from the pressures of work by frequenting a bar called Cheers. While he dated bar waitress Diane Chambers (Shelley Long), he married the somber-looking Lilith Sternin, who, according to Frasier, "rules the roost in her bra and panties." He collects first-edition books and considers himself "the solver of all problems personal." He conducts traveling self-help seminars called "The Crane Train to Mental Well-Being" and with Lilith had a son named Frederick (who was born in the backseat of a taxicab). He has a dog named Pavlov, Charles Dickens is his favorite author, and he has a spider collection. On *Cheers*, Frasier mentioned that his father, a scientist, was deceased and that he was an only child; on *Frasier*, his father, Martin, a retired police officer, lives with him, and he has a brother, Niles. As *Cheers* ended, Frasier and Lilith divorce (with Lilith retaining custody of Frederick, although Frasier has visiting rights), and Frasier moves back to Seattle (feeling that his life in Boston had become stagnant).

Place of Birth: Seattle, Washington, in December 1952.

Parents: Martin (John Mahoney) and Hester Crane (Nancy Marchand).

Education: Bryce Academy; Harvard University (majored in psychology with a minor in music; was a member of the crew team); Oxford University (acquired his degree). At Bryce, he accidentally joined the girls' soccer team when he signed up in the "F-List" (the "F" for "female," not "freshman," as he thought).

Occupation: Private-practice psychiatrist; host of *The Frasier Crane Show,* a daily (2 p.m. to 5 p.m.) call-in advice program on KACL 780 on the AM radio dial. He first ended his program with "Good day and good mental health"; later it was "Good day Seattle and good mental health." He was also the host of the TV series *A.M. Seattle* when his radio show was canceled for a program called *Car Chat.* A classical music piece, Bartok's "Concerto in C," opens his radio program.

Inspiration: Frasier attributes to his mother, Hester, his inspiration for becoming a psychiatrist. When Frasier was eight years old, the school bully threw his book *The Fountainhead* under a bus. When Frasier came home from school crying, his mother explained to him why children are so mean. It was then that he says, "I became a student of humanity." This is later contradicted when Frasier mentions that he hoped to become an actor but his father (when said to be a scientist on *Cheers*) persuaded him to become a psychiatrist.

Ancestry: Martin possesses an old clock that both Frasier and Niles consider hideous but is believed to be related to their ancestors and royalty (it was actually stolen by Frasier's great-great grandmother from the daughter of Tsar Alexander II, for whom she worked as a maid). It is later revealed that this relative also worked in Manhattan as a lady of the evening. Thus, they are not descended from royalty but are, as Frasier says, "from thieves and whores."

Address: The Elliott Bay Towers (Apartment 1901).

Favorite Strategy Game: Chess.

Musical Ability: Sings and plays the piano.

IQ: 129.

Awards: The Seattle Broadcaster's Lifetime Achievement Award; the Stephen R. Schaefer Lifetime Achievement Award.

Favorite Eatery: Stefano's Restaurant (where a caricature of him appears on the wall).

Favorite Coffeehouse: Café Nervosa.

Car License Plate: 330 WPT.

TV Commercial Work: Spokesman for Redwood Hot Tubs.

Belief: Eating a high-fiber breakfast, "so I can start the day off right."

First Love: His babysitter, Ronnie Lawrence (who is now his father's romantic interest).

Wives: Frasier was first married to Nanette Goodsmith (also called Nanette Guzman; played by Dina Sybey, Emma Thompson, and Laurie Metcalf), a woman who works as a children's entertainer called "Nanny Gee." He was next married to Lilith Sternin. After their divorce, he began dating Charlotte Connor (Laura Linney), a matchmaker (owner of Charlotte's Web) and leaves to join her in Chicago, as seen in the final episode.

Flashbacks: Young Hester (Rita Wilson).

David Hyde Pierce, Jane Leeves, Peri Gilpin, Eddie, Kelsey Grammer, and John Mahoney. *NBC/Photofest © NBC*

NILES CRANE

Parents: Hester Crane (a psychiatrist) and Martin Crane (a police detective).

Place of Birth: Seattle, Washington, in 1957.

Relationship: Frasier's younger brother.

Occupation: Psychiatrist (specializes in marriage and family; he says of his occupation that it is "the saving grace of my life"). He also serves on the board of the American Psychiatric Association.

Address: As a child, Niles mentions living on Wallace Lane in Seattle; at this time, he and Frasier wrote a series of detective yarns called "The Crane Boys Mystery Stories." He now lives at the Montana Hotel in Seattle.

Ex-Wives: The neurotic, well-dressed, very thin, very beautiful but never-seen Maris. Niles next elopes with Melissa "Mel" Karnofsky, Maris's plastic surgeon, but the marriage ends after two days when Niles realizes he loves Daphne Moon, his father's live-in physical therapist, and marries her in 2002 (as the series ends, Daphne and Niles become the parents of a baby they name David). During his divorce from Maris, Niles was forced to temporarily abandon his apartment and moved into Apartment 8 of the Shangri La Apartments at 52 Elm Street.

Pet Parrot: Baby.

IQ: 156.

Education: Bryce Academy (where he was an unusually sensitive child and picked on by bullies); Yale University (a member of the Phi Beta Kappa fraternity); Cambridge University.

Trait: Allergic to parchment. ("My ear itches. I sneeze and I have a tough time at the library.") He spends $250 for a haircut, has a fear of authority figures and phobias about insects, and is afraid of "Chair Clusters" (chairs being placed too close to one another). His nose tends to bleed if he lies, he faints at the sight of blood, and he suffers from stress (has panic attacks and hyperventilates). He is a master speller (almost won a national spelling bee as a child) and is annoyed by spelling errors (he will correct misspelled graffiti when he sees it).

Favorite Eateries: Stefano's Restaurant and Café Nervosa (where he often orders a latte "with a whisper of cinnamon" and sometimes adds nutmeg or chocolate shavings).

Character: Like Frasier, he is snobbish and fussy. He has gourmet tastes (especially for French cuisine) and likes fine wine, opera, classical music (plays the piano), and the theater. He is often seen in double-breasted suits (sometimes with Trafalgar suspenders).

Business: He and Frasier attempted to run their own eatery, the Happy Brothers Restaurant.

Car: A Mercedes-Benz with the license plate SHRINK.

Sports: While Niles and Frasier enjoy attending squash games, Niles is not sports inclined. He is, however, a proficient marksman and well versed in fencing. He has also taken lessons in kickboxing and karate.

MARTIN CRANE

Place of Birth: Seattle in 1932. He is the son of a police officer.

Marital Status: Widower. He met his late wife, Hester Palmer (a forensic psychiatrist), in 1952 at a crime scene where she was hired by the police to work on a profile of the killer. On their wedding anniversary, Hester, who passed away in 1987, would make gingerbread cookies shaped like corpses.

Brother: Walt (married to Zora, a Greek woman); nephew, Nikos (Walter and Zora's son).

Occupation: Retired Seattle Police Department detective (now disabled after being shot in the hip while investigating a convenience store robbery when he was 62). In his youth, he was a mounted police officer and rode a horse named Agadies. He was also with Vice Homicide. He now works as a security guard for Keckner Security. His injury prohibits him from living alone, and he accepted Frasier's invitation to live with him.

Romantic Interest: Ronnie Lawrence (Wendie Malick), a girl who once babysat Frasier and Niles. Ronnie plays the piano at the Rendezvous Room of the Wellington Hotel. She also recorded a record album for seven-year-olds called *Ronnie Lawrence—Mood Swings*; it sold seven copies.

Obsession: Solving a 20-year-old murder case called "the Weeping Lotus Murder" (a hooker was killed, and someone tried to stuff her body into a bowling ball bag; Martin feels he is overlooking a crucial clue but can't figure out what it is). He keeps the promise he made to the victim's mother (finding the killer) by eventually solving the case.

Military Service: The Korean War (he joined the army when he was 19 years old).

Favorite Sport: Fishing. Each year, he embarks on a trip to Lake Noomeheegen for the trout.

Secret: Martin has a shoebox that contains 30-year-old songs that he wrote for Frank Sinatra but never sent.

Pet Dog: Eddie, a Jack Russell terrier that has problems with Frasier and constantly stares at him. Eddie has a pigeon friend (Barney) who visits him on the patio, and the two stare at each other.

Apartment Disgrace: An eyesore of a recliner that Martin loves but Frasier hates (as it clashes with his decor).

Favorite Drink: Ballantine Beer.

Favorite Hangout: McGinty's Bar.

Sports: A fan of the New York Yankees, Seattle Seahawks, and Seattle Mariners.

Character: Completely opposite of Frasier and Niles (as they take after their mother). He is much more down to earth and often a bit gruff and has a difficult time expressing himself. He does not share the same interests as his sons and wishes they were more like him (loving sports and the great outdoors).

ROZ DOYLE

Relationship: Frasier's radio show producer.
Place of Birth: Wisconsin in 1964.
Mother: Joanna Doyle (Eva Marie Saint), a Wisconsin attorney general.
Sister: Denise (who Roz believes has the perfect life).
Character: Through dialogue, it is revealed that Roz has a very active social (and sexual) life (which can especially be seen through Niles's snide remarks). She has a tattoo of the cartoon character Tweety Bird on her upper thigh and is very worried about her physical appearance as she ages. Although she has numerous relationships, she also worries that she will never find the right man and get married (she even claims to have what men normally have—a "black book" of the men she has dated). By one such fling (with a 20-year-old college student), Roz becomes pregnant and gives birth to a girl she names Alice. She is close to Martin (and the only character who calls him "Marty") and joins him in his weekly poker games.
Final Episode: Roz becomes the station manager of KACL radio.

DAPHNE MOON

Place of Birth: Manchester, England, in 1969.
Parents: Gertrude (Millicent Martin) and Harry Moon (Brian Cox).
Brothers: Of the eight, only three are seen: Simon Moon (Anthony LaPaglia), Stephen Moon (Richard E. Grant), and Michael Moon (Robbie Coltrane).
Position: Martin's live-in physical therapist and housekeeper. On her arrival at Frasier's apartment, Niles is immediately drawn to her but is too insecure to even approach her (it took him more than six years to build up the courage to ask her out on a date); they married on September 24, 2002 (in a small ceremony in Reno, Nevada). Daphne left England to get away from her domineering parents. She found her way to Seattle and first worked in a convenience store.
As a Child: The star of *Mind Your Knickers*, a British sitcom wherein she played Emma, a 12-year-old girl attending a private all-girls boarding school. Her role ended when she began to develop and could no longer play a 12 year old.
Trait: A dart and billiards champion; a member of the Manchester Light Opera Works. She is also an expert shoplifter and earned money by training rats for shows.

Character: Easily exasperated but a kind, down-to-earth young woman. She has a habit of telling long, boring stories about her family; believes in the supernatural; and considers herself to have slight psychic abilities. While she is a good housekeeper, she is a poor cook. She can also be seen as a bit irritated by both Frasier's and Niles's snobbish attitude.

The Fresh Prince of Bel Air
(NBC, 1990–1996)

Cast: Will Smith (himself); Karyn Parsons (Hilary Banks); Alfonso Ribeiro (Carlton Banks); Tatyana M. Ali (Ashley Banks); James Avery (Philip Banks); Janet Hubert, then Daphne Maxwell Reid (Vivian Banks); Joseph Marcell (Geoffrey).

Basis: Will Smith, a teenager growing up on the wrong side of the tracks, is given a second chance when he is sent by his mother (Viola) to live with his uncle Philip and his wife, Vivian, in hopes of straightening out his life. Philip and Vivian are the parents of Hilary, Carlton, and Ashley.

WILLIAM "WILL" SMITH
Place of Birth: West Philadelphia on July 3, 1973.

Education: West Philly High School (it was so bad that he carried his books in a pizza box so no one would know he was attempting to learn something). In California: the Bel Air Academy, then the University of Los Angeles.

Jobs: Car salesman at Mulholland Motors; waiter at the Brawny Deep (dressed as a pirate); waiter at the Peacock Shop (the college hangout); waiter at Chesler's Touchdown (the off-campus sports bar); assistant talent coordinator (books guests) for the TV talk show *Hilary* (which stars his cousin Hilary Banks). During the summer of 1994 when Will returned to Philadelphia to visit his mother, he worked as a cook/waiter at Duke's House of Cheese Steaks. It was stated that when NBC brass "realized" the series title was *The Fresh Prince of Bel Air*, the NBC Retrieval Team went to Philly and returned him to Bel Air.

Member: The L.A. Recreational Center.

Residence: Will first lived in the Banks family mansion, then in the pool house out back. He calls Philip "Uncle Phil."

TV Appearance: Danced on *Soul Train*.

Author: Attempted to write a book called *Celebrity Houses at Night*.

Impressing Girls: Joined the Bel Air Poetry Club pretending to be the famous poet Raphael De La Ghetto.

Flashbacks: Young Will (Floyd Myers Jr.).

Joseph Marcell, Alfonso Ribeiro, Karyn Parsons, Tatyana Ali, Janet Hubert, James Avery, and Will Smith. *NBC/Photofest © NBC*

HILARY BANKS

Place of Birth: Bel Air, California, in 1969 (the oldest of the children).

Trait: Beautiful, always fashionably dressed, extremely feminine, but also extremely conceited and a bit dense.

Childhood: Hilary grew up in the lap of luxury and was given anything she wanted. She tried to become a ballerina but stopped dancing when "I thought I would get feet like Fred Flintstone." Her attempt to play the violin also ended in disaster ("It irritated my chin"). She was a cheerleader in high school but quit when "they expected me to cheer at away games and travel by bus."

Education: The Bel Air Academy; the University of California, Los Angeles (UCLA; dropped out when she found the work too difficult).

Measurements: 34-25-34. She stands 5 feet, 7 inches tall.

Jobs: Salesgirl at the Bel Air Mall; assistant to Marissa Redmond, a has-been movie star; a position with Delectable Eats Catering; weather girl on KFB-TV, Channel 8's *News in Action* program (Hilary dressed in skimpy outfits and had virtually no knowledge of weather forecasting; this fostered angry protests from viewers who formed the "I Hate Hilary Newsletter"). Her gorgeous looks, however, did get her the job as host of *Hilary,* her own TV talk show.

Favorite Beauty Salon: Black Beauty.

Magazine Layout: Hilary posed nude for a *Playboy* magazine layout called "Warm Fronts" showcasing weather girls (Hilary's breasts were covered by clouds).

Favorite Magazines: She and *Seventeen.*

Trait: A knack for losing her house keys (she has 30 copies made each month and hopes someone will return at least one set, as she has her address on each key). She never wears the same outfit twice.

Final Episode: Hilary relocates to New York City when production of *Hilary* is moved to Manhattan.

CARLTON BANKS

Date of Birth: August 4, 1974, in Bel Air, California (the second-born child).

Childhood Dog: Scruffy.

Education: Bel Air Academy (has a 3.9 grade-point average; a member of the poetry and glee clubs); the University of Los Angeles. He hopes to become a lawyer like his father and first mentions Princeton, then Harvard, as his dream school. He feels he has an advantage over other applicants, as he has been faxing Santa Claus for years asking for a Princeton entrance gift certificate.

Job: Manager of the Peacock Stop, the college bookstore.

First Crush: The character Tootie (from the series *The Facts of Life*).

Favorite Breakfast Cereal: Fruity Pebbles.

Belief: He is a great singer and hopes to break into show business as Carlton Banks, Soul Brother Number One; that the world has gone crazy "since M&M's introduced the blue ones." He also thought he was a great dancer but managed to embarrass himself with his weird dancing on *The Soul Train 25th Anniversary Show.*

Flashbacks: Young Carlton (Gary LeRoi).

ASHLEY BANKS

Place of Birth: Bel Air, California, in 1979 (the youngest of the children).

Education: The Hollywood Preparatory Institute; the Bel Air Academy. Ashley was said to be a brilliant student but transferred to the less prestigious (and easier) Morris High School. At this time, she held a job at a mall food court corn dog stand and attempted to become a fashion model.

Character: Not as dedicated to school work as Carlton (more like Hilary) and also more outgoing and fun loving than Carlton (more like Will). As Hilary says of her, "She is dating right and becoming as beautiful as I am."

Musical Ability: Plays the violin. Ashley is also a talented singer and dancer. She performed on *The Soul Train 25th Anniversary Show* and made a recording of a song she wrote called "Make Up Your Mind." Will became her manager but also ruined her chances at stardom when he had radio stations continually play the song (so much so that fans became sick of hearing it).

Favorite Video Game: Tetris.

Most Embarrassing Moment: Ashley, sitting with her legs crossed at an academic awards ceremony, was called on to receive an English citation. She got up, but her leg had fallen asleep, and she fell on her face.

Trait: Loves to throw parties (especially when her parents are not home).

Final Episode: Ashley decides to attend the School for the Performing Arts in New York City (where she becomes roommates with Hilary when her TV show is moved to Manhattan).

Flashbacks: Young Ashley (Anastasia N. Ali).

PHILIP ZEKE BANKS

Place of Birth: A farm in Yamcrow, Nebraska, on January 30 (year not mentioned; he is a Capricorn).

Parents: Hattie (Virginia Capers) and Joe Banks (Gilbert Lewis).

Childhood: Had a pet pig named Melvin and won the Young Farmers of America Pig Passing Contest four years in a row. In later years, he was the first black president of the Young Farmers of America.

Education: Yamcrow Elementary School; Princeton University; Harvard Law School. He also mentions that he was accepted into Yale University, Stanford University, and the University of Philadelphia.

Occupation: Attorney with the law firm of Furth & Meyer; he is later appointed a judge. He is also the part owner of a record store called the Sound Explosion.

Favorite Hobby: Pool (he has a pool cue he calls "Lucille").

Award: The Urban Spirit Award for his community work. As a lawyer, Philip fought for equal housing, affirmative action, and better health care for African Americans. He was also an activist in his youth, witnessing riots in Harlem and Birmingham.

Address: Not mentioned by name, but he lives two houses from former President Ronald Reagan and his wife, Nancy ("We even share the same pool man").

VIVIAN BANKS

Place of Birth: Los Angeles.

Parents: George and Madelyn Richards.

Sisters: Viola "Vy" Smith (Vernee Watson); Janice Smith (Charlayne Woodard, then Pam Grier); Helen Smith (Jenifer Lewis).

Education: The Bel Air Academy; UCLA.

First Meeting: The TV show *Soul Train* (where she and Philip danced). Sometime later, when they again appeared on the show, Philip used the program's game segment scramble board (to unscramble letters to identify a celebrity) to ask Vivian to marry him.

Occupation: Substitute teacher at the Bel Air Academy, the University of Southern California, the University of Los Angeles, and UCLA.

Favorite Ice Cream Flavor: Vanilla Swiss Almond.

Character: A strict parent (more so than Philip, who is stern but less inclined to punish his children, especially Hilary, who uses sob stories to win him over). As played by Janet Hubert, she was easily upset, very demanding at times, and not the typical sitcom mother. When Daphne Maxwell Reid became Vivian, the character mellowed somewhat, became more approachable for her family, and was more in line with the sitcom mothers of the past.

Note: Vivian gives birth to a fourth child, Nicholas Andrew, on February 22, 1993. Ross Bagley plays the role (in the final two seasons).

GEOFFREY
Born in England in the late 1940s, Geoffrey is the Banks's prim and proper butler. He is often cynical and sarcastic and calls Will "Master William" (Will calls him "G"), and it appeared he was most fond of Ashley. He is a graduate of Oxford University and first became a butler to a Lord Fowler. He also served as a butler to the rock band Led Zeppelin, was a sparring partner to film action star Chuck Norris, and was even an Olympic torch runner. Geoffrey's personality changes often, his attitude being set by which character he is interacting with at the time. Geoffrey enjoys "loosening up" at the Circle M Dude Ranch on his weekends off.

Friends
(NBC, 1994–2004)

Cast: Courteney Cox (Monica Geller), Jennifer Aniston (Rachel Green), Lisa Kudrow (Phoebe Buffay), Matthew Perry (Chandler Bing), Matt LeBlanc (Joey Tribbiani), David Schwimmer (Ross Geller).

Basis: Six friends (Monica, Rachel, Phoebe, Chandler, Joey, and Ross) and their experiences living in New York City. Central Perk, a coffeehouse in Manhattan, is their hangout.

MONICA GELLER

Parents: Jack (Elliott Gould) and Judy Geller (Christina Pickles).

Brother: Ross Geller. Because she and Ross often bickered, their father created "The Geller Cup," a trophy that was awarded to the winner of a series of events that were held each Thanksgiving and meant to ease the tension between them.

Place of Birth: Long Island, New York, in April 1969.

Nicknames: "Harmonica" (by her father); "Monicow" (in high school); "Mother Hen" (by friends).

Religion: Jewish.

Childhood Trauma: Overweight due to her love of food. It was when Chandler remarked about Monica's weight (225 pounds) that she took control of her life. She mentions she didn't learn how to tell time until she was 13 ("It's hard for some people").

Imaginary Friend: Jarrod.

Measurements: 35-24-34. She stands 5 feet, 5 inches tall; has blue eyes and brown hair; and wears a size 2 dress and a size 7 shoe.

Education: Lincoln High School.

Address: An apartment (20) at Grove and Bedford streets in Manhattan's Greenwich Village. Monica sublets the apartment from her grandmother (who moved to Florida).

Occupation: Chef. Her love for food was her inspiration, and she says, "It began when I got my first Easy Bake Oven and opened Easy Monica's Bakery" (Ross called her "the unbaked batter eater" because she couldn't wait for the lightbulb to cook her brownies and she would eat the raw dough). Monica worked as a chef at the Iridium Restaurant (quit due to poor wages), the Café des Artistes (fired for accepting a gift from a food vendor), Alessandrio's Restaurant (earned extra money as the food critic for the *Chelsea Reporter*; received a penny a word for her reviews), and the Javu Restaurant. She was also a roller-skating waitress (with blonde wig and padded bra) at the 1950s-themed Moon Dance Diner, partners with Phoebe in a short-lived catering business, and creative chef for an unnamed company (where she was hired to create meals from substitute food ingredients).

Character: Very frugal, competitive, and neat. She is also bossy, obsessed with cleanliness, and often talks loud. She makes her own household cleaner ("ammonia, lemon juice, and a secret ingredient"), cleans the cleaning supplies, and vacuums her large vacuum cleaner with a Dust Buster. She is famous for her Thanksgiving Day feasts. (Ross claims that Monica makes the best turkey sandwiches in the world. Her secret is "the moist maker—a gravy-soaked slice of bread in the middle of two slices of turkey and the outer bread.") She reads *In Style* magazine and numbers the bottoms of her coffee mugs ("so I can keep track of them"). The one thing she refuses to make is chocolate pie ("I ate so many of them that I got sick"). She loves to show cleavage and believes her breasts get her attention.

Secret Shame: A closet full of junk (where she stores items that make her apartment neat).

Pet Peeve: Detests seeing animals dressed as humans.

Boyfriend, Then Husband: Chandler Bing. They married on May 17, 2001, and later adopted twins (Jack and Erica). On January 15, 2004, they announced they were moving to Westchester, and the final episode shows them preparing to leave Manhattan. Joey presided over the marriage ceremony (became a minister of sorts when Monica couldn't find an appropriate minister). Chandler cringes when he and Monica are referred to as "the Bings."

Courteney Cox, Matt LeBlanc, Lisa Kudrow, Matthew Perry, Jennifer Aniston, and David Schwimmer. *NBC/Photofest © NBC*

Relatives: Grandmother, Althea (on her mother's side); nephew, Ben Geller; niece, Emma Geller-Green; cousin, Cassie Geller.

RACHEL KAREN GREEN

Parents: Sandra (Marlo Thomas) and Dr. Leonard Green (Ron Liebman).

Sisters: Amy Green (Christina Applegate), Jill Green (Reese Witherspoon).

Place of Birth: Long Island, New York, in May 1970 (1971 is suggested in another episode; February on Valentine's Day in another; she mentions being an Aquarius, which would make the February date correct).

Education: Lincoln High School.

Address: An apartment at Grove and Bedford streets in Greenwich Village (which she originally shared with Monica).

Character: A strikingly beautiful girl who cares about her appearance and what others think. She buys 30 fashion magazines a month just to keep up with what's in and what's not. Rachel is always elegantly dressed but fears that people will find out she is not perfect: as a teenager, she had plastic surgery to fix her nose; she felt it was not right for her face. She can be seen as somewhat spoiled and self-centered but sweet and gentle to her friends; some people see her as a pushover and take advantage of her.

Bra Size: 32C. She shows ample cleavage and says, "I'd get more attention if I were a 36D." She has blue eyes and brown hair and stands 5 feet, 5 inches tall.

Childhood Traumas: While playing, her hair became entangled in the chains of a swing. She cried for days after her mother had to cut her hair to set her free and made one side shorter than the other. As one of the most beautiful girls in high school, Rachel suffered a second trauma when Ross, liking Rachel but feeling she did not care for him, started the I Hate Rachel Green Club and spread a rumor that she had male and female reproductive organs that tagged her as "the hermaphrodite cheerleader from Long Island."

Plus Toy: As a child, Rachel had a pink pony she called "Cotton."

Occupation: Rachel has a flair for fashion but first worked as a waitress at Central Perk. She quit for a job a Fortunato Fashions. This opened the doorway for her position as a junior miss (assistant buyer), then personal shopper (helps people shop), at Bloomingdale's Department Store. She next worked as a fashion consultant (then merchandising head) for Ralph Lauren (where she received a 45 percent discount on clothes). When Rachel is fired from Ralph Lauren for not being a team player, she is hired by Louis Viton Fashions.

Failed Writing Attempt: A novel called *A Woman Undone.*

Favorite Movie: Weekend at Bernie's (although she tells people *Dangerous Liaisons*).

The Unexpected: After a one-night stand with Ross, Rachel discovers that she is pregnant. On May 16, 2002, she gives birth to a daughter whom she and Ross name Emma (although she had contemplated Isabelle or Delilah; Emma was born at St. Vincent's Hospital and won first prize in the Grand Supreme Little Darling Contest baby pageant). The final episode finds Rachel giving up a job offer in Paris to stay in New York with Ross to raise Emma.

Fear: Turtles.

Relatives: Grandmother, Ida Green; great aunt, Muriel.

PHOEBE BUFFAY

Parents: Phoebe and her twin sister, Ursula, were born to Frank Buffay and his mistress, Phoebe Abbott. When Frank's wife Lily saw that Phoebe was unfit to raise the twins, she and Frank adopted them. In another episode, Phoebe explains that she was raised by her grandmother after her stepmother (Phoebe), a drug dealer, killed herself (by placing her head in the oven) and her father (Frank) deserted the family before she was born.

Childhood: Phoebe grew up on the streets of Manhattan and by the age of 14 lived in the back of a burnt-out Buick La Sabre. Her "career" was mugging people (one of whom was Ross, from whom she took the comic book he created, *Science Boy*). Phoebe also mentions that she lived with "an albino man who washed windows outside the Port Authority" and "a guy named Sidney who talked to his hand." It was when she met and befriended Monica that her life changed for the better.

Twin Sister: Ursula Buffay (Lisa Kudrow). She is somewhat dim-witted, works as a waitress at Riff's Bar in Manhattan (as seen on the series *Mad about You*), and starred in the X-rated film *Buffay the Vampire Slayer*.

Half Brother: Frank. She became the surrogate mother for him and his wife Alice (giving birth to triplets named Frank Jr., Leslie, and Chandler). It was during her pregnancy that Phoebe had a craving for meat that forced her to temporarily give up her vegetarian lifestyle.

Place of Birth: New York City on February 16, 1968.

Nickname: Pheebs.

Address: 5 Morton Street, Apartment 14, in Greenwich Village.

Measurements: 36-26-35. She has blonde hair; stands 5 feet, 8 inches tall; and wears a size 6 dress and a size 9 shoe.

Occupation: Masseuse (works at the Lavender Days Health Spa). Prior to this, she was a waitress at Dairy Queen; a masseuse at Helping Hands, Inc.; a telemarketer (selling copy machine toner for Empire Office Supplies); partners with Monica in a failed catering business; and a Relax-a-Taxi driver (turning her catering van into a cab with a massage table in the back; 2X85 is the cab ID number). She also rides with her grandmother's ashes, which she has in a box under the front seat.

Character: Sweet but also a bit eccentric and vague at times. She has a tendency to shock people with her frankness and had her belief in Santa Claus shattered when Joey told her he doesn't exist. She is the most promiscuous of her friends in that she brags about casual sex. She can speak French, and her apartment features "Gladys," a three-dimensional painting she created of a woman (a doll glued against a city background) coming out of the frame. She claims to make the best oatmeal cookies in the world (but makes them only occasionally "because it wouldn't be fair to the other cookies"). She believes in reincarnation (but not the theory of evolution) and is somewhat of a psychic (things just happen by coincidence, but Phoebe believes it is due to her mystic powers). She pretended to be a vice cop with the 57th Precinct ("who worked undercover as a whore") when she found a police badge on the street.

Author: Phoebe has written 14 unpublished novels ("I've been the only one who has read them, and they have been well received"), plays the guitar, and composes folk ballads she calls "acoustic folksy stuff" ("Smelly Cat" being her most famous) that she sings at Central Perk.

Pets: Suzy (mouse) and Bob (rat), which visit her apartment on occasion.

Abilities: Can read Joey's mind, breaks up with boyfriends without hurting their feelings, recalls her past lives, reads tea leaves, and senses the auras of other people.

Secret: "I have a deep dark secret: I married a gay Canadian [Duncan] so he could get his green card."

Marriage: After dating numerous men, Phoebe marries Mike Hannigan on February 12, 2004, and it has to be assumed they will live happily ever after as the final episode has no conclusion for Phoebe.

Relatives: Aunts, Sylvia and Mary; adoptive grandmother, Frances; half sister-in-law, Alice Knight; father-in-law, Theodore Hannigan; mother-in-law, Bitsy Hannigan.

CHANDLER MURIEL BING

Parents: Nora Tyler-Bing (Morgan Fairchild, author of the erotic book *Mistress Bitch*) and Charles Bing (Kathleen Turner), his transvestite father, star of the burlesque review *Viva La Gayness* (he lives in Las Vegas and works under his cross-dresser name of Helena Handbasket; the show's most famous song is "It's Raining Men").

Place of Birth: Long Island, New York, in April 1968. He is half Scottish.

Education: Lincoln High School (voted "Class Clown"; was afraid of bras ["I can't work them"]); New York University (in a band called Way No Way).

Address: An apartment house at Grove and Bedford streets.

Occupation: Data processor (as he calls it "data configuration and statistical factoring") for a large, unnamed corporation, then as a copyrighter in a similarly unnamed company on Madison Avenue.

Character: A jokester who uses humor as a defense mechanism when he becomes uneasy. He has commitment problems (being estranged from his parents) and tends to make bad first impressions and often accents the wrong words in his sentences. He hides the fact that he had (since removed) a third nipple (that he called a "nubbin") and has *TV Guide* delivered to him under the name Miss Chandler Bong. He plays tennis and ping-pong well and was called "Sir Limps-a-Lot" after Monica accidentally dropped a knife that cut off the tip of his pinkie toe.

Fear: Dogs.

Favorite TV Shows: Baywatch, Wonder Woman, and *Xena: Warrior Princess.*

Wife: Monica Geller. Before marrying Monica, Chandler suffered through three stages when he broke up with a girl: the sweatpants stage, the strip club phase, and the envisioning-himself-with-other-girls phase. Prior to Monica, Chandler is most famous for his romance with Janice (Maggie Wheeler), a girl with an annoying laugh, a nasal voice, and an irritating catchphrase ("Oh . . . my . . . God!," which she says with pauses between each word).

Adoption: On Thanksgiving Day in 2003, Chandler and Monica learn that they will become adoptive parents (Monica is unable to conceive naturally) when their surrogate mother, Erica, gives birth to twins (whom they name Erica and Jack). On January 15, 2004, Monica and Chandler announce they are moving to Westchester.

Least Favorite Holiday: Thanksgiving. In 1978, when Chandler was nine years old, he learned that his parents were divorcing (so his father could be with the family's houseboy). It left a scar on Chandler, and he can no longer celebrate the holiday in a normal manner (his special dinner on Thanksgiving is tomato soup, grilled cheese sandwiches, and a large bag of snacks called "Funyuns").

JOSEPH "JOEY" FRANCIS TRIBBIANI JR.

Parents: Joseph and Gloria Tribbiani.

Place of Birth: Queens, New York, in 1968. He is Italian American.

Sisters: Gina, Dina, Tina, Mary Angela, Mary Theresa, Cookie, and Veronica.

Childhood: Had a Cabbage Patch doll named Eliza Mae Emory, and Maurice, an imaginary space cowboy friend.

Plush Penguin Toy: Huggsy (his "bedtime penguin pal").

Occupation: Actor. His idol, Al Pacino, inspired him. His big break came "when I got the part of the butt double for Al Pacino" (in a shower scene).

Joey also worked as a Christmas elf, Christmas tree salesman, Central Perk waiter, store cologne sampler, museum tour guide, and waiter at Alessandrio's Restaurant.

Representation: The Estelle Leonard Talent Agency. June Gable plays Estelle.

Character: A bit naive, good natured, and not too bright. Joey can drink a gallon of milk in 10 seconds and eat an entire turkey in one sitting. Sharing food is against his nature (if, for example, Joey takes a girl out for dinner and she helps herself to something that is on his plate, the relationship is over). He enjoys reading comic books and playing foosball and video games.

Shoe Size: 7 ("I have surprisingly small feet").

ATM PIN Number: 5639.

Catchphrase: "How 'ya doin'?"

Favorite Foods: Sandwiches and pizza (he created "the Joey Special"—two pizzas together).

Acting Roles: "An unnamed porn movie"; a regular (as Dr. Drake Ramore) on the actual TV soap opera *Days of Our Lives* (the character was named "the Most Dateable Neurosurgeon" by *Teen Beat* magazine); guest role on *Law and Order* (although most of his scene was edited out, leaving him to appear only as a corpse); infomercial spokesman for the Milk Carton Spout; the role of Victor in an unnamed Broadway play at the Lucille Cortel Theater; the part of Mac in the TV series *Mac and Cheese* (Mac was the human assistant to Cheese, a futuristic robotic crime fighter); host of the game show *Bamboozle*; a soldier in *Over There*, a Word War I film shot at Pier 59 Studios in Manhattan. He also made a commercial for Ichabon, a lipstick for men, for Japanese TV and auditioned for the role of Mercutio in *Romeo and Juliet* under the name Holden McGroin.

Address: An apartment (19) at the corner of Grove and Bedford streets in Greenwich Village (which he shares with Chandler; he has posters of director Alfred Hitchcock and the films *Hurricane* and *Scarface* on the walls). He calls his TV set "Stevie" and his favorite recliner "Rosita." He and Chandler also have a pet chicken Joey calls "Chicken" and a duck Joey calls "Duck." Chandler calls the chicken "Our Chick" and the duck "Little Jasmine" (after Yasmine Bleeth of *Baywatch*). Joey is most fond of the "big white dog" (a plastic greyhound) in the apartment.

Joey's Fate: In the series spin-off *Joey* (which begins where the final episode of *Friends* leaves off), Joey has given up his role on *Days of Our Lives* and moved to Los Angeles to further his career. He acquires an agent and moves into an apartment (7) that is close to his older sister Gina (Drea de Matteo) and Gina's 20-year-old son, Michael (Paulo Costanzo). He feels that his face is his fortune and acquires a role on the series *Deep Powder* ("*Baywatch* on snow").

ROSS GELLER

Parents: Jack and Judy Geller.

Place of Birth: Long Island, New York, on October 18. He is considered a medical marvel because Judy had been diagnosed with an inability to conceive.

Sister: Monica Geller.

Childhood: He and Monica would compete against each other for "the Geller Award" (a troll doll nailed to a piece of wood).

Character: Polite, caring, a bit clumsy, and socially awkward. He is intensely interested in science and as a teenager created a comic book called *Science Boy* (who had a superhuman thirst for knowledge). He is cheap, steals things like towels and soap from hotels, celebrates with inexpensive Israeli champagne, and has his hair cut at Super Cuts (a bargain hair salon). He hates to be wrong about something and has an annoying habit of correcting people's grammar.

Education: Lincoln High School (where he wore a jacket that proclaimed "Geology Rocks") and eventually developed an interest in dinosaurs. He majored in anthropology in college (New York University, where he played drums and created "wordless sound poems" [music with sound effects; each song ended with an explosion]).

Occupation: Paleontologist with the Museum of Natural History (also called the Museum of Prehistoric History); he later teaches paleontology at New York University.

Address: An apartment in Manhattan's West Village.

Obsession: Aviator Amelia Earhart (he is determined to find out what happened to her after her plane disappeared in the 1930s).

Dislike: Ice cream.

Fear: Spiders.

Pet Monkey: Maurice (later given to the San Diego Zoo when he became unruly).

Beeper Number: 555-JIMBO.

Marital Status: Divorced from Carol Willick (Jane Sibbett), the mother of Ben (Cole Sprouse). Carol left Ross for her female lover, Susan Bunch (Jessica Hecht). Ross then hooked up with Rachel, and together they had a daughter they named Emma (Heather Simms, then Noelle Sheldon).

Relatives: Grandmother, Althea; cousin, Cassie Geller.

Good Sports
(CBS, 1991)

Cast: Farrah Fawcett (Gayle Roberts), Ryan O'Neal (Bobby Tannen).
Basis: The relationship between Gayle Roberts and Bobby Tannen, the argumentative costars of an all-sports cable network program.

GAYLE ROBERTS

Place of Birth: California in 1951 (she is 40 years old when the series begins).
Real Name: Gayle Gordon (she changed her last name to Roberts to avoid being confused with Gale Gordon, Lucille Ball's costar on her TV series *The Lucy Show, Here's Lucy,* and *Life with Lucy*).
Address: An apartment at the Landmark Building in Los Angeles.
Measurements: 36-24-35. She is 5 feet, 7 inches tall and wears a size 6 dress and a size 8 shoe.
Occupation: Cohost (with Bobby) of *Sports Central,* an information program on the Rappaport Broadcasting System ASCN (All Sports Cable Network). Gayle also hosts *Sports Chat* (interviews) and *Sports Brief* (updates).
Called: "The Doris Day of the Sports World" (for her friendly smile and wholesome personality).
Childhood: Said to be a very beautiful baby "who grew up to become a very beautiful woman." She was a sports fanatic and tried to play baseball and football with the boys but was most often rejected. When she thought that her dream of playing sports could not happen, she turned her attention to modeling and appeared on the covers of such magazines as *Redbook, Mademoiselle, Vogue, Seventeen,* and *TV Guide.*
Life Changer: When Gayle's picture appeared on the cover of *Sports Illustrated,* the sexy pose so impressed ASCN owner R. J. Rappaport that he immedi-

ately hired her as the network's first female sportscaster. She was an instant hit with the channel's male sports fans.

Charity Work: Volunteers for the Los Angeles Mission.

Pet Goldfish: Frankie.

Favorite Poem: "Fog" by Carl Sandburg (her favorite poet).

Allergy: Gayle is allergic to goat cheese and will not eat baby back ribs.

Most Hated Word: "I hate the word 'bitch.'"

Opening Theme: Gayle is seen reading the book *The Burning Bed* (a film in which Farrah starred), while Bobby is seen reading *Love Story* (the film in which Ryan starred).

ROBERT "BOBBY" TANNEN

Age: 42 when the series begins.

Place of Birth: Miami Beach, Florida.

Occupation: Cohost (with Gayle) of *Sports Central* on ASCN. He also hosts *Sports Brief* and *Sports Chat* with Gayle.

Early Career: The number one draft pick from the University of Miami (wore jersey 12) but quit football after two years to manage the career of his wife, singer/stripper Yvonne Pomplona (Sheri Rose). Following his divorce three weeks later, Bobby made a comeback with the Los Angeles Rams (jersey 13). He was traded to the Oakland Raiders and, at this time, wrote a tell-all book called *Panty Raiders*. When team member Lyle Alzado read the book, "he broke Bobby's body and tore his face off." Bobby next appeared in bandages on the cover of *Look* magazine with the headline "Bye Bye Bobby." Thinking that he had a great singing voice, Bobby attempted to become a recording artist and became known as "Downtown Bobby Tannen" (his only album was *Downtown Sings "Downtown" and Other Chart Busters—Including the Hit Single, Wichita Lineman*). When this failed, he worked as a pizza delivery boy for the Friends of Pizza. R. J., ordering a pizza, discovered him and remembered him for his football career. He then teamed him with Gayle.

Address: The Landmark Building in Los Angeles (in an apartment opposite Gayle's).

Hobby: Collecting beer cans (he has 147 unopened brands from 98 countries).

Tribute: When Bobby scored a touchdown at Shea Stadium (in New York), the organist would play the song "Downtown."

Pet Goldfish: Valli (when combined with Gayle's, they produce the singer Frankie Valli). When Bobby needs medical help with Valli, he seeks out Dr. M'odsquad (played by Michael Cole; his role from the series *Mod Squad* is played as a joke here).

R. J. RAPPAPORT

R. J. (Lane Smith) runs the station like a military general (supposedly adapted by his attending Culver Military Academy and Amherst College). He also owns Rap-Ha-Port, a 24-hour comedy channel, and with his "yes man" John McKinney (Brian Doyle-Murray) had a morning radio program called *Mac and Rap in the Morning*. One of R. J.'s holdings, Rappaport Airlines, sponsors *Sports Brief* ("the airline with fewer fatalities than any bicoastal airline"). R. J.'s hobby is taking television sets apart (even if they do not need fixing) and trying to figure out how to put them back together again.

Grace under Fire
(ABC, 1993–1998)

Cast: Brett Butler (Grace Kelly); Kaitlin Cullum (Libby Kelly); Noah Segan, then John Paul Steuer, then Sam Horrigan (Quentin Kelly); Geoff Pierson (Jimmy Kelly); Dave Thomas (Russell Norton); Alan Autry (Rick Bradshaw); Casey Sander (Wade Swaboda); Julie White (Nadine Swaboda).

Basis: An independent woman (Grace Kelly) struggles to raise her children (Libby, Quentin, and infant Patrick) in an environment that is uncommon to most mothers (oil fields).

GRACE KELLY

Place of Birth: Huntsville, Alabama.
Maiden Name: Grace Burdette.
Mother: Jean Burdette (Peggy Rea).
Sisters: Faith Burdette (Valri Bromfield), Evie Burdette (Ashley Gardner).
Brother: Gil Burdette (Blake Clark).
Age: 36.
Ex-Husband: James "Jimmy" Kelly. They married after graduating from high school, and each had a problem: Jimmy was a womanizer, and Grace had a severe addiction to alcohol. They divorced after the birth of Patrick due to their incompatibility.
Education: Huntsville High School. Grace later attends Missouri State College to pursue a degree in English (the Equator Coffee House is the school hangout).
Estranged Son: Matthew (Tom Everett Scott). Nineteen years earlier, Grace (then 16) had an affair and after the birth of her son gave him up for adoption when she could not care for him. Jack Grayson, a college professor, is Matthew's biological father.

Address: 455 Washington Avenue in Victory, Missouri. She later moves to the home across the street (number 466) when the landlord sold the house she was renting.

Phone Number: 555-0159.

Measurements: 34-23-34. She stands 5 feet, 7 inches tall and has blonde hair and black eyes.

Occupation: Waitress at Stevie Ray's Bar; fieldworker in Section 7 of the CBD Oil Refinery; office manager of the Reliance Construction Company (later promoted to crew chief).

The Day the Drinking Stopped: "When I saw a big red dog jump out of my lingerie drawer."

Car License Plate: FX B 352 (later AEH 497).

Favorite Ice Cream Flavor: Strawberry.

Lingerie Shopping: A store called Bras, Bras, Bras.

Favorite Snack: Little Debbie Swiss Cake Rolls.

Favorite Breakfast: Eggs and Canadian bacon.

Volunteer Work: The Crisis Center (where she uses the name "Chris").

Videos: Grace rents movies at Video World.

Favorite Music: Opera.

First Boyfriend: Russell Norton, the owner of Smiley's Pharmacy on Third and Lakesburg (when he bought the store, he never changed the name). He has a dog named Phil and uses a cologne "that's cheap, chicks dig, and kills bugs dead." He mentioned his favorite restaurant as "where the girls stopped dancing on the tables five minutes before." He drives a 1984 LeBaron and he also dines (with Grace) on the *Delta Queen*, a gambling riverboat anchored offshore. Tom Poston played Russell's father, Floyd Norton, a retired pharmacist.

Second Boyfriend: Rick Bradshaw, head of the oil company. He lived in a house with the street number 1261, and their relationship became serious (less comical than with Russell), but Rick ended it when he moved to Alaska for a higher-paying job.

Relatives: Nan Lil, Grace's grandmother on Jimmy's side (Alice Drummond).

GRACE'S CHILDREN

Elizabeth Louise, nicknamed "Libby," is a very pretty young girl who is also somewhat of a tomboy. She attends Glenview Elementary School and is a member of the girls' soccer team. She is a *Star Trek* fanatic and has a doll named Helen, a pet squirrel (Spot), and a goldfish (Fishy Fisherman). Elizabeth won the fourth-grade essay contest with her entry "Why I Like Outer Space" and entered the Little Miss Muppet Pageant (she sang "Tomorrow") but came in last. She has a collection of Barbie and Ken dolls and is learning to play the trumpet.

Quentin, the eldest child, is the most trouble for Grace. He rebels against Grace's authority, and the roof outside his bedroom window provides the only serenity he knows. His first bout of trouble was accomplished by purposely trespassing on property owned by the Victory Country Club. Quentin looks up to his father (not the best influence in his life, as Jimmy is reckless), and for a show-and-tell assignment for class (at Glenview High School), he used empty beer cans that Jimmy crushed against his forehead.

GRACE'S NEIGHBORS

Wade and Nadine Swaboda live next door to Grace. Wade served as a marine during the Vietnam War and was called "Wade the Impaler." He worked as a telephone lineman, a traffic reporter for KPLG radio, a helicopter reporter for KQMO-TV Channel 6, and then as an officer with the Sixth District of the Victory Police Department. As a child, he had a tree house with the sign "No Girls or Communists Allowed" and as a baby won "The Little Mr. Man" title. He enjoys making pottery and believes digital clocks will mean the end of safe driving ("Kids will not know what ten and two o'clock are").

Nadine, Grace's best friend, is a waitress at Stevie Ray's Bar. Nadine mentions that her mother has been married so many times that she has been a younger sibling, an older sibling, and even a middle sibling. When Grace had each of her children, Nadine was always by her side because "Jimmy always had an excuse." Wade is Nadine's fourth husband; she has had very little consistency in her life. When Nadine gave birth to a girl whom she and Wade named Rose, Nadine had to have her focal point, Boo Boo Bear, when she went into labor. Although it appeared that Nadine and Wade were a good couple, Nadine leaves him during the final season to move to Colorado, leaving Wade to fend for himself; the series ended before any issues were explained or resolved.

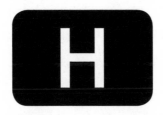

Harry and the Hendersons
(Syndicated, 1991–1993)

Cast: Bruce Davison (George Henderson), Molly Cheek (Nancy Henderson), Carol-Ann Plante (Sarah Henderson), Zachary Bostrom (Ernie Henderson).

Basis: A family of four (parents George and Nancy and their children, Sarah and Ernie) attempt to adjust their lives to accommodate a most unusual house guest: A Bigfoot named Harry. Based on the feature film, but information is based only on the TV series.

GEORGE AND NANCY HENDERSON

George and Nancy live at 410 Forest Drive in Seattle, Washington. It is a 2,000-square-foot home with 100 feet of copper piping. George is a marketing executive for the People's Sporting Goods Store but quit to become editor of a magazine called *A Better Life*. As a child, George had a dream to travel to Hollywood and meet his idol, Annette Funicello, and sing with her on TV's *The Mickey Mouse Club* (1955–1959). George is a graduate of Seattle State University. When George gave Nancy her engagement ring on June 26, 1972, he wrapped it in a piece of paper with a note attached saying, "Dear Nancy, will you *murry* me?" (the *murry* being a typo). He and Nancy have been married to each other for 19 years when the series begins; his car license plate reads 608 GHR.

Nancy Gwen Douglas, like George, grew up in Seattle and also attended Seattle State University. She works for the Student Council Exchange of Seattle and has more control over their children than George. As a kid, Nancy had a pet frog (Slimy) and played the triangle in her high school marching band. She claims that the most risqué thing she ever did was "not to wear a bra between 1972 and 1975" (she later says it was being arrested for civil disobedience for protesting in the nude on a public beach). When Nancy gets upset, she eats half a gallon of Breyer's Rocky Road ice cream.

SARAH AND ERNIE HENDERSON

Sarah, age 15 when the series begins, first attended Madison High School, then Northern College of the Arts. She is a member of the Madison track team and a talented singer and dancer. She wrote the song "Somewhere Out There" for the Homecoming Dance and was crowned its queen. Sarah is the only family member who is not too happy living with a Bigfoot. She fears her friends will find out and make her the talk of the town. She is, however, taking notes on everything that happens and is planning to write a book about Harry and her family—"but I'm going to use a pen name. I don't want anyone to think I'm nuts." Sarah's middle name is Nicole, and she aspires to become an actress (she starred in the Community Theater production of *Beauty and the Beast*, with Harry playing the Beast). She has a "special white lace bra" she calls "my lucky bra" and works at the Photo Quickie after school. Melissa is her pet hamster and she plays saxophone in the school orchestra.

Ernest, called Ernie, attends Madison Junior High School. He is closest to Harry ("Ernie" was the first word Harry spoke) and is a member of the Padres Pee Wee League baseball team. Although he doesn't like girls, he became friendly with Darcy Farg (Courtney Peldon), a very pretty and very rich but spoiled girl who moved next door. Ernie is not as studious as Sarah and finds himself getting into trouble with Harry more than he does on his own with Darcy. Darcy was originally introduced with the last name of Payne and has a cat called Damian ("the bird killer") and a sidewalk mineral water stand called Chez Darcy.

HARRY

Harry was born in Seattle and lived in its dense forest until he strayed from its safety, attempted to cross Interstate 5, and was struck by a car driven by George. Harry proved not to be vicious or afraid but sociable and sort of adopted the Hendersons as his family. He stands 8 feet, 1 inch tall and weighs 680 pounds. He lives in the loft of the Henderson home and is quickly learning how to become human. He has a Barry Manilow record collection and loves granola bars (which he calls "Num Num" and "Nummie Nummie"). The family's biggest problem is keeping Harry's existence a secret, although in final-season episodes he is exposed by a tabloid TV show. To protect Harry, George writes to the president of the United Sates requesting that the Bigfoot be declared a national park. The request is granted, giving Harry the freedom to live anywhere he wishes. He chooses to live with the Hendersons. George and Nancy wrote the book Sarah wanted to do called *My Life with Bigfoot* (originally called *Harry and Me*). When Nancy becomes upset with Harry, she calls him "Mister!" (e.g., "Go to your loft, Mister!"). Harry is voiced by Patrick Pinney and played by Kevin Peter Hall, Dawan Scott, and Brian Steele.

BRETT DOUGLAS
Brett (Noah Blake) is Nancy's brother. He assists George on the magazine and considers himself a ladies' man. He worked previously as a steward on a cruise ship (where he met and married a woman named Michelle; she left him after 25 days of marriage to star in the movie *Babes from Venus*; Brett refers to this as "the day she disembarked without me"). Brett hangs out at the Club 700 and calls George "G-Man," Nancy "Nance," Ernie "E-Man," and Harry "Hair Monger."

SAMANTHA GLICK
Samantha (Gigi Rice) and her daughter, Tiffany (Cassie Cole), were the Hendersons' original neighbors. Samantha works for the local TV station (Channel 10) and reports on *The News at 5*. She also hosts *Crime Time with Samantha Glick* and *Seattle Celebrities*. She and Tiffany are aware of Harry, and Samantha wishes that "the Hendersons would get a pet duck like a normal family." It was actually Tiffany who named the Bigfoot. When Tiffany, called "Tiffy" by her mother, first saw the Bigfoot, she called him "Hairy Guy." This prompted George to call him "Harry." Without explanation, Samantha and Tiffy are dropped and replaced by Darcy.

Hearts Afire
(CBS, 1992–1994)

Cast: Markie Post (Georgie Lahti), John Ritter (John Hartman), Beth Broderick (Dee Dee Star), Mary Ann Mobley (Mary Fran Smithers), George Gaynes (Strobe Smithers).

Basis: Political comedy about the relationship between a senator's aide (John Hartman) and his speechwriter (Georgie Lahti).

GEORGIA "GEORGIE" ANN LAHTI
Place of Birth: Chicago on November 4, 1950.
Father: George Lahti (Edward Asner), a disbarred attorney (spent two years in prison) and a former president of the American Trial Lawyers Association; Georgie's mother died shortly after her birth (later said when Georgie was three years old). Georgie was actually raised by Miss Lula (Beah Richards), the Lahtis' housekeeper, as George was too consumed with work to raise her. George took up ceramics in prison and is an excellent cook.
Childhood: Operated a sidewalk snow cone stand; won a Davy Crockett Bravery Award; wanted to wear her devil Halloween costume to school every day.
Education: Chicago University (acquired a degree in journalism). At her unnamed high school, she was singled out for writing the longest answers ever

given on a multiple-choice SAT exam ("I wasn't satisfied with E—none of the above").

Measurements: 37-23-35. She stands 5 feet, 6 inches tall and wears a size 6½ shoe.

Trait: A liberal feminist; easily excitable and upset; smokes but can't quit ("I smoke when I get upset, and I get upset a lot"); feels that because of her gorgeous figure and good looks, "I have a problem being taken seriously."

Occupation: Speechwriter for Strobe Smithers, a somewhat senile, conservative southern senator, then a newspaper reporter (for the *Courier*).

History: Georgie began her career in California as a question writer on the game show *Jeopardy* (she created the category "Potent Potables"). She wrote an episode of the TV series *Rhoda* before returning to Chicago to work as a reporter for the *Chicago Tribune*, then the *Chicago Post*. After eight years, she left the *Post* to write a book based on her life with Fidel Castro called *My Year with Fidel* (Georgie thought her story should be told, but the book didn't sell). Discouraged, she went to France and became "a cultural liaison in Paris" ("I worked at Euro Disney helping people on and off the teacup ride"). Before returning to the United States, Georgie traveled to Rome, "where I ran around the Trevi Fountain in my bra and panties." It was at this time that she secured a job with Strobe.

Author: Wrote romance novels under the name "Dusty Silver": *Naked Spring*, *Lust Beyond Tomorrow*, and *Flamingo Summer*.

Musical Talent: Plays the trumpet.

Favorite Breakfast Cereal: Kix.

Awards: A Pulitzer Prize and a Peabody Award for excellence in journalism.

DEE DEE STAR

Place of Birth: Amarillo, Texas.

Occupation: Office receptionist for Strobe Smithers in Washington, D.C. Prior to this, she was a beautician at the Beauty Pit Salon. Feeling that she was meant for better things, she left Texas and moved to Washington, where she found work at the local Foto Mat (it is not mentioned how she became Strobe's receptionist, but it is assumed that Strobe, a married ladies' man, spotted her and hired her on the spot).

Education: Amarillo High School (where she was voted "Class Beauty").

Character: Motivated by patriotism and a love of country (or, as most people put it, "She feels that any time a man plays an important role in world events, Dee Dee finds it her patriotic duty to throw her skirt over her head").

Biggest Fear: Losing her looks (as she bases her whole life around her beauty).

Reputation: Dee Dee's wild sexual activities have earned her the name "the Last Bimbo on the Hill."

Belief: Women are threatened by her looks, and she relishes the fact that she is thought of as a tease and easy ("It makes me happy").

Business: Mail Order Bras and Panties (like a Victoria's Secret franchise).

OTHER CHARACTERS

John Hartman, Strobe's assistant, lives at 1184 Arlington Drive (in Washington). He was born in the small town of Clay County and is now divorced from Diandra (who left him for another woman) and the father of Ben (Justin Burnette) and Eliot (Clark Duke). John has a dog (Rugboy), and 555-8663 is his phone number. He calls Georgie "Miss Lahti," while she calls him "Hartman." Ben and Eliot attend the Overland Elementary School; Eliot has a pet snake (Sam), and his first word as a baby was "moon."

As the series progressed, John and Georgie fell in love and married. The political aspect of the series was dropped when John, Georgie, Eliot, and Ben move to John's hometown to begin new lives. Here, John and his friend Billy Bob Davis (Billy Bob Thornton) take over the local weekly newspaper, the *Courier* (located on Main Street).

Billy Bob is married to Mavis Davis (Wendie Jo Sperber) and the father of Carson Lee (Doreen Fein). Mavis was Strobe's office secretary and left Billy Bob to get her master's degree at New York University. John and Georgia now live on Old Balboa Road; John becomes the paper's editor, Georgie the news reporter, and Billy Bob the society editor. Madeline Sossinger (Conchata Ferrell), a psychologist who rents space in the paper's building, joins the staff as the advice columnist ("Dear Madeline"). The paper later becomes the *Daily Beacon*, and Georgie gives birth to a girl (8 pounds, 10 ounces) she and John name Amelia Rose as the series ends.

Strobe and his wife, Mary Fran, have been married for 30 years. When introduced, it can be seen not only that Strobe has an eye for the ladies but also that he is becoming increasingly senile. Strobe was born into a political family, and during the 1940s (possibly after serving in World War II) he formed his own band (he played piano). Mary Fran was born in Sparta, Georgia, and took the beauty pageant path to get out of town. It was after her win in the Miss Tennessee Beauty Pageant that Mary Fran entered the Miss USA Pageant (where she sang the song "As Time Goes By"). It was here that Strobe, one of the judges, first saw Mary Fran, fell in love, and pursued her until she agreed to marry him. While beautiful, Mary Fran is also calculating and wants Strobe to retire so she can take his seat in the Senate ("It's my turn now after putting up with him for 30 years"). If Strobe doesn't step down, Mary Fran is threatening to air their dirty laundry in public. Strobe is in bed by 8:30 p.m., and he and John enjoy drinks at Harry's Bar. Strobe, Mary Fran, and Dee Dee were dropped when the program changed formats.

Home Improvement
(ABC, 1991–1999)

Cast: Tim Allen (Tim Taylor), Patricia Richardson (Jill Taylor), Richard Karn (Al Borland), Earl Hindman (Wilson Wilson Jr.), Jonathan Taylor Thomas (Randy Taylor), Taran Noah Smith (Mark Taylor), Zachery Ty Bryan (Brad Taylor), Debbe Dunning (Heidi Keppert), Pamela Anderson (Lisa).

Basis: Home improvement series spoof as seen through the activities of Tim Taylor (married to Jill and the father of Brad, Randy, and Mark) and the host of the Michigan-based TV series *Tool Time*.

TIM TAYLOR

Mother: Lucille (Bonnie Bartlett); his father is deceased.

Brothers: Jeff (Tom Sharpe) and Marty (William O'Leary).

Nieces: Gracie (Ashley Trefger) and Clair (Ashley Trefger), Marty's children (he is divorced from Nancy [Jensen Daggett]).

Address: 508 Glenview Road, Detroit, Michigan.

Education: Michigan State University.

Political Affiliation: Republican.

Garage Notice: "No Women Allowed" (as it contains his workshop and his Binford tools; it can be seen that when Jill gets angry at Tim and slams the door leading to the garage, his Binford tools fall off their pegboard hooks).

Occupation: Host of *Tool Time*, a local home improvement program that airs weekdays on cable Channel 112 (also given as Channel 8 and Channel 122); it is simulcast in Spanish on Channel 88. It is first mentioned that Tim was a salesman for Binford Tools when owner John Binford selected him to host *Tool Time* in 1988; it is later said that Tim came up with the show idea after taking two film courses in college. It is produced at WLNO-TV in Detroit; Sony monitors can be seen in the studio, and it is the fourth-highest-rated home improvement show in Michigan.

Nickname: Tim "The Tool Man" Taylor. His hard hat has the name "Timbo" on it.

Show Sponsor: Binford Tools.

Show Address: Tool Time, PO Box 32733, Minneapolis, Minnesota 42252 (actually the headquarters of Binford Tools).

Show Phone Number: 801-555-TOOL (later 555-0172).

Show Truck: A Chevy truck called "Blood Sweat and Gears."

Company Motto: "If it doesn't say Binford on it, somebody else makes it." A claw hammer was the first tool manufactured by Binford.

Catchphrase: "More power" (which Tim says when he has increased a power tool for better performance; it rarely works, causing more damage than good).

Hobby: Restoring classic cars (he spent two years restoring a 1933 Blue Goose Roadster hot rod [plate 2L TIME]; he later worked on a 1946 Ford). Tim was also the youngest person to ever join AAA.

First Car: A 1966 Corvair.

Dream Car: A 1933 Ford Roadster (the first car he is seen restoring).

Award: "Car Guy of the Year" (awarded by the Saganow Cheese Company, which appears to be an alternate sponsor of *Tool Time*).

Book: Tim wrote *How to Maintain Your Bench Grinder.*

Favorite Dinner: Trout almandine (although he mentions liking brockwurst, knockwurst, and liverwurst).

Favorite Breakfast: Chocolate chip pancakes.

Favorite Show Guests: Bob Vila (pioneering PBS host of *This Old House*); "The guys from K & B Construction Company."

Favorite Video Game: "Monkey Town."

Favorite Movie: Abbott and Costello Meet Frankenstein.

Noted For: His grunt (makes when something gets his attention; it can also be heard in the opening theme).

Favorite Sport: Football (he is often seen wearing a Detroit Lions sweatshirt).

Home Away from Home: The hospital's emergency room (as Tim is forever getting hurt during projects on *Tool Time*).

Christmas Tradition: Having the best light display and decorations for his home; hanging "car part ornaments" on the tree.

Videos: Tim and Al starred in a series of Binford Tools videos that spoof movie titles: *Silence of the Lamps, Glueless,* and *The Nutty Compressor.*

JILL TAYLOR

Parents: Lillian Patterson (Polly Holliday) and the Colonel (M. Emmet Walsh), her father, a retired army colonel.

Place of Birth: Texas.

Sisters: Linda (Carlene Watkins), Robin (Loryn Locklin), and Tracy (Maryedith Burrell).

Maiden Name: Jill Patterson.

Political Affiliation: Democrat.

Education: Michigan State University. As for prior schooling, Jill first mentions attending Adams High School, then the Huntley School for Girls and the Hockaday School for Girls (where she played Juliet in its production of *Romeo and Juliet*).

First Meeting: Jill and Tim met at college (their first date was at the Glitter Ballroom, where they danced to the song "Without You"). Tim proposed to Jill

Earl Hindman, Patricia Richardson, Tim Allen, Richard Karn, Taran Noah Smith, Jonathan Taylor Thomas, and Zachery Ty Bryan. *ABC/Photofest © ABC*

in a 1968 Dodge Dart; they married in 1978. On the program, Jill is three years younger than Tim, but in real life, Patricia Richardson is three years older than Tim Allen.

Occupation: Housewife. Jill originally worked as a researcher for *Inside Detroit* magazine. When it folded, she returned to school to get her master's degree in psychology.

Childhood: Called "Jilly Dilly" by her father; wore Tinker Bell perfume; had a dog named Puddles.

Expertise: Popular songs (she calls herself "The High Priestess of Pop Songs").

Kitchen Rules: "The blue sponge for the sink; the green sponge for the counter." Jill also has dinner ready by 6:15 p.m.

Car: A restored Austin-Healy.

Hobby: Pottery.

Favorite Restaurant: Sorentino's.

Favorite Magazine: Today's Woman.

Trauma: In final-season episodes, Jill has a hysterectomy due to a tumor.

Final Episode: Jill acquires her master's degree in psychology, and when a job opportunity arises for her to work at Family Practice in Indiana, Tim gives up his reluctance to move, and the home in which they lived is seen being transported to Indiana (by tugboat).

AL BORLAND

Place of Birth: Detroit.

Mother: Alma Borland (grossly overweight and never fully seen or heard; she has a pet turtle named Scooter).

Brother: Cal Borland (Keith Lehman).

Occupation: Tim's assistant on *Tool Time.* He was originally a heavy crane operator and a member of Local 324. He knows the right way to work on projects and is always saving Tim from his misguided way of doing things. Al also hosts *Cooking with Irma* (the show that follows *Tool Time*), has a home workshop, and called his first sawhorse Lily.

Girlfriend: Trudy McHale (Megan Cavanaugh); they married in the final episode in a ceremony performed by Wilson.

Military Service: Al joined the navy when he was 18 to travel the world (which did not happen; he was stationed in Nevada).

Education: Al mentions attending Gilmore High School (where he was the fencing champion of 1976).

Address: Apartment 505 (unnamed address; voted "Tenant of the Month" 11 times), then in a house he rents from Tim.

Trademarks: Wearing flannel shirts (and being teased by Tim for doing so) and his two-finger military-like salute to the home audience when Tim introduces him.

Invention: The board game "Tool Time." He also starred in a video called *How to Assemble Your Tool Box* (which was directed by Tim).

Hobbies: Appears to be dancing (he is taking a correspondence course called "Getting in Touch with the Square Dancer in You") and miniature golf (plays at Putt Putt Panorama).

Business: Owns 20 percent of his and Tim's favorite hangout, Harry's Hardware Store (originally called Kelly's Hardware Store); it is located at Third and Main Street in Royal Oak. It is later purchased by Tim.

Favorite Eatery: Big Mike's (also Tim's favorite).

Favorite Movie as a Child: The Sound of Music.

Favorite Meal: Shepherd's pie with double meat (he later says turkey).

Childhood: Al had a business called Little Al's Lemonade Stand (its slogan: "When It Comes to Lemons, I'm Your Main Squeeze"). His mother filmed virtually everything he did and presented him with a set of 12 eight-hour VHS tapes that highlight his life.

Complaints: While Al often complains about what Tim should not do during a *Tool Time* project, he is most upset when Tim leaves the cap off the epoxy cement tube.

Disgrace: Al bounced an $8 check at Cheese World in 1987.

WILSON WILSON JR.

Relationship: Tim's neighbor.

Marital Status: Widower (his late wife was named Kathryn). Wilson mentions that his father, Wilson Wilson Sr., was a scientist.

Niece: Willow Wilson (China Kantner), a college student who came to live with him in later episodes.

Address: 509 Glenview Road (his and Tim's backyards face each other).

Show Gimmick: Wilson's face is never fully seen, being partially obstructed by something wherever Wilson appears. The rather crude picket fence that separates Tim and Wilson's backyard is most often used (as it has been built too high for Wilson to see over it).

Greeting: "Hi-dee-ho, neighbor" (said to Tim); "Neighborette" when he address Jill. Tim calls him "Good Neighbor" (as he gives Tim advice to help him solve a problem).

Pet Mynah Bird: Mozart.

First Car: A British Morris-Miner (he keeps a picture of it in his wallet).

Quirks: Celebrates unusual holidays, like the end of the Punic Wars; uses a scarecrow (named Oliver) in his own image to protect his plants from birds; raises spiders; sings to his plants when he cross-pollinates them; plays the alpenhorn (used for sheepherding) in the Alpine and Yodel Festival; a fascination with insect mating; sculpts shrines out of yak butter; hangs ancient Crete bells in his backyard to attract friendly spirits; claims to be a feminist (stands up for women's rights); builds traps to catch porcupines (although none exist in the area, he claims, "You build the trap, they will come"); and doesn't have a TV set because "I just use my imagination and watch the pictures that are inside my mind." For barbecues, he enjoys grilled grasshopper and cricket kabobs (he found the recipe in the magazine *Aftermath*). He also enjoys taking herb baths (such as in rosemary and eucalyptus).

Education: The Greenville School for Boys (where he played Juliet in its production of *Romeo and Juliet* and was captain of the chess team); Oxford University.

Occupation: Appears to have had many jobs, but only several are mentioned: his writing the newspaper column "Rock Beat" (about rocks) for the *Wichita Star*; midwife; a minister with the Church of the Celestial; and circus juggler (he roomed with "the two-headed man," "Nicky, the Lobster Boy," and Margo, "The Human Cork Screw"). He is very well educated and quotes from many different books to make a point.

Mystery Possession: A shrunken head that he can't get rid of (no matter what he does to dispose of it, it always comes back).

As a Child: Was a bagpipe prodigy.

TOOL TIME ASSISTANTS

Lisa and Heidi assist Tim and Al (they open the program and bring the needed props for each project). Lisa is attending college, and while Pamela Anderson plays the role, she is not as prone to showing cleavage as she was in other projects (like *Baywatch* and *V.I.P.*). She left *Tool Time* to attend medical school. She opened *Tool Time* as follows: "Ladies and gentlemen, Binford Tools is proud to present Tim 'The Tool Man' Taylor."

Heidi, much sexier as the "Tool Time Girl," does show cleavage and has a peculiar nervous habit: her left breast twitches. She opens the show as follows: "Does everybody know what time it is? (audience yells, "Tool Time!"). Yes, Binford Tools is proud to present Tim, the 'Tool Man' Taylor."

The Hughleys
(ABC, 1998–1999; UPN, 1999–2002)

Cast: D. L. Hughley (Darryl Hughley), Elise Neal (Yvonne Hughley), Ashley Monique Clark (Sydney Hughley), Dee Jay Daniels (Michael Hughley).

Basis: Life with a family of four (parents Darryl and Yvonne Hughley and their children, Sydney and Michael) living in West Hills, California.

DARRYL HUGHLEY

Parents: Henry (Ellie Williams) and Hattie Mae Hughley (Marla Gibbs).

Address: 317 Crestview.

Occupation: Owner of the Hughley Vending Machine Company.

Background: Darryl was born into a lower-class Los Angeles family and lived at 135th and Avalon Street. His father was an airport janitor, but Darryl claims his family was so poor that they couldn't afford to buy a TV set that worked properly ("We had two sets—one for sound and one for picture"). Darryl was the shortest kid in his kindergarten class and called "Scooter" by his mother. At the age of 10, Darryl had a newspaper route and a lemonade stand; by age 16, he worked at his Aunt Jessy's beauty parlor, Kurls 'n' Knaps. A year later, during his junior year at South Central High School, Darryl felt inferior to other students and dropped out. Rather than be like his friends and hang out at the Jay Bones Pool Hall, Darryl acquired a job with the Perrymore Vending Machine Company (first as a delivery man, then as a repairman; the Vendamatic 86 was the first machine he serviced). Darryl saved his money, learned everything possible about vending machines, and then started his own business. He later attained his GED at Ulysses S. Grant High School.

Belief: "Computers will be the downfall of mankind."

Trait: Makes jokes about and insults people; hates to admit he is wrong about anything.

Greatest Fear: His wife (who is an intellectual and with whom he never argues).

Quirk: Always sits farthest from the front door "because you never know who is going to break into this place." He does not subscribe to the Playboy Channel but watches it anyway hoping for unscrambled moments.

Favorite Magazine: Ebony.

Barber Shop: Magic Shears.

Favorite Singer: Otis Redding.

Car: A Lexus.

Hates: Low-fat milk (but unknowingly drinks it because Yvonne tells him it is whole milk).

Relatives: Darryl's aunt, Jessy (Patricia Belcher); grandmother, called M'Dear (Virginia Capers); brother, JoJo Hughley (Miguel Nunez Jr.).

YVONNE HUGHLEY

Parents: James (Sherman Hemsley) and Paulette Williams (Telma Hopkins).

Sister: Shari (Adele Givens).

Place of Birth: Tucson, Arizona.

Education: University of Southern California (majoring in business administration).

Meeting: While attending college, Yvonne Williams met Darryl Hughley, working for Perrymore Vending Machines, by chance. They fell in love, married in 1987, and moved into an apartment above the Kurls 'n' Knaps beauty salon. It was at this time that Yvonne encouraged Darryl to follow his dream and start his own company. When Yvonne became pregnant with their daughter (Sydney), they moved to Los Angeles, then to the suburbs after the birth of their son, Michael.

Nickname: Darryl calls Yvonne "Vonnie." While dating, he romanced her with "poetry borrowed from Barry Manilow songs."

Jobs: Darryl's receptionist; fund-raising director at West Hills Hospital; marketing executive at the Staples Sports Center in Los Angeles.

Member: The West Hills School District PTA; the Car Pooling Mothers; the Neighborhood Safety Committee.

Favorite Book: Catcher in the Rye.

Trait: Loves to help people; an excellent cook; addicted to gambling (seen when she and Darryl go to Las Vegas and she becomes obsessed by slot machines).

SYDNEY AND MICHAEL HUGHLEY

Sydney is 10 years old when the series begins. She has two dolls (Jasmine and Heather) and is 6 inches taller than most of the boys in her class. She attends West Hills Elementary School, is a member of its hockey team, and is also a Brownie Scout. Darryl calls her "Sugar," and she claims that becoming a teenager has been difficult for her (while purchasing her first bra went well, her first period was horrific: Darryl celebrated "her womanhood" by hosting a party and inviting all her friends).

Sydney snores, and even before she was born, Darryl embarrassed her: he took a picture of Yvonne in mid-contraction seconds before Sydney's birth and used that picture as their 1988 Christmas card. While Sydney is considered the good child, she shocked her parents by drinking beer, piercing her navel, and dressing too provocatively (showing cleavage at age 13). She uses the computer screen name "Sydney 2002."

Sydney is enrolled in the accelerated program at school, while Michael (later attending West Hills High School) is having difficulty due to dyslexia. He is a member of the school soccer team, the Scary Spiders, but is also mischievous and has VIP seating in detention hall. As a child, Darryl mentioned that Michael had a talent "for getting his head stuck in things" (like the banister railing) and enjoys going with Darryl to Jiffy Lube. Michael suffers from a fear of heights and attempted (but failed) to become a rap star called "L'il Spooner."

Just Shoot Me
(NBC, 1997–2003)

Cast: George Segal (Jack Gallo), Laura San Giacomo (Maya Gallo), Wendie Malick (Nina Van Horn), David Spade (Dennis Finch), Enrico Colantoni (Elliot DiMauro).

Basis: A behind-the-scenes look at the operations of a Manhattan-based fashion magazine as seen through the experiences of its editor (Jack Gallo) and his off-the-wall staff (Maya, Nina, and Dennis).

JACK GALLO

Occupation: Editor/publisher of *Blush*, a magazine that Jack started in 1967 to encourage women to express their sexuality and "drop their mops and pick up a briefcase." In one episode, Jack's middle name is said to be Gilbert.

The Problem: Although *Blush* was the first magazine to give a voice to women, most women see it as just another magazine that treats women as trophies.

Marital Status: Divorced from his first wife, Eve (Jessica Walter), and currently married to Allie (Kristen Bauer van Straten), a woman almost 30 years his junior.

Daughters: Maya (by Eve); Hannah (by Allie).

Blood Type: B-positive (as Jack says, "I run my magazine by my blood type").

Home: A penthouse at 60 Park Avenue.

Blush *Address:* 45 West 41st Street in Manhattan.

Blush *Phone Number:* 555-9887.

Favorite Eatery: The Carnegie Deli.

Favorite Seafood: Soft-shell crabs "because it makes me feel powerful like a shark."

Fascination: Electronic gadgets.

Favorite Movie Comedians: The Marx Brothers.

Coffee: Black but sweetened with Sweet'N Low.
Racehorse: Tax Dodge (as he rarely wins a race).
After-Shave Lotion: Meadow After a Rainstorm.
Column: "From the Publisher."
Author: Wrote the book *Don't Back Down* (about his success as a publisher).

Rena Sofer, George Segal, Laura San Giacomo, David Spade, Wendie Malick, and Enrico Colantoni. *NBC/Photofest © NBC*

MAYA GALLO

Position: Articles editor at *Blush*. She previously worked in the newsroom of Manhattan's Channel 8 but was fired for "making an anchorwoman cry" when she tampered with her teleprompter. In the final episode, she becomes the editor of *Blush* when Jack retires.

Place of Birth: Manhattan on January 1.

Childhood: Wore her hair in pigtails, was overweight, and was not very pretty ("I was called Crisco [referring to the cooking shortening] by my schoolmates because 'I was fat in the can'").

Adulthood: A beautiful woman who is not afraid to be who she is and a fighter for women's rights. She has a tendency to dress provocatively (especially showing cleavage), and despite what she is now, she says, "People see me as a straight-laced, uptight school teacher. But I'm not. I like to have fun."

Measurements: 39-25-35. She is 5 feet, 2 inches tall and wears a size 6 shoe.

Education: The Westbridge School; the Columbia School of Journalism; Stanford University (majored in Shakespeare; starred in 10 productions).

Pets: Othello (a cat, after Shakespeare's character); Amelia Earhart (a turtle; after the pilot); Rags (a dog).

Blood Type: B-negative.

Address: Apartment 803 in a building on Gramercy Place in Manhattan.

Telephone Number: 555-4343.

Activities: Takes pottery classes and tutors children in her spare time; enjoys playing video games.

Career Change: Maya hoped to launch her own magazine (*Emily*, named after her favorite poet, Emily Dickinson) but was unable to because the market could not support another magazine, especially an intellectual one.

Award: The Our Guardian Angel Award for her work at the Avalon Foundation charity. Maya also heads *Blush*'s charity wing.

NINA VAN HORNE

Position: Former model turned fashion editor for *Blush*.

Magazine Covers: Vogue, Blush, Redbook, and *Mademoiselle.*

TV Spokeswoman: Noxema Skin Cream. She auditioned for Simple Time Stuffing but was rejected for "not being motherly enough."

TV Appearances: Guest on *Jeopardy*; a Fembot on *The Bionic Woman*; suspect on *Cops* ("But you can't see me; they pushed my face into the grass"); *Wake Up, New York* (giving makeup advice).

Measurements: 36-26-37; she stands 5 feet, 6 inches tall and wears a size 6 shoe.

Wardrobe: Sexy and alluring outfits ("Because that's all I own"). Nina mentions that as a child, she loved to try on party dresses and pretend to be a model. She bases her entire life on her looks and fears growing old and losing them.

Address: The Plaza Apartments on East 64th Street.

Nina's Past: Nina was a top model during the 1970s and 1980s. Before changing her name to Nina Van Horn, she was known as Claire Noodleman. She is unaware of who her parents are and is hoping to one day find them. She was abandoned as an infant in 1953 and placed in a feed trough of a farm family named Noodleman in Colby, Kansas (the note attached to her said, "Allergic to bananas"). She was raised by the Noodleman family, who gave her the first name of Claire (after their cat, which had run away). She grew up on the farm and developed a special skill: milking two cows at once using her feet. But Claire also had a special look. When she was 12 years old, her picture appeared on the cover of Blumgarten's Seed Catalog. The catalog found its way to a talent agent who was impressed by her picture. He became her agent and changed her name to Nina Van Horn (after a porn actress who lived in his building). In 1969, Nina became a sensation with her bikini poster "Jungle Beach"; she next starred in the feature film *Foxy Trouble* and its sequel *Cop Full of Trouble*. She starred in a regional theater production of *A Doll's House* and in 1977 was host of the TV series *A.M. Milwaukee*. Claire later remembers a different history. She was abandoned and did grow up on a farm but was a naughty girl. She had an affair when she was 15 and a year later gave birth to a child she named Chloe (whom she gave up for adoption). She was now allergic to peanut butter ("My lips swell up") and had a different farm talent: "They called me 'The Horse Calmer Downer'" (made horses feel at ease during storms). Claire yearned for the fast life and left the farm to pursue a modeling career. She changed her name to Nina Van Horn and began her career by modeling hats in Boston. She was crowned "1974 Model of the Year" and hosted the cable E! channel's *American Awards Pre-Show*. By the late 1970s, Nina fell on hard times. She was working as a mermaid at a boat show when Jack Gallo, the publisher of *Blush*, saw her and hired her.

Addiction: Alcohol (dates back to her modeling days when she drank, partied all night, and became hooked on drugs; she has great knowledge of hallucinogenic compounds, uppers, downers, and mood regulators). She is now clean but still has access to drugs.

Best Friend: The always talked about but rarely seen Binnie (Leann Hunley).

DENNIS FINCH

Father: Red Finch (Brian Dennehy).

Position: Executive assistant to Jack Gallo. Jack sees his magazine as his castle and Dennis as his gargoyle. Dennis was previously a gift wrapper at Bloomingdale's, then a movie theater usher. His middle name is mentioned as Quimby.

Place of Birth: Albany, New York.

Education: Hudson Valley High School; Hudson Valley Community College.

Trait: A schemer who also sees *Blush* as an opportunity to meet beautiful girls. He fears owls and in his youth entered figure skating contests. He appears to know what Jack is thinking and has the ability to hack into foreign banks and manipulate the tax code for his own benefit.

Wife: Dennis marries Adrienne Barker (Rebecca Romijn), a fashion model in third-season episodes; they divorce a year later.

Favorite Song: "Time in a Bottle."

Columnist: Writes "Dear Miss Pretty."

Hobby: Collecting old TV action figures (for the money he can get for them) and ceramic kittens (which he loves and saves).

Pet Cat: Spartacus.

Computer Password: Finch Fry.

Favorite Magazine: Teen Scream.

Trait: As Jack says, "Dennis spends his time thinking about women's breasts and bottoms and has a gift for hearing words like 'nude' and 'sex' from great distances." Dennis is a yuppie and honestly believes (despite all his shenanigans) that he works hard, gets little pay, and is given no respect.

ELLIOT DIMAURO

Elliot is a photographer for *Blush*. He was born in New Jersey and attended Hawthorne High School. Although talented as a photographer, he could never achieve elite status and began selling his photographs on the streets of Manhattan. It was here that Jack first met him and hired him for *Blush*.

Elliot gets along with everyone at the magazine except Nina. They constantly insult each other, and the only thing they have in common is an old blues singer named Cholera Joe Hopper, a recording artist with such "hit" songs as "Swollen Glands," "Chin Hair Mama," and "A Pebble in My One Good Shoe." Elliot has a brother named Donnie (Dennis Cross), who is pretending to be handicapped (as children, Elliot and Donnie were playing Frisbee when the disk landed in a tree; Donnie went to retrieve it, fell out of the tree, injured his head, and, seeing this as an opportunity, faked a brain injury to be babied and get everything for free).

The King of Queens
(CBS, 1998–2006)

Cast: Kevin James (Douglas Heffernan), Leah Remini (Carrie Heffernan), Jerry Stiller (Arthur Spooner).

Basis: Events in the lives of a working married couple (Doug and Carrie) and Carrie's sarcastic father (Arthur) who lives with them.

DOUGLAS "DOUG" STEPHEN HEFFERNAN

Parents: Janet (Jenny O'Hara) and Joe Heffernan (Dakin Matthews); Joe owns a hardware store.

Sister: Stephanie Heffernan (Ricki Lake).

Place of Birth: Queens, New York, in 1965.

Address: 3121 Aberdeen Road in Rego Park, Queens. Prior to marrying Carrie, Doug lived in Apartment 5 at 63rd Street in Queens.

Education: St. Gregory's High School (also said to be St. Griffin High School; a member of the football team and called "Heifer Legs" due to being overweight).

Childhood Dog: Rocky.

Dream: Having a pet monkey.

Ability: A knack for making sandwiches (yearns to open a sandwich shop).

Occupation: Delivery man for IPS (International Parcel Service). Doug's father had hoped he would follow in his footsteps and take over the family hardware store. One day while helping his father, an IPS delivery man brought a package to the store, and Doug was hooked; he wanted to become an IPS driver (which he did in 1990). Doug was originally assigned to Zone 12 ("The Boonies"), then the more prestigious Zone 8. At IPS, Doug has the ID number 62287 and posed as Mr. April for the "Men of IPS" calendar. He holds the company record for the fewest lost packages, the most deliveries, and a perfect time record. To make extra money, Doug took a job as a limo driver and sold Sparkle Top Water Filters.

Best Friend: Deacon Palmer (Victor Williams), his coworker at IPS. Deacon and his wife, Kelly, have two children, Major and Kirby, and live in Apartment 16C of the La Frak Apartment Complex in Queens.

Religion: Catholic.

Car License Plate: 428 DIP.

Shoe Size: 11.

Hangouts: Murray's Bar; Brother's Pizzeria.

Favorite Snack: Pringle's Potato Chips.

Favorite Movie: Risky Business.

Sports: Bowling (bowls at Bowl-A-Rama on a team sponsored by Cooper's House of Ale); softball (on a team sponsored by Brother's Pizzeria; he is called "Moose").

Favorite Movie Theater: Loyola Theater (also seen as Cinema Village).

Secret: Hides his collection of adult films on VHS tapes labeled "The Bad News Bears Go to Japan."

Most Hates about Carrie: Wearing her hair in a bun (makes her look old and unattractive).

Relatives: Doug's cousin, Danny Heffernan (Gary Valentine); uncle, Stu (Gavin MacLeod).

Flashbacks: Young Doug (Tyler Hendrickson).

CARRIE HEFFERNAN

Parents: Arthur and Lily Spooner. Arthur is divorced from Lily, and it is later said that Carrie is the daughter of Arthur's deceased first wife, Sophia. Arthur also mentions having a wife, now deceased, named Theresa.

Sister: Sara Spooner (Lisa Rieffel).

Place of Birth: Greenwich Village in New York City in 1969. The family moved to Queens when Arthur became a decorative ribbon salesman. Carrie later discovers that her real name is Simone, but Arthur changed it to Carrie when, during a poker game, he put Simone's name up as stakes and lost it to his Uncle Chester (who wanted the name Simone for his daughter).

Maiden Name: Carrie Spooner.

Childhood: Carrie learned to knit from her mother and pick fights and yell from her father. She was a Brownie Scout and at the age of one developed a severe case of croup. As a preteen during the summer of 1977, she attended Camp Unity, where she picked fights and mooned truckers off Route 9.

Religion: Catholic.

Education: St. Clair's Elementary School; Monsignor Scanlon High School (when her shop teacher threatened to fail Carrie, she stole his car).

Leah Remini, Kevin James, and Jerry Stiller. *CBS/Photofest © CBS*

Occupation: Checker at Foodtown on Northern Boulevard; legal secretary in a mid-Manhattan firm called Haskell and Associates (later Kaplan, Hornstein and Steckler). Carrie arranges the muffins at the morning meetings, and a good day for her is getting positive feedback from the tight (and expensive) skirts and cleavage-revealing blouses she wears. She loses her job due to downsizing but becomes a secretary at the Dugan Group, a real estate development firm in Manhattan (prior to this, she attempted a rather disastrous homemade cell phone case company).

Measurements: 35-25-35. She stands 5 feet, 3 inches tall and wears a size 2 dress and a size 6 shoe.

Meeting: Carrie met Doug at a nightclub called Wall Street in 1992 (Doug was the bouncer; another episode claims they met over Jell-O shots on Foxy Boxing Night). They married in 1995 and lived in a small apartment before moving in with Arthur to save money for the house they currently own.

Character: Very pretty but very bossy and often overbearing. She is actually "the man of the house," and Doug fears any confrontation with her. She is not a happy person by nature and believes that dressing elegantly for work (and spending a great deal of money on her clothes) is a necessary part of their household budget.

Best Friend: Kelly Palmer (Merrin Dungey), the wife of Doug's friend Deacon.

Final Episode: Doug and Carrie, who were told they could not have children, adopt a Chinese baby girl, then learn that Carrie has become pregnant. Doug has also acquired a new job as a salesman at Finelli Home Furnishings.

Flashbacks: Young Carrie (Madison Lance, then Rhiannon Leigh Wynn).

ARTHUR EUGENE SPOONER

Place of Birth: New York in 1925. He lived on a farm from age seven to age 10.

Wife: Originally said to be Sophia, now deceased (who is Carrie's mother). He mentions being married to Lily (now divorced) and, also deceased, Theresa. He later marries Veronica Olchin (Anne Meara), the mother of Doug's friend Spence Olchin (Patton Oswalt), but the marriage ends after a few months.

Character: Obnoxious, loud, and stubborn. Arthur developed a habit of screaming and yelling at people who annoy him and fears he will lose his voice and no one will hear him (Doug calls him "a demented circus monkey"). Arthur is not a happy person and claims that the happiest day of his life occurred when he received a pair of 3-D glasses (although his older brother, Skitch, took them away from him). Arthur is 75 years old when the series begins and lives in the basement of Doug and Carrie's home (he burned down his house by cooking on a hot plate). He cheats at board games and was, at one time, addicted to nasal spray and gambling.

Military Service: Veteran of World War II (served with the 7th Infantry).

Occupation: Claims to have held the following jobs: riveter on the Empire State Building (1931; impossible, as he would have been six years old); owner of a trout farm; decorative ribbon salesman; assembly line worker at the Corbin Bowling Ball Company; crab cannery worker in Maryland; typist for former New York Mayor Abe Beame; marketing salesman; production assistant on the TV series *Sesame Street*; publishing company employee (under the name

"Clark Gable"); and entertainment director at the local senior citizen center. After retiring, he worked as a counter clerk at the Big Hot Pretzel, then at Angelo's Pizza Parlor. He tried to invent an alternate screw and driver called "Arthur's Head." He also failed at three businesses: Arthur Spooner, Music Teacher; Arthur Spooner, Candle Maker; and Rent a Senior (for people who need someone to use in car pool lanes).

Musical Ability: Plays the harmonica but failed in an attempt to start a blues band.

Favorite Song: "Tijuana Taxi."

Quirks: He has a collection of 78-rpm vinyl records and exercises to the song "Hello Mudder, Hello Fadder." He hangs out at OTB (Off Track Betting) and the Nudie Nude Bar. Arthur is notorious for stealing fruit from the neighbor's lemon tree and claims someone stole his idea for moist towelettes. He has a problem with long plane flights ("I tend to panic and scream like a woman").

Pet Parrot: Douglas.

Catchphrase: "You wanna a piece of me?" (when he loses his temper and threatens people).

Favorite Coffee Shop: Java Hut.

Exercise: Because Arthur does not keep fit, Carrie hired Holly Shumpert (Nicole Sullivan) as Arthur's dog walker (she walks him along with other dogs at the Corona Dog Park).

Flashbacks: Young Arthur (Erik Per Sullivan).

King of the Hill
(Fox, 1997–2010)

Principal Voice Cast: Mike Judge (Hank Hill/Jeff Boomhauer), Kathy Najimy (Peggy Hill), Pamela Adlon (Bobby Hill), Johnny Hardwicke (Dale Gribble), Brittany Murphy (Luanne Platter), Stephen Root (Bill Dauterive), Ashley Gardner (Nancy Gribble).

Basis: Life with family man Hank Hill (married to Peggy and the father of Bobby) and his close friends, Dale, Bill, and Boomhauer, living in Arlen, a suburban Texas town.

HANK RUTHERFORD HILL
Parents: Cotton and Tillie Mae Hill.

Place of Birth: The Bronx, New York. Hank always believed he was born in Texas until his mother revealed that she was attending a ball game at Yankee Stadium and literally gave birth to Hank in the ladies' room (this would be impossible, as Hank's time of birth is mentioned as 3:07 a.m., when the stadium would be closed). Just as inconsistent is Hank's birth year: 1953, 1954, 1955, 1956, 1959, and 1961. Hank believed he was an only child until he learned that his father, who served as a soldier during World War II, had more than 270 affairs, leaving Hank with numerous half siblings.

Address: 123 Rainey Street in Arlen, Texas (in the county of Heimlich); the living room wall reflects the state of Texas as a clock.

Pet Dog: Ladybird (a bloodhound).

Education: Arlen High School (star player on the football team). He later taught shop class at Tom Landry Middle School.

Church: Arlen First Methodist Church.

Physical Appearance: Tall (6 feet, 2 inches) and a bit overweight. He has brown hair and wears large eyeglasses.

Character: Friendly, outgoing, but afraid of taking a risk. He is very conservative and opposes lying, but when he does, he turns his head and looks around the area he is in. He prides himself on being a do-it-yourself projects expert.

Catchphrase: "I'm gonna kick your ass" (when annoyed, but just a threat).

Favorite Drink: Alamo Beer. Tuesday nights are special, as he "drinks beer with the guys in the alley."

Occupation: Salesman then assistant manager of Strickland Propane (he is so work oriented that he introduces himself to people as "Hank Hill, Strickland Propane" and answers the telephone with the company slogan, "Strickland Propane, taste the meat, not the heat"). His boss is Buck Strickland (who is addicted to gambling, drinking, and womanizing). Hank was working at the clothing store Jeans West when Buck, seeing what a great salesman he was, hired him. He is also a member of the Arlen Zoning Commission.

Awards: "Blue Flame of Valor" and "Propane Salesman of the Year."

Favorite Music: Bluegrass and country and western (idolizes Willie Nelson).

Dislikes: Alternative fuel sources, such as butane (which he calls "bastard gases").

Hobby: Caring for his lawn.

Favorite Sport: Football.

Political Party: Republican.

Red Car License Plate: 4D3 170.

Shoe Size: 12.

MARGARET "PEGGY" HILL

Parents: Doc and Maddy Platter.

Place of Birth: A Montana cattle ranch in 1959 (the family later moved to Texas).

Brother: Hoyt Platter.

Education: Arlen High School (where she met and dated Hank).

Physical Appearance: Matronly; wears eyeglasses; distinguished by large feet (size 16½). Her feet appeared on the Internet in a series of fetish videos called

Bobby, Hank, and Peggy Hill. *Fox Broadcasting/Photofest © Fox Broadcasting*

"Peggy's Feet Dot Com" (Peggy was tricked by a foot doctor to believe she was making empowerment videos to help women with large feet).

Occupation: Housewife; substitute teacher at Arlen High School and Tom Landry Middle School; reporter for the Arlen *Bystander*; agent with Seizemore Realty; proprietor of Sugarfoot's Barbecue Restaurant; customer service representative for Alamo Beer.

Favorite Pastime: Playing Boggle (won the Texas State Boggle Championship).

Character: A kind and gentle person who is completely devoted to her family; believes people can do anything if they make a commitment. If she becomes tense, she suffers from headaches.

Blood Type: AB-negative.

Sports: Member of the Lady Giants softball team.

Award: Won "Substitute Teacher of the Year" three times in a row.

Car License Plate: 416 2AS.

LUANNE LEANNE PLATTER

Relationship: Peggy's niece (the daughter of Hoyt and Leanne Platter).

Character: A very sweet young woman who came to live with Hank and Peggy when her alcoholic mother was jailed for stabbing her father with a fork during an argument and their trailer was repossessed. Peggy sees her as the daughter she never had; Hank first sees her as a bother, then as a vulnerable woman who is just looking to be with a loving family; Bobby looks on her as his sister rather than as a cousin (he considers her "the coolest person I know").

Attributes: Blonde and busty and considered a very beautiful woman.

Religion: Christian. When religion became a big part of her life, she became what she calls "a born-again virgin" and taught her own Bible study class. When she faces a tough situation, she always tells herself, "What would Jesus do?"

Dream: To become a beautician (specifically a Hollywood makeup artist). She attends the Arlen Beauty Academy, then Arlen Community College (an unspecified major). She drops out (poor grades) to work at the La Grunta Hotel (serving drinks), then as a hairstylist at the salon Hottyz.

Entertainer: Known as "Luanne and the Manger Babies." Luanne found a box of sock puppets at a garage sale and created a Christian-themed puppet show that told the story of the animals who witnessed the birth of Christ. She was hired by Arlen TV Channel 84 to perform her show for children (but was canceled when she changed the theme to a gangster-based saga).

Husband: Lucky Kleinschmidt, a lazy 38-year-old who fakes accidents to acquire money by suing. They become the parents of Gracie, a girl who most resembles Luanne.

DALE ALVIN GRIBBLE

Dale, Hank's best friend and neighbor, was born in Texas in 1949. He is married to Nancy (a TV reporter for Channel 84) and the father of Joseph (although he is unaware that Joseph is the result of an affair that Nancy had with his neighbor John Redcorn). Dale, the owner of an extermination company (Dale's Dead Bug), has been smoking Manitoba cigarettes since the third grade and uses a Zippo lighter, drinks Alamo Beer, and is not only paranoid but also a hunter, gun fanatic, and believer in urban legends and conspiracy theories. He drives a white Dodge Caravan (that he calls "The Bug-e-bago") that is distinguished by a large plastic queen ant on the roof and has the license plate LXD 352. He is a musician (electric keyboard) with the Dale Gribble Bluegrass Experience and raises show turtles. *What's Happening!!*, *Sanford and Son*, and *Fantasy Island* are his favorite TV shows. He has three locks on his front door.

Dale stands 5 feet, 10 inches tall and is distinguished by his orange cap (with "Mack" on the front) and eyeglasses (with the flip-up sunglasses on a hinge). Dale is also a bounty hunter, and when he acquires a job, he wears a blue cap with "Bounty Hunter" on it. He reports on neighborhood activities through his newsletter, "The Gribble Report," and has no athletic ability (in high school, he was the locker room towel manager). He is president of the Arlen Gun Club and believes the government is out to get him (especially the IRS, as he doesn't pay taxes and has managed to trick the government to get unemployment benefits under his alias of "Rusty Shackleford"; he claims he has not used his real name since middle school, where his name was on his library card). Dale enjoys lollipops and Mountain Dew soda and dislikes Peggy.

WILLIAM "BILL" FONTAINE DE LA TOUR DAUTERIVE

Bill, Hank's clinically depressed neighbor, was born in Louisiana in 1949 to a wealthy Cajun family (he lived on an estate called Chateau D'Haute Rive; translates as "Castle on the High Bank"; his last name means "William Fountain of the Tower of the High Bank"). Bill is divorced (from Lenore) and overweight, speaks fluent Cajun French, and plays the accordion. He was abused by his father (regularly spanked; placed in a rabbit hutch and made to wear dresses for punishment) and has the only copy of the family's secret barbecue sauce. Like Hank and Dale, he enjoys drinking Alamo Beer and engaging in discussions with them. Years of depression have changed him into a self-pitying middle-aged man. His 1949 birth date is questionable when it is seen that in 1974 he scored the most career touchdowns as a member of the Arlen High School football team (he wore jersey 72 and was called "Bill Dozer"; he would have also been a 25-year-old senior).

Bill suffers from a foot fetish and is driven insane when he sees Peggy's abnormally large feet. During his military career with the army (H Company of the 10th Infantry at Fort Blanda), he was an excellent barber and is now the local base barber. He also worked with Luanne at Hottyz, a women's hair salon, as a professional hairstylist (where he pretended to be gay so as not to offend women but was fired when it was discovered he was straight).

ROBERT JEFFREY "BOBBY" HILL

Bobby, age 13 (but also said to be 11), attends Tom Landry Middle School. Hank wanted to name him Butch, but Peggy objected. He hopes to become a stand-up comedian (like his idol, comic Celery Head) and has disappointed Hank in that he has no interest in propane. Bobby has the ability to communicate with people (especially girls), who see him as cute and charming. He cannot master a do-it-yourself project and is not as athletic as his father (which leads Hank to often say, "That boy ain't right"). Bobby does show expertise in golf and is an excellent marksman. As the series progressed, Hank and Bobby became closer, especially in their love for Texas (which Hank believes is the greatest state in the nation), food (especially meat), hunting, and even propane. Bobby then considered Hank his hero. He has the ability to make great cookies by adding extra butter, can be seen reading *Teen People* magazine, and held a job as a caddie to Buck Strickland (Hank's boss) at the Everwood Country Club. Bobby's greatest thrill (accidentally seeing Luanne nude) is also his greatest regret (as she is his cousin).

JEFFREY "JEFF" BOOMHAUER

Jeff, Hank's friend, is a ladies' man and distinguished by his incoherent southern style of speech (although through his mumblings, some words can be understood). Hank and Bill have no problem communicating with him. He idolizes classic cars (drives a 1969 Dodge; as a teenager, he drove a Ford Mustang he called "Miss Sally"). His exact occupation is unknown; he was engaged to a woman named Katherine, but his sleazy brother, Patch, stole her away from him.

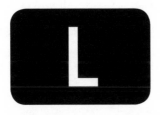

Law and Order
(NBC, 1990–2010)

Cast: Sam Waterston (Jack McCoy), Jerry Orbach (Lennie Briscoe), S. Epatha Merkerson (Anita Van Buren), Jesse L. Martin (Edward Green), Benjamin Bratt (Rey Curtis), Chris Noth (Mike Logan), Steven Hill (Adam Schiff), Alana de la Garza (Connie Rubirosa), Carolyn McCormick (Dr. Elizabeth Olivet), Anthony Anderson (Kevin Bernard), Leslie Hendrix (Dr. Elizabeth Rodgers).
Basis: Incidents in the lives of personnel with the New York Police Department (NYPD).

JOHN "JACK" McCOY
Jack, the son of Irish immigrant parents, was born in Chicago. His father, a police officer, abused both him and his unnamed mother and later died of cancer resulting from his addiction to cigarettes. Jack, raised as a Catholic (taught by the Jesuits), grew up during the era of the Vietnam War, despising it and President Richard Nixon's policies. He rides a Yamaha motorcycle and is a fan of punk rock bands. With a desire to become a lawyer, Jack attended New York University (1970) and acquired a job with the Manhattan district attorney. He eventually worked his way up to become the district attorney. As a teenager, he delivered newspapers to make money and played on his high school basketball team.

Jack is not one for adhering to the rules and breaks them to enable a conviction (he is often found in contempt of court for doing so). His time with the district attorney's office found Jack involved with three women: Diana Hawthorne (jailed for suppressing evidence); Sally Bell, a defense attorney; and Ellen, whom he married and with whom he had a daughter (Rebecca). Despite his unethical ways, Jack is responsible for prosecuting the most corrupt police officers during his time in office.

LEONARD "LENNIE" BRISCOE

Lennie, a detective with the NYPD, was born in 1940 (January 2 is given in one episode) in Manhattan. He attended P.S. 21 and mentioned parking cars as a teenager at the Atwater Hotel. Lennie's badge number is 8220, and he first began working as a beat (street) cop for three years with the 116th Precinct in Queens, before being transferred to the 27th Precinct in Manhattan. He is also said to have worked with the Manhattan 29th, 31st, 33rd, and 36th precincts as well as the 110th Precinct in Queens. He worked with the Homicide Bureau until 2004, at which time he resigned and became an investigator for the Manhattan district attorney's office; he passed away the following year. Lennie was an honest cop and known for his sarcastic sense of humor. He likes 1950s and 1960s popular music, is an expert at playing pool, and had a drinking problem, and although raised as a Catholic (his mother's side), he also considers himself Jewish (by his father's heritage). He was a corporal during the Korean War (his father, who later developed Alzheimer's disease, served in World War II; his grandfather was a bootlegger during the 1920s). Lennie was married twice (wives not named) and had two daughters: Cathy (deceased) and Julia.

ANITA VAN BUREN

Anita is a lieutenant with the Manhattan 27th Precinct of the NYPD. She is divorced from Donald Van Buren (a hardware store owner) and the mother of Ric and Stefan; she is currently engaged to Frank Gibson. She spent five years patrolling the streets and seven years as an undercover narcotics agent before being transferred to the Homicide Division. In 2010, Anita revealed that she was suffering from cervical cancer, and although not actually stated, treatments appear to have cured her. She also appears to have retired shortly after (as her position as head of the Two-Seven unit was taken over by Toni Howard; Anita had taken over the position when Captain Donald Cragen transferred). Anita was involved in shootings that resulted in death but was exonerated each time. Her efforts to file a lawsuit against the police department for discrimination (a white policewoman with less experience was promoted over her) was dismissed (but caused extra work on her and her squad in retaliation). She is a graduate of John Jay College and sometimes called by the nicknames "L.T." and "Lieu" (both referring to her rank). She was said to have served during the Vietnam War and was severely wounded during a battle.

EDWARD "ED" GREEN

Ed, badge number 3472, began working as a uniformed police officer in 1993; in 1997, he became a member of the Mid-Manhattan Narcotics Unit. He was next assigned to the 27th Precinct and partnered with Lennie Briscoe for five years (after which he became a senior detective). Nina Cassidy (Milena Govich), then Cyrus Lupo (Jeremy Sisto), whom he calls "Loops," became his partners. Ed appears to work by his own rules. When he is involved in a shooting that leads to questions about his tactics, he chooses to leave the station, citing his disenchantment. Lupo is then teamed with Kevin Bernard (Anthony Anderson), the Internal Affairs Bureau detective who investigated Ed's shooting incident. Ed is seen as having an addiction to gambling and mentions, because of his father's occupation as an oil field engineer, that he has lived in several cities around the world while growing up; his father is now suffering from Alzheimer's disease. Ed, a vegetarian, can speak Spanish and some French and Russian. He received the NYPD Meritorious Police Duty Award and the American Flag Breast Bar for his service.

REYNALDO "REY" CURTIS

Rey, married to Deborah and the father of Isabel, Olivia, and Serena, is a homicide detective with the 27th Precinct. He was originally with the Organized Crime Control Bureau but left when he felt his female superior was trying to seduce him. He is a Catholic and works strictly by the book, believing that if someone breaks the law, that person needs to be punished (even with the death penalty). Rey and Deborah married in 1989, and Deborah's recent medical condition (multiple sclerosis) forced Rey to retire from the force to care for her. Rey mentioned having a sister (who died in a car accident when she was 10 years old) and is of a mixed heritage (Native American, German, Peruvian, and English). Big Brother and the Holding Company and Oasis are mentioned as his favorite bands.

MICHAEL "MIKE" LOGAN

Mike, born on New York's Lower East Side in 1958, is the son of a working-class Irish-Catholic family. He attended Our Lady of Mercy (grammar school) but was mischievous and spent much time in detention. Mike was not typical of his fellow officers, as he was depicted as a womanizer and a man with a short fuse (referred to as Mike's "famous temper" by Captain Cragen). It is revealed that Mike was abused by his alcoholic mother as a child, and this, coupled with sexual abuse by his parish priest (at Our Lady of Mercy), manifested to create the short-tempered person he is today. Because of his position in life, he truly dislikes upper-class professionals (especially lawyers), is pro-choice, and favors drug legalization. He first served with the Homicide Division of the NYPD's 27th Precinct, then the Domestic Dispute Unit of the 128th Precinct on Staten Island, and finally the Major Case Squad Unit of the 27th Precinct.

ADAM SCHIFF

Adam, a graduate of Columbia University (served on the *Law Review*), is the New York County district attorney (he began his career in 1973 as an assistant district attorney). He is a Democrat but never lets that affiliation affect his decisions. Adam is morally opposed to capital punishment but will seek it if that is the will of the people he represents. Adam can be seen associating with many powerful judges, businessmen, and politicians—many of whom are corrupt and whose unethical practices he rejects. Adam is married but becomes a widower when his wife suffers a massive stroke and he takes her off life support when he learns there is no hope for a recovery. They have a son named Joshua (never seen). Adam mentions being a fan of baseball (Boston Red Sox) and football (Columbia Lions). He resigns in 2000 (replaced by Nora Lewin [Diane Wiest]) to become the coordinating commemorations director of the Holocaust Project.

CONSUELA "CONNIE" RUBIROSA

Connie, a graduate of Swarthmore College, is the daughter of a Spanish immigrant (a doctor) and a Mexican mother. She mentions having a sister (the victim of an abusive relationship) and a brother (married with two children). Her parents are divorced, although her mother has remarried. After graduating from college, Connie taught kindergarten for one year before pursuing a law degree. She acquired a job as an assistant district attorney with the Manhattan district attorney's office and worked her way up to executive assistant district attorney. In 2011, three years after her stepfather's passing, her mother suffered a stroke, forcing Connie to relocate to Los Angeles to care for her. Here, she acquired the position of a Los Angeles County deputy district attorney.

DR. ELIZABETH OLIVET

Elizabeth, a clinical psychologist, performs consultation work (usually providing psychological profiles of suspects) for the Manhattan district attorney's office and the 27th Detective Squad. Her duties also involve determining whether murder suspects are legally sane. Elizabeth is not an easy woman to understand. Her methods appear a bit complex and often frustrate Jack McCoy, whose prosecutions rely on Elizabeth's findings (Elizabeth sides with compassion, suggesting incarceration in a mental facility or psychotherapy sessions rather than imprisonment). She later resigns from the police department to begin her own practice.

KEVIN BERNARD

Kevin, an Internal Affairs Bureau detective, wears badge number 1954 and joined the department to become a homicide detective. He was born in Compton, California, where as a child he witnessed how illegal immigrants are treated, with farmers hiring them as cheap labor. He supports the pro-life movement and is not overly fond of dogs (as in his Catholic grammar school he was nicknamed "Saint Bernard"). His personal life is virtually a mystery with the exception of the revelation that while at the police academy, Kevin had an affair with a fellow cadet that resulted in the birth of a boy. The boy, raised by his mother (who later marries someone else), believes that this man is his father (as Kevin is not a part of his life).

DR. ELIZABETH RODGERS
Elizabeth, a medical examiner for the Manhattan coroner's office, is often frustrated by her job, as the answers that detectives need are not readily available after an autopsy. It is revealed that Elizabeth hoped to become a surgeon but found that performing surgery on a live person dramatically upset her; she then changed her career to pathologist. Elizabeth loves classical music and considers herself an amateur sleuth (based on the knowledge she gains from reading detective novels). She is totally dedicated to her job (even eats her lunch in the morgue next to bodies) and later becomes the New York City assistant chief medical examiner.

Law and Order: Special Victims Unit
(NBC, 1999–2017)

Cast: Mariska Hargitay (Olivia Benson), Chris Meloni (Elliot Stabler), Dann Florek (Don Cragen), Ice T (Odafin Tutuola), Kelli Giddish (Amanda Rollins), Diane Neal (Casey Novak), Richard Belzer (John Munch), Raul Esparza (Rafael Barba).

Basis: A profile of the detectives attached to the Special Victims Unit (SVU) of the New York Police Department (NYPD).

OLIVIA "LIV" MARGARET BENSON
Olivia is a lieutenant with the 16th Precinct's SVU. She was born in 1968 and joined the NYPD in 1992, being assigned first to the 55th Precinct. She worked as beat cop for six years, was promoted to detective in 1998, and became a sergeant in 2013 and a lieutenant in 2015. She worked with Elliot Stabler for 12 years and took over the SVU when its incumbent head, Captain Donald Cragen, retired.

Olivia's birth resulted from a rape (Serena, a teenager working in the Columbia University cafeteria, was attacked by Joseph Hollisater, a food salesman, in 1967). Joseph later committed suicide, while Serena, who abused Olivia, was an alcoholic and died in 2000 when she sustained injuries from a fall down a subway staircase (being drunk at the time).

While Elliot can be seen feeling for the victims of a sexual assault, Olivia appears to be very sympathetic to them (perhaps because of what happened to her mother). She can speak French, Italian, and some Spanish and is thus able

Mariska Hargitay and Christopher Meloni. *NBC/Photofest © NBC*

to read culprits their *Miranda* rights in different languages. Olivia has A-positive blood and has not been wounded during her time with the department (although she has been exonerated from several police-involved shootings).

ELLIOT STABLER

Elliot, a detective with the Manhattan 16th Precinct's SVU, was born in Bayside, Queens, in 1966 and married a woman named Kathy in 1984. They are the parents of Maureen, Kathleen, Elizabeth and Richard (twins), and Elliot Jr.

Elliot is from an Irish American family and is the son of Joseph and Bernadette Stabler. Joseph, a police officer, lost his pension when he refused to testify against dirty cops; Bernadette suffered from bipolar disorder. Elliot has three brothers and two sisters (all unnamed) and attended the Sisters of Mercy High School and Queens College. He served a hitch with the U.S. Marines before joining the police department (while in the service, he got a tattoo on his forearm that depicts an eagle, an anchor, and a globe); he also did a tour in Operation Desert Storm in 1991. Elliot wears badge number 6313 and is noted for his case closure rate (solves 93 percent of his assignments) and was partners with Olivia Benson for 12 years (he retired in 2011 after being a cop for 22 years, 19 of which were with the SVU; he joined the NYPD in 1986). It is mentioned that as a child, Elliot showed interest in being an architect but wanted to become a police officer like his father (who was also abusive to him).

DONALD "DON" CRAGEN
Don has a long and distinguished career with the NYPD. He was born in the late 1940s (April 1, 1947, is mentioned in one episode) and served as the commander of both the 27th Precinct and the SVU. He began his career in the mid-1960s as a beat cop (after serving in the army as a Green Beret), then as a detective and captain. He was associated with the 16th and 24th precincts, the Anti-Corruption Task Force, and finally the SVU. He was married to Marge, a flight attendant (killed in a plane crash), and was addicted to alcohol (using liquor to help him get over the horrors of his job). Although he is a captain, he is listed as a lieutenant in the credits. A poster of the Lone Ranger can be seen on the window to Don's office door.

AMANDA ROLLINS
Amanda, born in Atlanta, Georgia, served with the SVU of the Atlanta Eighth Precinct. A serial rape case brought her to New York, where, after capturing the culprit, she landed a job with the Manhattan 16th Precinct. Very little is revealed about her. She is the daughter of Beth Ann and an unnamed father and has a sister named Kim. She has a daughter, out of wedlock, named Jesse and had (and appears to have under control) a gambling problem (she attends Gamblers Anonymous meetings).

ODAFIN "FIN" TUTUOLA
Fin is a sergeant with the Manhattan 16th Precinct's SVU. He was born in Harlem in 1962, and is divorced from Teresa Randall and the father of Kwasi (nicknamed Ken), a gay who is now married (to Alejandro), and through a surrogate they are expecting a baby boy (who Odafin wants to be called "Fin"). Fin served with the U.S. Army's 75th Ranger Regiment and joined the NYPD in 1985. He was assigned to the Narcotics Division in 1992 (in an undercover capacity) and in 2000 became a member of the SVU (where he served with John Munch for seven years). Fin is an avid fan of video games and attends such annual conventions (video games, he says, give him the release he needs from the pressures of his job).

CASEY NOVAK
Casey is an attorney who first worked as a clerk for a judge named Mary Clark. She is a graduate of Harvard Law School and investigated white-collar crimes as a member of the White Collar Bureau of the Manhattan district attorney's office before joining the 16th Precinct's SVU. Casey is Catholic, and based on her mention that her birthstone is a sapphire, she was born in September. She lives on Manhattan's Upper East Side and is a member of the precinct's Sex Crimes softball team. Casey often becomes too close to the victims of rape cases, thus

letting her emotions interfere with her judgment. She prides herself on a 71 percent successful conviction rate, and she too became a victim of rape (beaten so severely that she required treatment in the intensive care unit).

JOHN MUNCH

John, born in Maryland and a graduate of Pikesville High School, began his career in law enforcement with the Baltimore Police Department (as seen on the 1983 NBC series *Homicide: Life on the Street*, where the character first appeared). In 1995, he was promoted to senior detective. He joined the NYPD's 16th Precinct in 1999 and served with the SVU (first as a senior detective, then as a sergeant) until his retirement in 2013 (at which time he became a special investigator of the Manhattan district attorney's office). Due to inconsistencies in dialogue, John mentions that he also grew up on the Lower East Side of Manhattan and that his birth year could be either 1944 or 1951.

John is Jewish and can speak Russian, Hebrew, Greek, and Yiddish. He was married four times; two of his ex-wives are seen: Gwen (Carol Kane) and Billie Lou (Ellen McElduff). John mentioned that his grandfather worked in the garment industry and that his father was physically abusive to him (which made John resent him; it is learned that John's father suffered bipolar disorder and later committed suicide; his mother is currently living in a retirement community). John also appears to have two brothers: Bernie (owns a funeral parlor) and David (owner of a drywall business). He also has two uncles: Lee (a bar manager) and Andrew (Jerry Lewis), the latter suffering from severe depression and living on the streets of Manhattan. At some point in the late 1960s, John used his love of music to write reviews for an alternative magazine called *The Paper*. By the early 1970s, John considered himself "a dangerous radical" (although the police found him not to be a threat) due to his anti–Vietnam War protests and left-wing political views. John mentions owning a bar (the Waterfront) while living in Baltimore and has high hopes of opening one in Manhattan. During his tenure with the NYPD, John earned several awards: Firearms Proficiency, Excellent Police Duty, and the American Flag Breast Bar.

RAFAEL BARBA

Rafael, a Cuban American, was born in the Bronx (grew up on Jerome Avenue). He attended an unnamed Catholic high school and earned a law degree at Harvard University. He first worked at the Kings County (Brooklyn) district attorney's office, then for the Manhattan district attorney's office, where he was assigned to the Sex Crimes Bureau of the 16th Precinct. Rafael is a stickler for following the rules (often too meticulous, as it hinders his thinking). Lauren Sullivan, an 11th-grade classmate, was his first love; in later life, he was in a relationship with a woman named Yeline Munoz. Although his parents are not named, his mother was the principal of a charter school; his father passed away sometime in the 1990s. His grandmother Catalina Diaz recently passed at the age of 85. Rafael enjoys skiing and attending Broadway plays and later becomes a district attorney, although he is still referred to as an assistant district attorney.

Living Single
(Fox, 1993–1997)

Cast: Queen Latifah (Khadjah James), Kim Fields (Regine Hunter), Kim Coles (Synclaire James), Erika Alexander (Maxine Shaw), John Henton (Overton Jones), T. C. Carson (Kyle Barker).

Basis: A behind-the-scenes look at the operations of a magazine as seen through the experiences of cousins Khadjah and Synclaire James.

KHADJAH JAMES

Khadjah was born in East Orange, New Jersey, and is a graduate of Howard University. She was editor of the school's newspaper and worked in a rat costume at Chuckie Cheese. After graduating, she moved to New York to establish *Flavor*, a monthly magazine dedicated to African American women. She chose the title *Flavor* "because we've got taste."

Khadjah lives in a brownstone in the Prospect Heights section of Brooklyn in an apartment with changing numbers (A, 1A, and 3A). *Flavor* is located in Manhattan above the Chemical Bank Building, and the tacky (as Khadjah calls it) *Savor* magazine is her competition. Khadjah often takes on too much work (being the owner and editor) and is often stressed out by the end of the day. She hates to borrow money and can't sleep or eat until she pays it back. While she dated, she never found a man who could meet her standards until she reconnected with her childhood friend and found romance with Terrence "Scooter" Williams (Cress Williams). Rita Owens played Khadjah's mother, Rita James.

SYNCLAIRE JAMES

Synclaire was born in Missouri and also attended Howard University. She is now Khadjah's receptionist at *Flavor* but worked previously as a supermarket cashier, telephone solicitor, babysitter, and order taker at the Turkey Burger Hut. She has a dream of becoming an actress and shares an apartment with Khadjah.

Synclaire feels that her head is too big for her body ("I applied for a job at Chuckie Cheese but lost it because my head was too big to fit the rat head") and has devised a unique office filing system she calls "an emotional filing system"

Queen Latifah, Kim Coles, Kim Fields, and Erika Alexander. *Fox/Photofest © Fox*

("Things that make Khadjah happy are in the front, the things that make her weary are in the back, and the things that upset her are not within her reach"). When Synclaire feels blue, she wears wind chime earrings; she decorates her desk (and the office) with troll dolls ("to spread joy and happiness in the office"; she calls the largest doll "Crispis Attucks"), and the least favorite time of the day for her is quitting time ("I have to say good-bye to the makeup that got me through the day"). Her Christmas gifts are also unique: made from the plastic egg in which Leggs pantyhose are sold. As a child, she had a pet turtle (Fred) and a plush cat (Mr. Jammers). As the series ended, Synclaire joined a comedy troupe and came to the attention of a Warner Bros. TV executive who offered her the role of a nun in a sitcom he was developing.

REGINE HUNTER
Regine, Khadjah's friend, also lives with her and Synclaire. She was born in East Orange, New Jersey (grew up with Khadjah), and has the real first name of Regina, "but that is not classy enough for me." Regine is a clothing buyer for the Boutique in Manhattan. As the series progressed, she turns her love of fashion into a job as a costume designer for a Spanish TV soap opera (*Palo Alto*), then a wedding planner. When Regine becomes engaged to Dexter Knight (Don Franklin), she moves in with him. Ira Lee "Trip" Williams III (Mel Jackson), a songwriter, becomes Khadjah's and Synclaire's new roommate.

Regine is extremely feminine and a fanatic about clothes. She was a beautiful child and uses her beauty to get what she wants. She is self-centered and self-absorbed and wants to have children—"These genes are too good to waste." She is well endowed and called "loud and busty" by her friends. She attended MIT and claims that "my double D's" got her in and that "my breasts also made me Homecoming Queen."

Regine is on a mission to marry a man "who knows that fine wine doesn't come with a twist-off cap." She believes that she is irresistible to men and that "sometimes life is not fair to me. That's why bras come in different sizes." Regine must have a man by her side at all times. If she is in a room and a man doesn't look at her, she eases her fear by saying, "He must be gay." Being without a man for long periods of time (two or three days) causes Regine to panic, as she believes she is losing her looks and goes on a chocolate-eating binge. She lives by a code she calls "The Three C's of Men: Catch, Control, Conquer." Regine mentions she is a vegetarian, but she can be seen eating fish sticks. Chip Fields (Kim's real-life mother) played her mother, Laverne Hunter.

Kim Fields's real-life breast reduction surgery was incorporated into the series, changing her Regine character somewhat. She became less obnoxious and more caring; showing ample cleavage didn't matter as it once did.

MAXINE "MAX" FELICE SHAW
Maxine is a lawyer with the firm of Evans, Bell and Associates in Manhattan. She is a friend of Khadjah, Synclaire, and Regine and later became an attorney for the public defender's office. She was born in Philadelphia and met Khadjah at Howard University. She has her own apartment (address not given) but considers Khadjah's apartment her second home.

OVERTON WAKEFIELD AND KYLE BARKER
Overton and Kyle are best friends (grew up in Cleveland, Ohio) and now share an apartment in the Brooklyn brownstone where Khadjah lives. Overton is the building's maintenance man and lives by the handyman's code "I won't rest until it's fixed." He is dating Synclaire (who calls him "Obie"), and the two later marry. Overton has "a secret shame" (a fear of clowns), a dog (Sanford; named after his favorite TV series, *Sanford and Son*), three fish (Cocoa, Kyle, and Maurice), and shops at a hardware store called the Hardware Hacienda. Sundays are special for him and Synclaire—"It's flea market shopping day."

Kyle is a stockbroker and believes that he is irresistible to women. He was in a band called Water ("the missing element in Earth, Wind and Fire") and has a love–hate relationship with Max.

Mad about You
(NBC, 1992–1999)

Cast: Helen Hunt (Jamie Buchman), Paul Reiser (Paul Buchman).
Basis: Events in the lives of Jamie and Paul Buchman, a diverse New York couple.

JAMIE BUCHMAN
Parents: Gus (Carroll O'Connor, John Karlen, Paul Dooley) and Theresa Stemple (Carol Burnett, Penny Fuller, Nancy Dussault).
Place of Birth: New Haven, Connecticut, in 1962.
Sister: Lila Stemple (Anne Ramsay).
Maiden Name: Jamie Stemple.
Nickname: Called "Peanut" by her father.
Education: Yale University.
Address: 142 West 81st Street (Apartment 11D) in Manhattan.
Pet Dog: Murray.
Occupation: Regional vice president of the Ferrah-Ganz public relations firm on Madison Avenue in Manhattan. When she is laid off, she first works as a press agent for the mayor of New York City. She then joins with her friend Fran Devanow (Leila Kenzie) to begin their own public relations firm (Buchman-Devanow). Fran is married to Dr. Mark Devanow (Richard Kind), a gynecologist and called "Snookie" by Fran; they live on Second Avenue. In her youth, Jamie was a counselor at Camp Winneway.
Quirk: Likes to be liked by other people and goes out of her way to impress them so they will like her (in high school, Jamie was known as "the Stemple sister who showed a boy her boobs to be liked"). She also has a knack for telling pathetic stories about herself and having people believe her.
Measurements: 36-25-35. She stands 5 feet, 8 inches tall and wears a size 8 shoe and a size 2 dress.

Helen Hunt and Paul Reiser. *NBC/Photofest © NBC*

Comic Book: Her image appears in *Mega Void* as the evil Queen Talin.
Birth: In 1997, Jamie and Paul become the parents of a girl they name Mabel
(played in a flash-forward at age 18 by Meredith Bishop).

PAUL BUCHMAN

Parents: Burt (Louis Zorich) and Sylvia Buchman (Cynthia Harris). When Burt
enters Paul and Jamie's apartment, he says, "It's me, Burt, Burt Buchman,
your father."

Siblings: Debbie Buchman (Robin Bartlett) and Ira Buchman (John Pankrow).
Place of Birth: Manhattan.
Occupation: Documentary filmmaker (owner of Buchman Films). When the company folded, he became a producer and director for the Explorer Channel.
Favorite TV Show As a Kid: Spy Lady (mythical).
Career Inspiration: The first movie he saw: *Attack of the 50 Foot Woman* (made in 1958 with Allison Hayes as the star).
First Documentary Film Made: A Day in the Life of a Button.
Famous For: His "classic" film *Hooter Vacation.*
Education: New York University School of Film.
Address: Prior to moving into Jamie's apartment, Paul lived at 129 West 81st Street (Apartment 5B); he now sublets the apartment to Kramer (from the series *Seinfeld*).
Favorite Eatery: Riff's Bar. Ursula (Lisa Kudrow), the absentminded waitress, is Phoebe's cousin from the series *Friends.*
Movie Rentals: Paul and Jamie are members of Video Village.
The Meeting: It was a Sunday morning in December of 1989 when Paul, at a newsstand and about to buy the last copy of the *New York Times*, meets a girl (Jamie Stemple) who is also seeking the *Times*. She tells him that she needs the paper because it contains her parents' obituary ("beams fell on them during an earthquake"). Paul believes her and lets her buy the paper. As Jamie departs, she drops a dry-cleaning receipt with her name on it. That night, while with friends, Paul checks the obituary page of the *Times* and sees no Stemple. The following day, Paul picks up Jamie's dry cleaning (pretending to be Coco, Jamie's houseboy) and tracks Jamie down. The two fall in love and marry in 1992 (five months before the series begins).
Relatives: Uncles Phil (Mel Brooks) and Julius (Al Ruscio).

Note: In the pilot film, Jamie and Paul have the last name Cooper.

Moesha
(UPN, 1996–2001)

Cast: Brandy Norwood (Moesha Mitchell).
Basis: Incidents in the life of a teenage girl (Moesha) from high school through her acceptance into college.

MOESHA DENISE MITCHELL
Parents: Frank (William Allen Young), the owner of a car dealership, and Deidre "Dee" Mitchell (Sheryl Lee Ralph), her stepmother, the vice principal of

Crenshaw High School; her biological mother is deceased. Frank married
Dee three months before the series begins. Dee, who enjoys shopping for
clothes at the Swap Meet, is desperately seeking to win Moesha's love but
finds it difficult, as Moesha believes no woman can replace her real mother.
Brother: Miles Mitchell (Marcus T. Paulick). He has a Chicago Bulls poster on his
bedroom door along with a sign that reads, "Caution: No Trespassing." He

Countess Vaughn, Lamont Bentley, Brandy Norwood, William Allen Young,
Shar Jackson, and Marcus T. Paulick. *UPN/Photofest © UPN*

is a talented dancer but also has a knack for getting into trouble and hearing "go to your room." His most defiant act was smoking weed in his bedroom.

Birthday: May 17, 1981 (she is 15 years old when the series begins).

Nickname: "Mo" (by friends) and "Pumpkin" (only by her father).

Favorite TV Show As a Child: The mythical *Spunky's World.*

Address: 6653 West Post Road in Los Angeles.

Education: Crenshaw High School (a straight "A" student). In 1999, after graduating from Crenshaw, Moesha put college aside to become a part of the workforce (she was accepted into Columbia University, Northwestern University, the University of Southern California, Harvard University, and Spellman College). When this failed, she chose to attend Columbia University (although she previously mentioned Northwestern as being her dream college).

Wardrobe: Moesha always tries to be in style but is stopped from wearing cleavage-revealing tops and midriff blouses by Frank (who, along with Dee, feels she is too young to be showing skin; when Moesha shows cleavage, Frank has "a heart attack," as he claims. He believes his gray hairs "are a part of raising a beautiful teenage girl").

Flaw: Moesha believes "my only flaw is that I have a big butt."

Character: A sweet, kind, and obedient daughter until she grew older and balked at parental authority and faced constant punishment for doing so (which changed the focus of the show from typical high school girl to rebellious high school girl). She is very friendly and likes to help people she believes are in trouble (and always makes situations worse). She hates to hear the words "Moesha, we have to talk" from Dee (as she knows she is in trouble).

Hangout: The Den.

Jobs: Salesgirl at Class Act (a clothing store); receptionist at *Vibe* magazine. Moesha hoped to become a writer and overstepped her bounds (interviewing Maya Angelou without permission) and was fired from *Vibe* (prompting her to attend college).

Failed Business: Unforgettable Vitamins (a supplement to help people remember).

The Nanny
(CBS, 1993–1999)

Cast: Fran Drescher (Fran Fine), Charles Shaughnessy (Maxwell Sheffield), Lauren Lane (C. C. Babcock), Nicholle Tom (Maggie Sheffield), Madeline Zima (Gracie Sheffield), Benjamin Salisbury (Brighton Sheffield), Daniel Davis (Niles).

Basis: A nanny (Fran) attempts to care for the children (Maggie, Gracie, and Brighton) of a widowed Broadway producer (Maxwell) while at the same time hoping to become his wife.

FRANCINE "FRAN" JOY FINE

Parents: Sylvia (Renee Taylor) and Morty Fine (Steve Lawrence, then Mort Drescher).

Sister: Nadine (Ellen Ratner); she is married to Barry Cooperman.

Place of Birth: Flushing, New York, in 1964 (later said to be November 26, 1970). She mentions being a Libra.

Education: P.S. 19 (also given as P.S. 165); Flushing High School (also said to be Hillcrest High School); here, she was a member of the Cosmetology Club and played the Reverend Mother in the school play *The Sound of Music.*

Childhood: Lived in Apartment 11 in Flushing; had her sweet 16 party in the Half Shell Room at Benny's Clam Bar; attended Camp Kindervelt in 1974 (making the 1964 date correct); had a pet goldfish named Goldie.

Occupation: Beautician, then Nanny. Fran attended the Ultisima Beauty Institute (later mentions the Barbizon School of Modeling). Her fascination with beauty led her to become an expert on hair, makeup, and clothing (she wears size 2 miniskirts, cleavage-revealing blouses, and bright colors; as she says, "Some women believe I'm a hooker by the clothes I wear"). Fran was a foot model for two years, then a salesgirl at the Bridal Shoppe in Flushing.

She was fired for rejecting her boss's advances and became a door-to-door salesgirl for Shades of the Orient Cosmetics. At the home of Maxwell Sheffield, she was mistaken for an agency nanny and hired when she impressed Maxwell's children. It is later revealed that the spirit of Maxwell's deceased wife (Sara) sent Fran to Maxwell, as she knew she could take her place and raise her children.

Measurements: 34-26-34. She stands 5 feet, 7 inches tall and wears a size 7 shoe.

Favorite Music: Jazz.

Pride and Joy: Her collection of "pilfered memorabilia."

Favorite TV Shows: The Young and the Restless; Jeopardy (where she was a contestant); the fictional *Edge of Life* (as a child). She is an expert on 1960s TV shows.

Favorite Hair Salon: The Chatterbox.

Favorite Actress: Barbra Streisand. *Yentl,* starring Barbra, is her favorite movie, and she claims "Barbra is my spiritual leader." She paid $200 for bubblegum (now framed) stepped on by Barbra and taken from the bottom of her shoe and feels she and Barbra have a lot in common—"We share the same heritage and an unusual voice."

Membership: Shopper's Anonymous (she shops when depressed).

Acting: Played Juliet in Maxwell's off-Broadway production of *Romeo and Juliet.*

Title: Voted "Miss Subways of 1989"; appeared as "America's Favorite Nanny" on *The Rosie O'Donnell Show.*

Character: Loves to give advice and solve problems with flair, style, and street psychology. Her voice is nasal and high pitched and is annoying to some people. She mentions becoming a TV weathergirl as her greatest desire.

Final Season: Fran and Maxwell marry and become the parents of twins Eve Kathryn and James Samuel.

Relatives: Fran's grandmother, Yetta Rosenberg (Ann Morgan); grandma, Netta (Marilyn Cooper); cousin, Tiffany (Jaclyn John); aunts, Rose (Sylvia Drescher), Sparkle (Ann Berger), and Frieda (Lainie Kazan); foster daughter, Mei Ling (Jennie Kwan); great uncle, Manny (Milton Berle). Unseen were Shiomo Rosenberg (Yetta's husband) and Marsha Rosenberg (Fran's niece).

Flashbacks: Young Fran (Jamie Renee Smith).

MAXWELL SHEFFIELD

Parents: James (Robert Vaughn) and Joan Sheffield (Joan Collins). James was first married to Elizabeth, now deceased (Dina Merrill in flashbacks). He also says his first wife's name was Sara (Bess Armstrong in flashbacks).

Place of Birth: England; raised by Clara Mueller (Cloris Leachman), a strict nanny.

Sisters: Jocelyn (Sophie Ward, then Twiggy); she called him "Mopsey"; half sister (by Joan and James), Conception (Maria Conchita Alonso).

Nicholle Tom, Fran Drescher, Charles Shaughnessy, Benjamin Salisbury, and Madeline Zima. *CBS/Photofest © CBS*

Brother: Nigel Sheffield (Harry Van Gorkum).
Address: "A fashionable 19-room home on Park Avenue."
Education: The Eton School; Oxford University.
Occupation: Broadway producer and owner of Maxwell Sheffield Productions.
Productions: The Sound of Music (produced in England when he was 17), *The Widower, Annie II, Moby* (based on the novel *Moby-Dick*), *Norma* (a musical

based on the film *Norma Rae*), *Whodunit, The Widower, Loves Me Not,* and *Regardless.* He has won three Tony Awards.

Regrets: Not backing such plays as *Cats, Sunset Blvd.,* and *Phantom of the Opera,* which he felt were lame ideas and would never make it as successful Broadway plays.

Recognition: Listed as one of the most eligible widowers by *Esquire* magazine.

Trademark: Wears blazers with nautical symbols and gold buttons.

Relatives: Mother-in-law, Roberta (Diane Baker); father-in-law, Ernest (George Coe) (both are Sara's parents); grandmother, Eloise; great-grandmother, Eve Catherine; great aunt, Isobel; great uncles, Philip and Bill.

Flashbacks: Young Maxwell (Christopher Marquette).

Final Episode: Before moving to California to produce a TV series, Maxwell produced *Yetta's Letters,* a play based on Fran's grandmother's love letters. The somewhat senile Yetta believes that Maxwell and Fran are Rob and Laura Petrie (from *The Dick Van Dyke Show,* where Ann Morgan, then Ann Morgan Guilbert, who plays Yetta, was Rob and Laura's next-door neighbor, Millie Halper).

CHASTITY CLAIRE "C. C." BABCOCK

Parents: Stewart (Robert Culp) and B. B. Babcock (not seen).

Position: Maxwell's business partner after he changed the name of his company to Sheffield-Babcock Productions.

Place of Birth: New York City to a wealthy family and is second in line to inherit a fortune (her mother is first).

Siblings: Sister, D. D. Babcock; brother, Noel Babcock (Michael McKean).

Address: 407 East 86th Street.

Character: C. C. believes that people think of her as a "self-centered, cold-hearted witch." She tries to be nice, sincere, and sensitive, "but my nasty attitude can't make that happen." She has a terrible memory for names, especially when it comes to Maxwell's children (whom she calls "Macy," "Bob," and "Nancy"; she calls Fran "Nanny Fine").

Pampered Pet Dog: Chester.

Computer Password: Good and Plenty (after the candy).

Infatuation: C. C. tries to impress Maxwell with her business knowledge in the hope that he will one day propose marriage to her (which failed when Maxwell married Fran).

MARGARET "MAGGIE" SHEFFIELD

Maggie is Maxwell's 14-year-old daughter. Although very pretty, she does not see herself as such or even in a positive light. She feels, "I'm too tall and a worthless, pathetic unlovable thing." She also believes she has no personality and will never fall in love. Fran's intervention with makeup and sexier (but conservative) clothes gave her a positive outlook. As the series progressed, Maggie considered Fran her best friend, not her nanny.

Maggie attends Holy Cross Grammar School, Lexington Academy High School, and finally Columbia University. She enjoys school, rarely complains about homework, and is taking figure skating lessons. Her gorgeous looks came to the attention of the Chloe Simpson Modeling Agency, and Maggie was tested for a series of stylish teen ads, but her test results found her to be "vacant and lifeless." Her first job was a volunteer candy striper at Bellmont Hospital. As the series progressed, Maggie met a male model named Michael (Andrew Levita), and the two married. What made this unusual was that Andrew was the cousin of James Brolin, who was married to Fran's idol, Barbra Streisand. At one point, Maggie was seen as an activist and involved in a "Save the Planet" campaign.

GRACE "GRACIE" VICTORIA SHEFFIELD

Gracie, six years old when the series begins, is Maxwell's youngest child and called "Angel" by Fran. She appears wiser than her age but has been classified as "a complicated girl with multiple issues." She is introverted and insecure and, for one so young, attends therapy sessions. She likes school but can't enjoy it (she worries that the polar ice caps are melting and could upset the balance of the globe). She first attends Holy Cross Grammar School (where she played the Itsy Bitsy Spider in the school play *Mother Goose on Broadway*), then the Lexington Academy.

Gracie believes the gorgeous showgirls that audition for her father are "giant Barbie dolls." She is a member of the scout troop the Red Robbins, takes ballet lessons, has a teddy bear (Mr. Fuzzy; later called Teddy), two hamsters (Mr. Sheffield and Miss Fine), and an invisible friend she calls "Imogene." Gracie is very obedient and very close to Fran, whom she considers a substitute mother.

BRIGHTON SHEFFIELD

Brighton, age 10, is the middle child and quite mischievous when the series begins. He has a keen interest in sports (especially baseball; the New York Mets are his favorite team) and attends the same schools as Gracie. He shared his first kiss with Fran's cousin Tiffany, and living with Fran and becoming exposed to Fran's overly protective mother sort of rubbed off on him, as he became a member of Fran's mother's elderly canasta team, the Flushing Queens. He and Fran enjoy watching *Gilligan's Island* marathons to see the theme change from "And the rest are here on Gilligan's Island" to "The Professor and Mary Ann, here on Gilligan's Island." His one bad habit is overindulging on junk food. He later develops an overactive interest in girls and plays right field on his Little League team. Final-season episodes see Brighton attending Yale University.

NILES

Niles, like Cher, has only a single name. He has been in Maxwell's service for 25 years in 1999 (his father was a butler to Maxwell's father, James). He is a member of the Professional Butler's Association, and although he does cook and clean, his favorite part of the job is watching the beautiful showgirls audition for a part in a play. He is also Maxwell's chauffeur (driving his limousine) and has written the play *Love, Valet, Companion*, which he hopes to convince Maxwell to produce. In his all-boys high school play *The Sound of Music*, Niles played the Baroness. His favorite food is Belgian waffles (which Fran calls "Eggos") and has a love–hate relationship with C. C. (they continually insult each other but marry in the final episode); Niles is also a compulsive gambler.
Flashbacks: Young Niles (Preston Wamsley).

Nash Bridges
(CBS, 1996–2001)

Cast: Don Johnson (Nash Bridges), Cheech Marin (Joe Dominguez), Jodi Lyn O'Keefe (Cassidy Bridges), Yasmine Bleeth (Caitlin Cross), James Gammon (Nick Bridges).

Basis: Detectives Nash Bridges and Joe Dominguez investigate cases on behalf of the Special Investigative Unit (SIU) of the San Francisco Police Department (SFPD).

NASH BRIDGES

Place of Birth: San Francisco on December 7, 1955.

Sister: Stacy Bridges (Angela Dohrman), an assistant district attorney who is also a lesbian.

Daughter: Cassidy Bridges.

Wife: Nash is divorced from Lisa (Annette O'Toole), his first wife (Cassidy's mother), a food caterer, and from his second wife, Kelly (Serena Scott Thomas), a socialite.

Brother: Bobby Bridges (John Walcott), a drug dealer (later killed).

Address: 86 Sacramento Street (where he lives with Cassidy and his retired father, Nick).

Education: Bay High School (wore jersey 55 as a member of the football team); San Francisco State College. After graduation, he entered the police academy.

Childhood: Had a dog named Old Jimbo and developed an interest in magic (especially sleight of hand).

Car: A 1971 yellow Plymouth Barracuda he calls "the Cuda." In some episodes, Nash claims the car was made in 1970.

License Plate: GQD 685.

Occupation: Inspector (received a Gold Star for bravery), then captain of the SIU branch of the SFPD.

Badge Number: 22.

Car Code: 5-George 51.

SIU Headquarters: An old warehouse in downtown San Francisco, then a docked ferry boat off Hyde Street called the *Eureka,* and finally a 177-foot-long barge (once housing the Allied Cannery Company, then a rave club; it is believed to be haunted).

Character: Nash tends to call people "Bubba," balks at having to follow the rules, and hates sharing information with the FBI ("They're too damned sure about everything," he says). Doing things his way causes friction with his superiors but gets the job done.

Side Business: Nash and Joe moonlight as private investigators in a business called Bridges and Dominguez—Private Investigations (located at 427 Grey Street in an office building occupied by psychiatrists).

JOE DOMINGUEZ

Relationship: When first introduced, Joe was Nash's ex-partner who had quit the force to become a private detective; he is then back on the force and Nash's partner.

Rank: Inspector, then lieutenant.

Businesses: Partner with Nash in Bridges and Dominguez—Private Investigations; owner of the Tender Loin, a gay bar he acquired in a get-rich scheme that backfired; part owner (with his family) of Loco Joe's Salsa, a dip made from a family recipe (he receives 1 percent of the profits).

Nickname for Nash: "The Nashman."

Wife: Inger (Caroline Langerfelt); she and Joe later become the parents of an infant they name Lucia.

Address: 4665 Laguna.

Character: More respectful of the law than Nash (laid back and prone to following the rules, unlike Nash's shoot-first-and-ask-questions-later approach).

CASSIDY BRIDGES

Relationship: The only child of Nash and Lisa Bridges.

Place of Birth: San Francisco.

Education: Union Bay High School; Berkeley College.

Career Choice: Originally, Cassidy had aspirations to become an actress (she appeared topless in an avant-garde play called *Tears of the Monkey*). Having been raised by Nash, she found an interest in law enforcement and joined the police academy. After graduating, she was assigned to Nash's unit.

Favorite Ice Cream Flavor: Chocolate.

Measurements (in 2000): 36-25-34. She stands 5 feet, 10 inches tall and has blue eyes and brown hair.

Character: Cassidy is rarely defiant and loyal to both her father and her mother (Lisa). If she does become angry or upset, she takes her frustrations out on a police gym punching bag.

Final Episode: Cassidy is seen leaving for Paris, undecided about her future.

CAITLIN CROSS

Occupation: Inspector with the Internal Affairs Division of the SFPD.

Place of Birth: San Francisco (grew up in the posh Sea Cliff section).

Childhood: An uncanny interest in watching crime dramas on TV led her to become a law enforcement officer.

Education: Union Bay High School; San Francisco State University.

After College: Caitlin joined the San Francisco Police Academy and graduated with top honors. She first worked for the FBI but quit "when I couldn't tell the lies from the truths." She next worked as an analyst for the CIA, Russian Intelligence Division ("I analyzed documents all day long"; as a result, she can speak and read Russian). She resigned five years later when the mayor of San Francisco hired her to oversee the procedures of the SIU.

Address: 440 California Avenue.

Measurements: 37-26-38. She stands 5 feet, 5 inches tall; has "sultry blue eyes" (as seen on her driver's license), and wears a size 7 shoe.

Nickname: Called "the Grand Inquisitor" by Nash (who is not too pleased with having his unit investigated).

Character: Totally self-sufficient. Caitlin is beautiful and knows it—but she never uses that asset to accomplish things. She has a difficult time asking for help, and Nash calls her "Sister" (e.g., "I've got a hot lead for you Sister, trust me"). Caitlin is very sure of herself ("I find things out, that's what I do") and becomes angry when Nash tries to keep something from her (but "I'll find out," she says). She is also coach of a Police Athletic League soccer team called the Cougars.

Car: An electric Xebra Roadster.

License Plate: XEBRA.

Caitlin's Fate: In 2000 (joining the SIU in 1998), Caitlin leaves for a job in Boston.

NICHOLAS "NICK" BRIDGES

Nick, Nash's father, is a widower and a former longshoreman. He is suffering from the early stages of Alzheimer's disease and previously lived at the Three Oaks Retirement Home (he couldn't get along with management and was evicted; he now lives with Nash and Cassidy and cares for the house). His late wife is mentioned as being a librarian. During World War II, he served aboard the battleship USS *Phoenix*.

Northern Exposure
(CBS, 1990–1995)

Cast: Rob Morrow (Joel Fleischman), Janine Turner (Maggie O'Connell).
Basis: A young doctor (Joel) attempts to begin a medical practice in a town (Cicely) of 214 people in the remote regions of Alaska (in the borough of Arrowhead, hundreds of miles from Anchorage).

JOEL FLEISCHMAN
Place of Birth: Flushing, New York.
Twin Brother: Jules Fleischman (Rob Morrow).
Religion: Jewish (although he celebrates Christmas; he believes in the spirit of the holiday and enjoys decorating a tree).
Childhood: Attended Camp Indian Head.
Education: Richfield High School; Columbia University Medical School.
Internship: Beth Sinai Hospital in New York City.
Predicament: Joel was rejected 74 times for a medical school scholarship and thus had to take out $125,000 in student loans. When Joel learns that his loan will be paid off if he agrees to become a doctor for four years in Cicely, he agrees.
Practice: Established in the abandoned Northwestern Mining Company Building.
Nurse: A native woman named Marilyn Whirlwind (Elaine Miles).
Character: Compassionate and caring about his patients. He always gives of himself to help others, although he often has a difficult time understanding the customs of the people he treats.
Reading Matter: *Golf Digest* and the *New Yorker* magazines and the town's only newspaper, the *Cicely World Telegram*.
Hangouts: The Brick Bar (for a beer); Rosalyn's Café (for lunch).
Shopping: Ruth's General Store (owned by Ruth Anne Miller [Peg Phillips]).
Truck License Plate: 5792 H2.
Girlfriend: Maggie O'Connell (see below). They dated for three years, but after their relationship ended, Joel became depressed and retreated to the remote fishing village of the Manonash tribe to get over his lost love (the village is located "upriver from Dead Man's Gorge"). Joel returned several months later and was let out of his contract (at which time he returned to New York and set up his own practice).
Prior Girlfriend: Elaine Schulman (Jessica Lundy).

Rob Morrow and Janine Turner. *CBS/Photofest © CBS*

MARGARET "MAGGIE" MARY O'CONNELL

Parents: Frank (John McCann) and Jane (Bibi Besch) O'Connell.
Place of Birth: Grosse Pointe, Michigan.
Education: Grosse Pointe High School.
Occupation: Bush pilot and property agent (she is Joel's landlady).
Business: Owner of the one-plane O'Connell Air Taxi Service in Cicely.
Plane ID Number: N41492.
Pickup Truck License Plate: 8346 MA.
Address: The south corner of Katunick and Washington.
Curse: Maggie believes what people say: "I am cursed when it comes to boy-friends." Prior to losing Joel, she dated Harry (choked to death at a picnic on potato salad); Bruce (fishing accident); Glen (took a wrong turn in his Volvo onto a missile firing range); Dave (fell asleep on a glacier and froze to death); and Rick (killed by a falling satellite).
New Life: Maggie is elected the mayor of Cicely after Joel departs.

CICELY FACTS

Town Threat: Jessie, a great bear that roams the area (the bear is missing two toes, which were shot off by Holling Gustav Vincoeur [John Cullum], the owner of the Brick Bar). Holling, age 68, is married to 23-year-old Shelley Marie Tambo (Cynthia Geary), the waitress at the Brick Bar. Shelley was born in Saskatoon, Saskatchewan; won the beauty pageant title "Miss Northwest Passage"; and attends the Lady of Our Refuge Church. Holling is mentioned as being born in both Quebec and the Yukon. Anthony Curry played Shelley's father, Gordon; Wendy Schall is her stepmother, Tammy.

Legendary Creature: A man-beast named Adam (Adam Arkin) is believed to be living in the great woods that surrounds the town (revealed to be a mountain man; he married Eve [Valerie Mahaffey] in the episode of May 11, 1992).

Town Founder: Maurice Minifield (Barry Corbin), a former astronaut who ar-ranged the writing off of Joel's debt. Maurice served with the U.S. Marines and was stationed on Parris Island. He owns 15,000 acres of land, drives a classic Cadillac (license plate 39-759), and likes gourmet cooking and show tunes. As a kid, he had a dog named Buddy. His unseen brother, Malcolm, died owing him $8,000. His goal is to make Cicely the next boomtown. He is assisted by Ed Chigliak (Darren E. Burroughs), a half Native Alaskan who was raised by the local Tlingits people. He drives a Jeep (license plate JR 38LC) and reads *Teenage Mutant Ninja Turtles* comic books. Ed is also a shaman in training. One-Who-Waits is his invisible spirit guide; Low Self Esteem is his personal demon (resembles a leprechaun).

Town Radio Station: KBHR (57 on the AM dial). Chris Stevens (John Corbett), born in West Virginia, is the only deejay on the town's only radio station.

It is called Great Bear Radio and is owned by the Minifield Communications Network. Chris is an ex-convict and conceptual sculptor who, through an ad in *Rolling Stone* magazine, became a minister with the Universal Life Church (he is also the town's only clergyman).

Quirks: Cicely is virtually crime free except when the ice breaks (during the spring thaw); people go crazy and steal things. At the Brick Bar (telephone number 907-555-7328), the book *The Rainbow* by D. H. Lawrence is under the leg of the kitchen table to keep it from wobbling.

Parker Lewis Can't Lose

(Fox, 1991–1993)

Cast: Corin Nemec (Parker Lewis), Maia Brewton (Shelly Lewis), Melanie Chartoff (Grace Musso), William Jayne (Mikey Randall), Troy Slaten (Jerry Steiner).

Basis: Life with Parker Lewis, a seemingly normal teenager with an uncanny knack of never losing; no matter what happens to him, he always comes out on top.

PARKER LEWIS

Parents: Martin (Timothy Stack) and Judy (Anne Bloom, then Mary Ellen Trainor). They own Mondo Video (VHS tape rentals are $2.99 each), and, according to Parker, "asking them for advice is like looking for gasoline with a match—you're lucky to get out alive."

Sister: Shelly Ann Lewis (see below).

Place of Birth: Santo Domingo, California.

Address: 101 Durning Place.

Education: Santo Domingo High School.

Character: The "cool kid" with an ingenious plan for every situation. He resists authority and lives by his own rules. He dreams of attending college and is a master of self-promotion. He records people (on both videotape and audiotape) for "blackmail purposes." He claims that the earliest he ever arrived at school was 7:52 a.m.

Headquarters: An abandoned room above the boys' gym at school.

Radio Host: Plays "Dr. Retro" on the school station, WFLM (89.9 FM).

Favorite Eatery: The Atlas Diner; Sparky's Hamburgers.

Favorite Wristwatch: A Swatch watch (model 150 M).

Favorite Movie Theater: The Multi Plex Cinema.

SHELLY ANN LEWIS

Relationship: Parker's 13-year-old sister, a freshman at Santo Domingo High School.

Character: Shelly appears very sweet but is feared by students as she assists school principal Grace Musso (her idol) in an effort to get the goods on Parker and bring him down (Parker refers to her as "Grace's pretty, two-faced, sugarplum freshman obedience trainee"). He also calls her "Shelly Belly" and "Santo Domingo's Hell Hound" (as he believes she must be adopted).

Affiliation: The Vogues, a snobbish clique of girls who hold themselves in high esteem.

Dates: Parker explains, "My sister is capable of many things: humiliating me in public, reading my diary, selling my baby pictures; but getting a date, that's a different story." Shelly is so feared that boys will not approach her. Hoping to get on Shelly's good side, Parker tried to bring out her natural beauty in what he called "Operation Pretty Woman—changing a 72-pound swamp monster into Julia Roberts."

Curfew: 11:00 p.m. (quite late for a 13-year-old).

Favorite Movie: Fatal Attraction (an R-rated movie she has seen 15 times).

Hobby: Collecting "My Little Pony" dolls (according to Parker, "the world's largest collection on the continent").

Video Warning: If it appears that Shelly is trying to help Parker in any way, a red warning light is flashed on the screen.

GRACE MUSSO

Position: Principal of Santo Domingo High School. According to Parker, "She is a psychopath with tenure." She is always called "Ms. Musso."

Main Goal: Get the goods on Parker "and take him down."

Parker File: Grace has a record of every infraction caused by Parker and has labeled it "File SN2935-59." All she asks for "is a cup of coffee and a little peace and quiet in the morning."

Salary: $38,000 a year (but lives in a $600,000 home and has a cabin at Sky Lake).

Wardrobe: Very attractive and often dresses in tight skirts and blouses that cause havoc when she attends school sports events (where the guys leer at her and never win).

Past: In 1969, when Grace was a junior at Santo Domingo, she was the obedience helper to its principal. When she graduated a year later, she was slimed with 60 gallons of lime Jell-O on the night of her senior prom. To make up for what happened, she runs the school like a military prison (her detention room punishment is forcing students to watch a home video of her life—from infancy).

Favorite Singer: Donny Osmond (she claims to have written thousands of letters to him since 1970).

TV Appearance: The game show *The Dating Connection* (where she failed to get a date); as of October 13, 1991, Grace had had 1,357 blind dates.
Turn-On: Men with beards and the rock group the Bee Gees.
Bank: Santo Domingo Trust Bank.

OTHER CHARACTERS

Gerald "Jerry" Steiner and Michael Patrick "Mikey" Randall are Parker's "best buds." Mikey is a fan of actress Molly Ringwald and worked as a counter boy at Dog on a Stick fast food. He plays the guitar (especially in his parents' bathtub—"great echo effects") and is a freshman (Parker and Jerry are sophomores) and calls them "Sirs" and "Mr. Lewis and Mr. Randall." He yells "Eeek" when he sees Grace, collects *Star Trek* figurines, carries a Big Bird (from *Sesame Street*) thermos to school, and has his coat Scotchgarded (a spray-on cloth dirt protector) twice a month. He also keeps a jar of monkey brains on his desk at school.

Jerry has a pet ant named "Sparky" and, being brilliant in math, was called "Mr. Calculator." He carried a *Family Ties* TV series lunchbox in grade school and became depressed when Jetsons (from the TV series) chewable vitamins were discontinued. He has a Spoons of the World collection and loves video games (is a member of Video Games Anonymous—an addiction that began with the board games "Candy Land," "Chutes and Ladders," and "Monopoly"; when "Pac-Man" came out, he was hooked, scoring 3,000,020 points on his first try). Jerry and Mikey also attend Santo Domingo High School, and when Parker sets out on a mission, he says, "Gentlemen, synchronize your Swatches." He also possesses a file of excuses he calls "The Musso Excuse File."

Lawrence "Larry" Francis Kubiac (Abraham Benrubi) is 20 years old and has been a junior at Santo Domingo High for seven years. He is not bright, weighs 270 pounds, and stands 6 feet, 7 inches tall. He is mean and, as Parker says, "the most dangerous force ever to squeeze into a high school football uniform" (jersey 77). Larry's only pleasure is eating, and he is very protective of his school lunch (which he carries in a large paper bag with a misspelled "Lary's Lunch" on it). His catchphrase is "Eat now!" His "office" is "School Bathroom 12," *Field and Heifer* is his favorite magazine, and in honor of his tenth year at school, the cafeteria named a sandwich after him: "The Kube" (pizza and French fries on sourdough bread).

The PJs

(Fox, 1999–2000; WB, 2000)

Voice Cast: Eddie Murphy (Thurgood Stubbs), Loretta Devine (Muriel Stubbs), Michele Morgan (Juicy), Ja'net Dubois (Mrs. Avery), Cheryl

Frances Harrington (Mambo Garcelle), Crystal Scales (Calvin), Pepe Serna (Sanchez), Shawn Michael Howard (Smokey). Phil Morris voiced Thurgood in two episodes.

Basis: A puppet animation project filmed in Fomation that relates events in the life of Thurgood Stubbs, a lazy, unmotivated apartment house superintendent ("supa").

THURGOOD ORENTHAL STUBBS

Occupation: Maintenance engineer of the 13-story Hilton Jacobs Building in the Projects ("The PJs") in an unnamed, corrupt, and crime-ridden city. The building is named after *Welcome Back, Kotter* actor Lawrence Hilton-Jacobs.

Age: 48 when the series begins but claims "to look 60."

Wife: Muriel.

Character: Overweight, obnoxious, and rude (he buys exercise videos to lose weight but never watches them). He avoids tenant complaints and rarely fixes anything. His wardrobe is mainly a white short-sleeve shirt, blue overalls, and brown shoes.

Eating Habits: Loves fried, fatty foods and takeout and junk snacks.

Place of Birth: The Projects, where he grew up in a very poor family.

Current Life: Lives in the building's basement. It is furnished with other people's discards. In his youth, Thurgood was a professional wrestler called "The Conquistador" with the NWA (Negro Wrestling Association).

Favorite TV Series: Wheel of Fortune.

Favorite Magazine: Jet.

Favorite Drink: Mule 40 (an alcoholic beverage). Thurgood attempted to make his own wine and called it "Baron von Thurgood's Spring Frolic."

Favorite Place: The Boiler Room (finds serenity from everything that annoys him).

Belief: He is the world's greatest gumbo chef. He also makes his own chocolate milk by combining Coco Puffs with milk in a blender.

Cologne: Old English 800 Cologne.

Favorite Days: "Rent day and eviction days."

Pet Rat: Whiskers. In another episode, he claims that black rats frighten him.

Hero: Action star Jackie Chan. Thurgood served as the technical adviser on his film *Hell Hole 2*, which was being made in the Projects.

Band: Thurgood and the Stub Tones.

Radio Program: With his friend Smokey, Thurgood had a radio show called *Thurgood and Smokey's Laugh Riot* (on the Projects station WHJS).

Investment: Bought the abandoned movie theater on Al Sharpton Boulevard (for $1 from HUD) and turned it into the Thurgood Stubbs Neighborhood Theater.

OTHER CHARACTERS

Muriel Stubbs, Thurgood's wife (maiden name Muriel Warren), is totally devoted to him. She is always seen in a pink blouse with "Paris" on it. She keeps a daily record of her activities in her journal and is president of Women United to Save Our Projects.

Juicy Hudson and Calvin Banks are children who idolize Thurgood. Calvin is slim and intelligent, while Juicy, the son of obese parents, is short, fat, and slow witted. Juicy has a sign attached to him that reads "Do Not Feed."

Florence Avery is the elderly woman whom Thurgood calls "a dried-up old gargoyle." She suffers from numerous illnesses, is forever hitting Thurgood with her cane, and worked as a con artist in her youth. She has had several heart attacks and sleeps with a shotgun she calls "Mrs. Jones" under her bed. She has a pet dog named Lucky. In later episodes, Sharique (Wanda Christine), a teenage runaway, comes to live with her.

Garcelle DuPris, called "Mambo Garcelle," "Haiti Lady," and "Voodoo Queen" by Thurgood, is a Haitian immigrant who appears to have actual powers of a voodoo priestess, but her threats to use them on Thurgood do not faze him.

Emilio Sanchez, always called Sanchez, is Thurgood's friend. He was born in Cuba and was a promising opera singer whose passion for cigarettes now forces him to speak through a throat microphone. His late wife was named Esperansa, and he is most often seen in a blue and white hat with the word "Nevada" written on it.

Smokey, a homeless man and crack addict, lives in a cardboard box and is always picked up with the trash. He once had a job as a rat trainer called "Ratman Crothers." Although friends, Thurgood calls him "Mr. Crackhead" and "Mr. Crack" (in later episodes, it is seen that Smokey is trying to get his life back together by giving up drugs).

Bebe Ho (Jenifer Lewis) is Muriel's sister, a woman who truly despises Thurgood.

By dialogue, it appears that Bebe was a slut in high school and slept with many of her teachers. Jimmy Ho (Michael Paul Chan), Bebe's fifth husband, is a Korean who considers himself part of the African American community (which displeases Thurgood, especially when Jimmy speaks and refers to himself as a black person).

Profiler
(NBC, 1996–2000)

Cast: Ally Walker (Samantha Waters), Jamie Luner (Rachel Burke), Robert Davi (Bailey Monroe), Caitlin Wachs (Chloe Waters), Erica Gimpel (Angel Brown).

Basis: Forensic psychologists Samantha Waters (1996–1999), then Rachel Burke (1999–2000), each possessing a unique ability to feel for the victims of crime and understand the human mind, solve baffling crimes as members of the Violent Crimes Task Force (VCTF), an Atlanta, Georgia–based unit of the FBI.

SAMANTHA "SAM" WATERS

Place of Birth: Atlanta, Georgia.

Address: 501 Alameda (in a converted firehouse).

Marital Status: Widow.

Daughter: Chloe.

Measurements: 36-27-24. She stands 5 feet, 10 inches tall and has light brown hair.

Occupation: Profiler for the FBI.

Character: Samantha is not a psychic. Her highly developed intuition allows her to think in pictures and visualize the frame of mind of both the killer and the victim. She looks beyond the obvious and rarely guesses. Samantha cannot sleep when she is working on a difficult case and sometimes feels scared, "but I'm not going to quit." She is a workaholic and often burns the candle at both ends. Her hobby of photography seems to relax her: "It offers me an escape from the dark corners."

Best Friend: Angel Brown (who helps care for Chloe; Angel is an artist, and Chloe has a dog named Denzil).

Childhood: Samantha and her mother enjoyed solving puzzles. It made Samantha feel alive, as she felt that each puzzle was a mystery to be solved. As she grew, she developed an interest in solving mysteries and chose law enforcement as her career.

Education: Atlanta State University; Atlanta Police Academy.

Career: Her abilities at profiling brought her to the attention of Bailey Monroe, head of the VCTF, who recruited her in 1991 (in the pilot episode, Bailey is said to be head of the FBI Investigative Support Unit; he is divorced and the father of Frances [Heather McComb]). Samantha performed brilliantly until 1993, when it all came to a tragic end. Samantha was about to reveal the identity of a killer the FBI labeled "Jack of All Trades" when he turned the tables on her: he killed her husband and sent Samantha on a downward spiral. She quit the FBI and with Chloe moved to the country to live an anonymous life. Strangely, Jack also disappeared. In 1996, a series of killings believed to be perpetrated by Jack prompt Bailey to ask for Samantha's help. Samantha is reluctant to help until Bailey persuades her to rejoin his team. Three years later, one of the greatest confrontations in television history occurs when Samantha tracks Jack, faces him, and, in an extremely tense and unexpected moment, shoots him dead at point-blank range. Although unethical but justified, Samantha's nightmare was over. But so was her job. On October 21, 1999, Samantha resigned "to do what I need, what Chloe needs—each other." Rachel Burke replaced her.

Jack of All Trades: Samantha had encountered evil in its purest form—Jack of All Trades, the most sinister character in the history of television up to that time. Jack killed to draw Samantha close to him. He considered himself the ultimate tormentor and monitored Samantha's activities by tapping into the FBI's computer systems via his password "Jack O. Trades." Jack was later revealed to be Albert Newquary (Dennis Christopher); in the opening theme, his credit reads "and Jack." Traci Lords played his "kill mate" Sharon Lesher, who was known as "Jill of All Trades."

RACHEL BURKE

Place of Birth: Arlington, Virginia.

Occupation: FBI profiler.

Childhood: At the age of 10, Rachel had a vision of a young girl whose parents wished they never had a child. The girl felt that her life was empty and ran away from home. Rachel envisioned the girl's death but was too late to help when the girl was found dead at the bottom of a well. Rachel believed that her vision was a gift—to see what others could not—and, although quite young, made a vow to help people with her abilities.

Education: University of Virginia (a degree in psychology).

Early Career: Instructor for special agents at the FBI Training Center in Virginia; agent for the Senate Bureau; field agent with the Houston, Texas, field office of the FBI ("because I was sick of seeing criminals beat the system; they should be behind bars").

Measurements: 34-25-32. She stands 5 feet, 6 inches tall.

Address: An unidentified apartment on Melrose (in Atlanta).

Telephone Number: 555-0192.

Character: Rachel can think in pictures and visualize the frame of mind of both the killer and the victim ("I can see into the criminal mind and explain the unexplained"). She is not a psychic but rather a forensic psychologist and does not have to be at a crime scene to receive images: "I could be brushing my teeth or grinding coffee when they come." Rachel has an 88 percent accuracy rate, "but it's that other 12 percent that bothers me." And, like Samantha, "I can't sleep when I'm working on a tough case."

Relic Hunter
(Syndicated, 1999–2002)

Cast: Tia Carrere (Sydney Fox).

Basis: A beautiful young woman (Sydney Fox) risks her life battling a different type of criminal—those who steal and seek to profit from ancient relics.

SYDNEY FOX

Occupation: Professor of ancient studies at Trinity College (also called Trinity University) in California. In her spare time, she teaches tai chi classes.

Assignments: Recover lost treasures on behalf of the university museum.

Motivation: "Part of what I do is search for relics. Every relic tells a human story and gives us an insight into our lives."

History: Sydney is the daughter of Randall Fox (Fred Dryer), a dam builder who believes in defying everything. Sydney would follow in his tradition as an adult, but her interest in relics began when she was a student at St. Theresa's Catholic School for Girls. It was here, after befriending a teacher who hunted for relics as a sideline, that Sydney learned that "relics don't belong to people or individuals." She next attended Franklin High School, where she apparently acquired an interest in the theater (played Maria in her senior play production of *West Side Story*); no mention is made of her interest in relics. It appears that when Sydney was a student at Trinity College (majoring in ancient civilizations), her interest in relics was piqued, and she chose to pursue her current field.

Goal: Find relics and save them from unscrupulous characters who want to possess them.

Favorite Baseball Team: Boston Red Sox (indicating that she may have been born and raised in New England).

Trait: Can be either a temptress or an Amazon—"Whatever it takes to get the job done."

Assignments: Sydney travels the world, usually the remote corners of the globe. The first thing she does after (sometimes during) a case "Is to go to a hotel, take a bath, and have a glass of whatever they call wine."

Character: Depicted as gorgeous, but on assignments that attribute often becomes lost, as she is no lady. She can take care of herself, but sweating, being overcome by the enemy, and exploring the least desirable places are not uncommon to her.

Measurements: 35-24-36 (she is seen in her bra in the opening theme). She stands 5 feet, 8 inches tall and wears a size 4 dress and a size 10 shoe.

Abilities: Martial arts expert; sharpshooter (likes to use her crossbow).

Birth Sign: Scorpio.

OTHER CHARACTERS

Nigel Bailey (Christien Anholt) is Sydney's teaching assistant and partner on assignments. He is working on his master's degree (attended Oxford in England) and says, "All I wanted was a nice little teaching job in a nice little library surrounded by books." He is a Taurus (born May 10) and was originally said to have attended England's Cambridge University. He can speak a dozen languages and read ancient scripture and is an expert on weapons technology. He hates for Sydney to use the words "boarding school," as it reminds him of his youth when "I was incarcerated"; he called the headmistress "Dragon Lady."

Claudia (Lindy Booth) is Sydney's gorgeous blonde secretary. She measures 34-24-34; stands 5 feet, 7 inches tall; and has no love of history (she acquired the job "because my father is a friend of the college"). Claudia is a vegetarian and loves to eavesdrop (when Sydney catches her at the door, Claudia responds with "I was looking for my contact lens"). When Sydney tells Claudia something, she always responds with "Got ya." Claudia is an expert on tarot cards ("Do you think I would leave who to date and what to wear to chance?") and believes she had a past life (as Eves, a handmaiden to Cleopatra). Claudia likes to experiment with her computer (placing her picture in a program to see how she looks in clothes, especially pastels: "I hate cucumber color; it makes me look icky"). She also believes that online shopping is dangerous ("I buy too much and then have to figure out what half to return"). Claudia left at the end of the second season for her dream job as a model in New York.

Karen Petresky (Tanja Reichert) is a blonde (measures 34-24-35 and stands 5 feet, 5 inches tall) who replaces Claudia and works as Sydney's administrator (Karen's "talent" is showing ample cleavage to get what she wants from men). Unlike Claudia, Karen is genuinely interested in relics and helps Sydney accomplish her assignments.

Sabrina, the Teenage Witch
(ABC, 1996–2000; WB, 2000–2003)

Cast: Melissa Joan Hart (Sabrina Spellman), Beth Broderick (Zelda Spellman), Caroline Rhea (Hilda Spellman), Nick Bakay (Voice of Salem).

Basis: Sabrina, a 16-year-old girl who is half witch and half human, struggles to conceal her true identity while attempting to live the life of an ordinary human teenage girl.

SABRINA SPELLMAN

Parents: Edward Spellman (Robbie Benson, then Doug Sheehan), a warlock, and Diane Becker (Pamela Blair), a mortal woman (an anthropologist).

Address: 133 Collins Road in Westbridge, Massachusetts (the upstairs hall closet is the door to the Other Realm, a home to witches).

Birthday: March 29, 1981 (as seen on her passport); also given as April 22, 1981, and in September on the opening day of school.

Measurements (from 2001): 34-25-35. She is blonde; stands 5 feet, 2 inches tall; and wears a size 2 dress and a size 6½ shoe.

Education: Westbridge High School (writes for the school newspaper, the *Lantern*; is a school safety monitor; produced a movie called *The Blood of Mindy Adelman*; and wore jersey 35 as a member of the Marauders basketball team; the Fighting Scallions is the football team); Adams College (journalism major; writes for the school newspaper, the *Adams Advocate*). At Adams (founded in 1891), she cohosted (with Roxy) *Chic Chat*, a call-in radio program (WAC, 98.9 FM) that airs from 8 to 10 p.m.

After-School Hangout: The Slicery (a pizza parlor; high school); Eve's Diner (college).

Favorite Other Realm TV Show: When Good Witches Go Bad (airs on the "Witch Channel." She appeared on *Sabrina's World*, a reality show that depicted her life in the mortal world).

Requirement: Other Realm jury duty (witches deliver bad news as the Grim Reaper).

Physical Flaw: An overbite.

Occupation: Student. She worked as the "Lovely Assistant" to Magic Jolly at the World of Wonder, pizza maker at the Slicery, waitress at Pork on a Fork (fast food), and waitress at the coffee shop Three Bean Brew (making $5.25 an hour; it later becomes Hilda's Coffee House). Through the Other Realm Employment Agency, Sabrina became a Sandman ("I put people in my neighborhood to sleep"). After graduating from Adams College, Sabrina becomes an apprentice for the *Boston Citizen* (a newspaper) and a staff writer/ reporter for *Scorch* (a music industry magazine), then a freelance writer.

Character: A very beautiful girl who never uses that asset to her advantage. She is ticklish behind the ears and always finds trouble when she uses her magic to help people (something she is not supposed to do, as it could expose her). When Sabrina catches spring fever, her daydreams can be seen by anyone.

Powers: Levitation was her first ability, followed by casting spells, zapping, invisibility, changing appearance, and influencing mortal minds. She cannot use her powers for profit, turn back time, or eat pancakes ("If a Spellman eats a pancake, it becomes addictive"). She is forbidden to duplicate products (e.g., when Sabrina tried to conjure up the candy M&Ms, they became N&Ns). Every 25 years, she must have a magic checkup, and when she prepares meals, she uses *The Magic Meals Cookbook*. She is assisted in her magic with spells contained in the book *The Discovery of Magic*.

Favorite Drink: A Polar Freeze smoothie.

Favorite Cookie: Gingerbread.

Favorite Lip Gloss: Strawberry Swirl.

Incurable Trait: Being a busybody (when her "Gyro" ["the part that makes her busy body work"] malfunctions, she needs tuning at "Buddy's Busy Body Parts").

Other Realm Computer Password: Sabrina Is Hot.

Habit: Stealing cookies from the cookie jar.

Lingerie Purchases: Victoria's Secret.

Family Secret: "Every member of the Spellman family is born with a twin."

Evil Twin: Katrina (Melissa Joan Hart). Sabrina is good, while Katrina is devious (Jezabella, played by Beth Broderick, is revealed to be Zelda's evil twin; currently jailed in the Other Realm with Katrina).

Catchphrase: "Woo Who" and "Gotta Go."

Band: The Gal Palz (with friends Roxie and Morgan; they appeared on the TV show *National Superstars*).

Loves: Harvey Kinkel (Nate Richert) was actually Sabrina's one true love (his father runs a company called Termite King). They dated in high school but drifted apart after graduation (he was also the only mortal to learn Sabrina's secret; he accidentally caught her performing magic and promised never to reveal it). Josh (David Lissauer), a reporter for the *Citizen*, became her next romantic interest. When Josh receives a transfer, Sabrina falls for Aaron Jacobs (Dylan Neal), a band promoter who proposed marriage. She accepted but had doubts, especially when Harvey came back into her life. On her wedding day, Sabrina realized that Harvey was her true love and returned to him.

Family Matriarch: Great aunt, Irma (Barbara Eden), a beautiful witch who is "the dreaded holy terror of the Other Realm" and the first witch to transport herself from one place to another (via "a large Brazil nut") before the broom was introduced.

Cousin: Amanda Wickham (Emily Hart). She is the daughter of Harold and Marigold and from the Fourth Galaxy in the Other Realm. She is attending Witchright Hall, an Earth-based boarding school, and doesn't mean to be evil, but things just happen when she casts spells.

Girlfriends: Valerie Birkhead (Lindsay Sloane) is a bit unsure of herself and often becomes the victim of one of Sabrina's spells. Roxie King (Soleil Moon Frye) is a sociology major at Adams College, where she hosts *The Roxie King Show* on radio station WAC, 98.9 FM (originally with Sabrina as *Chic Chat*). Kate Jackson plays her mother, Candy. Morgan Cavanaugh (Elisa Donovan) attends Adams College and rooms with Sabrina and Roxie. She is pretty but dense and hopes to become a fashion designer (she creates a clothing line called Morgan Ware). She worked at Hilda's Coffee House and formed a band called Girl Palz with Sabrina and Roxie.

Relatives: Cousins, Susie (Sonje Furtag), a witch with green skin and warts; Larry (Joel Brooks), an emperor; Roland (Phil Fondacaro) and Pele (Kellye Nakahura); aunt, Sophia (Melissa Joan Hart); uncles, Danny (David Alan Graf) and Monty (Dana Gould).

Flashbacks: Sabrina as a girl (Emily Hart).

ZELDA SPELLMAN

Relationship: Sabrina's aunt (also Princess of the Other Realm country of Massapequa Park; she was born in the Northern Sector).

Zelda and Hilda's Mother: Lydia (Shirley Jones).

Age: "500 plus years old"; grew up in the fourteenth century.

Education: The Other Realm University (has a four-digit IQ; a degree in quantum physics; three degrees in intergalactic studies). She also graduated from Harvard University in 1873 with three science degrees.

Caroline Rhea, Melissa Joan Hart, and Beth Broderick. *The WB/Photofest*
© *The WB*

Occupation: Scientist (teaches at Adams College).
Awards: The Other Realm Science Fair and "Outstanding Student of the
    Decade."
Political Party: The Social Democratic Do-Gooder Party.
Interests: Psychiatry, slug reproduction, and art (she was an intern for Leon-
    ardo da Vinci and a model for Goya; nude portraits of her sold at the Art
    Museum).
Discovery: Credited with identifying 17 moons.
Computer Password: Chem Kitten.
Favorite Drink: Bottled water.
Favorite Food: Honey calf marrow.
Favorite Magazine: The Other Realm's *By Enchanted.*
Childhood Interest: Bees. She was a child prodigy (violin; took lessons for 200
    years).
Romance: Will date only intellectual mortals (although she did date the West-
    bridge High School vice principal, Willard Kraft [Martin Mull]).
Teenage Zelda: Judith Jones.

HILDEGARD "HILDA" ANTOINETTE SPELLMAN

Relationship: Zelda's younger sister. A third sister, Vesta, is mentioned but never seen.

Place of Birth: The Other Realm (Northern Sector).

Age: Contradicts Zelda. Although younger, she first mentions being 620 years old, then 650. During the fourteenth century, she shared an apartment with Vlad the Impaler (Dracula). She also says she was beheaded in the sixteenth century for being a witch.

Education: The Other Realm High School; Clown University (she dislikes its being called "clown school").

First Use of Magical Powers: Zapped a grotesque clay horse.

Occupation: Musician (plays the violin). In her youth she worked as a blacksmith, donkey walker, fisherman, and, with Zelda, an Earth-like Wild West singing duo called the Spellman Sisters. She first opened her own business, Hickory Dickory Clock (where she and Zelda helped lost travelers in time through the Lost in Time Clock), then, when Sabrina attended Adams College, Hilda's Coffee House.

Favorite Dessert: Devil's food cake.

Favorite Food: Deviled ham.

Favorite Holiday: Halloween (she and Zelda decorate the house and sing Halloween carols).

Least Favorite Holiday: Thanksgiving ("because the Puritans that started it were not fond of witches").

Zelda's and Hilda's Fate: At the end of the 2002 season, Hilda had married, and Zelda left to pursue new goals (did so to focus more on Sabrina and her new friends, Roxie and Morgan, who move from the college dorm to Sabrina's home).

Teenage Hilda: Alexandra Johnet.

SALEM SABERHAGEN

Mother: Unnamed, played by Louise Sorel.

Daughter: Annabell Saberhagen (Victoria Jackson).

Relationship: A human turned into a cat that Zelda and Hilda must care for. In 1966, Salem was a powerful warlock who not only dreamed of taking over the world but actually acted on it. The Witch's Council stopped him but in punishment sentenced him to serve 100 years as a black American short-haired cat. Hilda was a follower of Salem's teachings about world domination, and for punishment she was sentenced to care for him. Salem believes that if he can get a mortal woman to kiss him, the spell will be reversed.

Weakness: Tassels.

Favorite Bar: Earth-based Hooters (for the gorgeous girls; he despises the Other Realm Hooters because the "girl" waitresses are literally hooting owls).

Favorite TV Show: V.I.P. (a real series starring Pamela Anderson).

Enjoyment: "The sound of the can opener makes me feel alive"; people talking baby talk to him; helping Sabrina with her problems.

Favorite Food: Squid (although he has learned to speak dog and tricks the neighbor's dog, Silky, into getting meat for him). It is also seen that the family's leftovers are today's lunch for him.

Favorite Dessert: Chocolate syrup in his milk bowl. He also takes Metamucil, a laxative, in his iced tea.

Favorite Game: Chess.

Quirk: Paints to make money (although Hilda takes the credit, as who would believe that a cat was responsible?); when he is upset, he eats ("but when I'm happy I eat"). The song "What's It All About, Alfie" makes him cry.

Bedtime: Although 8:30 p.m. is mentioned, it rarely happens.

Education: The Other Realm High School. It is here that he casts a spell that made the mortal world forget the holiday "Bobunk." In 1999, when Sabrina became depressed by Christmas, she accidentally pressed the erase button on the Other Realm TV remote control and erased Christmas. December 25 was just another day until she realized that Christmas was a special time for families and it was reinstated. It is also learned that St. Nick, alias Santa Claus, is a distant cousin of Sabrina's.

Shame: Ostracized for eating a rat in public. It pains Salem to be sincere.

Trait: A coward who will run and hide at the first sign of trouble. He also uses Zelda's computer to get into online chat rooms (where he pretends to be a woman).

Seinfeld
(NBC, 1990–1998)

Cast: Jerry Seinfeld (himself), Jason Alexander (George Costanza), Julia Louis-Dreyfus (Elaine Benes), Michael Richards (Cosmo Kramer), Wayne Knight (Newman), Heidi Swedberg (Susan Ross).

Basis: Billed as "a show about nothing" that is actually the events that befall four friends living in New York City: Jerry, George, Elaine, and Kramer.

JEROME "JERRY" SEINFELD

Parents: Morty (Phil Bruns, then Barney Martin) and Helen Seinfeld (Liz Sheridan).

Place of Birth: Queens, New York.

Education: Edward R. Murrow Junior High School; J.F.K. High School; Queens College.

Occupation: Stand-up comedian. At one point in his life, Jerry sold umbrellas on the street (where he claims he invented "The Twirl," twisting the umbrella to make it attractive).

Address: 129 West 81st Street (Apartment 3A, then 5A). The building, serviced by Plaza Cable, is opposite Almo's Bar and Grill. Magnets of the Statue of Liberty, the New York Mets, the Comedy Central TV logo, and Superman adorn his refrigerator.

Phone Number: KL5-2392 (later 555-8583).

Favorite Eatery: Monk's Café.

Favorite Sports Teams: New York Mets, New York Knicks, New York Jets.

Membership: The New York Health Club.

Barbershop: Three Brothers Barbers.

Suit Size: 40.

Computer: An Apple Mac (the video game "Red Baron" is next to it).

ATM PIN Code: Jor-El (Superman's father).

Car: A 1992 Saab (plate JUN 728).

Catchphrase: "That's a shame" (said when something goes wrong).

TV Appearances: The Tonight Show and *The Today Show.* His segments on the Japanese TV series *The Super Terrific Happy Hour* earn him 11 cents in royalties when they air. He also performs at colleges and improv clubs across the country.

Pilot Film: Jerry and George wrote a TV pilot based on Jerry's life (later picked up as an NBC series) called *Jerry* ("a show about nothing"). They were initially paid $13,000, but George's efforts to negotiate for more money netted them only $8,000. When asked of his past writing credits, George mentions writing the off-Broadway play *La Cocina*, a comedy about a Mexican chef named Pepe.

Favorite T-Shirt: Golden Boy (when it didn't make it through its last washing, Jerry replaced it with Golden Boy's son, Baby Blue).

Relatives: Uncle Leo (Len Lester); grandma, Nana (Billye Raye Wallace). Jerry mentions having a sister (unnamed); his cousins, Jeffrey (works for the Parks Department), Douglas (addicted to Pepsi Cola), and Artie; uncle, Mac; aunt, Sylvia; and Isaac and Manya, an elderly Polish couple whose relationship to Jerry is not spelled out.

GEORGE LOUIS COSTANZA

Parents: Frank (Jerry Stiller) and Estelle Costanza (Estelle Harris).

Place of Birth: Queens, New York (where he lives with his parents at 1344 Queens Boulevard). He later acquires an apartment (609) on 86th Street in Manhattan. In one episode, George mentions growing up in Brooklyn.

Michael Richards, Jason Alexander, Julia Louis-Dreyfus, and Jerry Seinfeld.
NBC/Columbia TriStar Television

Character: Somewhat dishonest, insecure, and neurotic; he is also a bit manipulative, seeking to get people to do what he wants.

Trait: Sometimes refers to himself in the third person (most often, "George is getting upset!"); claims to have two personalities, "Relationship George" and "Independent George"; and describes himself as "a short, fat, bald man who lives with his parents."

Education: Edward R. Murrow Junior High School; J.F.K. High School; Queens College.

Dream Job: Architect (he uses the name Art Van Delay, architect, to impress people).

Actual Jobs: Real estate broker for Rick Bahr Properties (quit when his boss refused to let him use his private bathroom; George has an obsession with quality bathrooms); proofreader at Pendant Publishing (fired for having sex on his desk with the cleaning lady); assistant to the traveling secretary for the New York Yankees (fired when he pretended to be a hen supervisor for

Tyler Chicken to impress a girl); executive at Play Now, a playground supply company (pretending to be handicapped cost George his job); executive at Kruger Industrial Sanding (where he had the nickname "Koko," then "Gammy"), a company that sands and smoothes anything.

Girlfriend: When George and Jerry teamed to write the *Jerry* pilot, he fell in love with NBC executive Susan Ross. They planned to marry, but George, stingy with money, bought expired wedding invitations from Melody Stationary. The envelopes contained toxic glue and killed Susan (as she licked them to seal them). To remember Susan, her parents (unnamed; played by Warren Frost and Grace Zabriskie) established the Susan Ross Foundation with George assigned to distribute money to worthy causes.

Favorite Candy: Twix bars (on which he considers himself an expert).

ATM PIN Code: Bosco (after his favorite chocolate drink).

Membership: The Champagne Video Club (where he is most famous for renting the supposedly risqué film *Raquel, Raquel*).

Favorite Eatery: Monk's Café.

Family Holiday: Festivus ("for the rest of us"). Held at Christmastime (and invented by George's father), it involves performing feats of strength.

Accomplishment: Scored 860,000 on the video game "Frogger" at Mario's Pizza Parlor.

Car: A 1976 Chevy Impala (plate QAG 826).

Wish: To become an adult film star named Buck Naked.

Relatives: Cousins, Shelly and Rhisa; uncle, Moe; aunt, Baby.

ELAINE MARIE BENES

Place of Birth: Towson, Maryland.

Parents: Alton Benes (Lawrence Tierney), a famous author; her mother is not named. Alton deserted the family when Elaine was nine years old.

Address: Apartment 2G on 16 West 75th Street in Manhattan (she uses the Tri-State Wakeup Service), then Apartment 3E on 78 West 86th Street. She moved to Manhattan in 1986 and mentions living with a roommate named Tina.

Education: Five unnamed eastern universities (where she was a debate and equestrian champion); a finishing school and undergraduate work at Tufts University.

Allergy: Allergic to cats.

Favorite Baseball Team: Baltimore Orioles.

Occupation: Proofreader for Mr. Lippman (Richard Fancy) at Pendant Publishing; personal assistant to author Justin Pitt (Ian Abercrombie), who hired her because she reminded him of his idol, Jacqueline Kennedy; product description writer for J. Peterman (John O'Hurley), owner of the J. Peterman mail-order catalog.

Character: Has to have things her way; takes her anger out on people if something goes wrong; hates people smoking and women wearing fur coats; is a horrible dancer.

Sensation: Called "the Nip" by Jerry (a Christmas card photo, taken by Kramer, revealed that Elaine was braless, and her open blouse revealed her nipple); a life-size mannequin of Elaine appears at Renitzi's clothing store; she was "Best Man" at a lesbian wedding.

Measurements: 34-25-35. She stands 5 feet, 3 inches tall and wears a size 7½ shoe and a size 2 dress.

Favorite Eatery: While Elaine frequents Monk's Café, she enjoys take-out orders from the China Panda restaurant.

Weakness: Juicy Fruit candy.

Favorite Toothpaste: Close-Up.

Catchphrase: "Get out!" (said when she becomes excited).

Favorite Punctuation: Exclamation point (which she wrongly uses to highlight sentences that do not require it).

Fear: Dogs.

Favorite Movie: A Streetcar Named Desire (she hates *The English Patient*).

Rival: Sue Ellen Mischke (Brenda Strong), a rich schoolmate (heiress to the Oh Henry! candy bar fortune) who never wears a bra (Elaine calls her "the Braless Wonder").

Relatives: Elaine mentions a sister, Gail; her grandma, Mema; cousin, Holly; and uncle, Pete.

COSMO KRAMER

Mother: Babs Kramer (Sheree North), a restaurant restroom attendant; his remark that he is the last male member of the family indicates that his father has passed.

Background: Kramer, called Kessler in the pilot, reveals that he was brought up in a strict household (had to be in bed every night by 9 p.m.) and ran away from home at the age of 17 (stowed away on a ship bound for Sweden). He never attended high school but did acquire his GED. He mentions having a deaf cousin from whom he learned American Sign Language and serving time in the army (although his service record "is classified").

Address: Apartment 3B, then 5B (Jerry's across-the-hall neighbor). Kramer's apartment is anything but usual. Jerry's one-night experience there revealed creaks in the middle of the night, tiny footsteps, and an irritating red glow from the neon sign across the street. Kramer would like levels in his apartment (like the Egyptian pyramids). His rummaging through dumpsters netted him the set from the 1960s TV series *The Merv Griffin Show*, which he set up in his apartment and treated visitors like guests on a talk show. He also enjoys making figures out of pasta.

Occupation: A self-styled entrepreneur (he did admit to having one job, a "bagel technician" [makes bagels] at H&H Bagels in Manhattan; he has been on strike for 12 years). He conceived a company called Kramerica (where he hopes to develop a rubber bladder system for oil tankers to prevent spillage into the sea). He devised PB&J's, a restaurant chain that sells only peanut butter and jelly sandwiches, and a store where one can make his own pizza pie. He "worked" as a broker for Bryant-Leland when he was mistaken for an employee and decided to stay on (fired for not knowing what he was doing). With George's father, he developed "the Mansierre, a bra for men." He was Santa Claus at Coleman's Department Store (fired for spreading communist propaganda), a lifeguard, a "line-up decoy" for the New York Police Department, a stand-in for the father of an eight-year-old child on the soap opera *All My Children*, a medical actor (performs illnesses for interns to identify), a ball boy for the U.S. Open tennis tournament, and author of *The Coffee Table Book of Coffee Tables* (published by Pendant Publishing). He invented a cologne called The Beach, was an underwear model for Calvin Klein, had one line ("Boy, these pretzels are making me thirsty") in the Woody Allen movie *The Alternate Side*, and appeared on the TV series *Murphy Brown* (as one of Murphy's secretaries). He sold his life story to J. Peterman (Elaine's boss) for $750.

Volunteer Work: The overly protective bodyguard to actress Bette Midler (playing herself); personal coach to Karen Hanson (Marguerite MacIntyre), "Miss Rhode Island" in the Miss America Pageant; responsible for keeping mile 114 of the Arthur Burkhardt Highway clean as part of the Adopt-A-Highway campaign.

Favorite Foods: Fresh fruit, Kellogg's Double Dip Crunch cereal, and hot dogs from Papaya King. When he wanted eggs from cage-free chickens (as opposed to "sweatshop chickens"), he bought a rooster (by mistake) and named it "Little Jerry Seinfeld." He also likes extra monosodium glutamate in his Chinese food.

Membership: The Polar Bear Club (swims in freezing water).

Fear: Clowns, mice, and being in tight spaces.

Favorite Activity: Golf (where, while playing on a beach, hit a hole in one—landing in the blowhole of a whale).

Favorite Sport: Canadian football.

Obsession: Smoking Cuban cigars. At one point, he set up his apartment as a smoking club.

Favorite Drink: A milkshake.

Affliction: Seizures when he hears Mary Hart speak (as seen when he watched her show, *Entertainment Tonight*).

Catchphrase: While Kramer has no official word or statement, he does say "Giddyup" when expressing his feelings about something.

Dream: To drive the rear end of a hook-and-ladder fire truck (he feels he knows the shortcuts firemen don't).

Habit: Snooping into other people's medicine cabinets; shopping at the airport's duty-free shop.

Lawyer: Jackie Chiles (Phil Morris), a famous fast-talking attorney Kramer retained in several lawsuits, suing Java World for giving him a cup of coffee with a loose lid (settled for a lifetime supply of free coffee); the tobacco industry for acquiring yellow teeth from smoking cigarettes (settled for his image appearing on billboards as the Marlboro Man); a girl (Sue Ellen Mischke) he saw on the street in her bra and crashed his car, claiming she was a distraction (lost and had to pay his own car repair bills).

Car License Plate: ERB 224 (although he was mistakenly issued one that read ASSMAN).

Phone Number: 555-3455 (then 555-8643).

Favorite Eatery: Monk's Café.

Painting: Famous for posing in a portrait called *The Kramer* (where he was described as "a loathsome, offensive brute").

Alter Ego: Kramer uses the names H. E. Pennypacker and Dr. Martin Van Nostrand.

Never-Seen Friend: Bob Saccamano.

Distrust: Alarm clocks (Kramer claims that he uses his "mental alarm clock," as it never fails).

NEWMAN

Newman (no first name given) lives on the east side of Jerry's building (Apartment 5E). He is best friends with Kramer and on a cautionary friendship with Jerry, whom he despises because "he and his friends frolic it up on the west side of the building." Newman works as a letter carrier for the U.S. Postal Service (he dreams of being transferred to a route in Hawaii). He rarely abides by the postman's code, places undelivered mail in a storage unit, and doesn't deliver the mail when it rains. Jerry greets Newman with a not-so-friendly "Hello, Newman" (Newman responds in a similar manner with "Hello, Jerry"). He has a weakness for Drake's Coffee Cake snacks and avoids going to the beach (fears getting freckles). He became partners with Kramer on several failed moneymaking ventures: selling used vinyl records, recycling soda cans to Michigan for a 10-cent return deposit (as opposed to New York's five cents a can), and hiring homeless people as a taxi service using rickshaws.

Newman hates junk mail, feels that ZIP codes are meaningless, and often becomes overwhelmed by his job: "The mail never stops! It just keeps coming and coming and coming, there's never a let-up! It's relentless!"

FRANK AND ESTELLE COSTANZA

Frank, who is gruff and appears threatening, is now retired. He worked as a Christian artifacts salesman and can speak Korean (as a result of being stationed in Korea during the war). He was an army chef and served with the Fighting 103rd Squadron. One bad experience—poisoning his fellow soldiers (trying to revitalize expired meat with spices)—has since left him fearful of cooking.

Frank's hobby is collecting *TV Guide* magazines and listening to Latin American music on vinyl records. With Kramer, he developed the Mansierre, a male bra. He despises household infestations (like mice) and also has a collection of silver dollars.

Estelle is simply obnoxious and overbearing. She is forever complaining about Frank and George to the point that George finally moves out and Frank and Estelle briefly separate. She is mentioned as being retired.

MORTY AND HELEN SEINFELD

Morty, jovial and fun loving, made a living selling raincoats. He invented "the Beltless Trenchcoat" (which, also called "the Executive," apparently never sold well). He and Helen now live in retirement at Del Boca Vista in Florida (where he is president of the tenant's board). He is very generous with his money and always sides with Jerry on issues. Helen believes Jerry is the perfect son ("How could anybody not like him?"). When Jerry is seen talking to Helen on the phone, Morty is also seen talking on an extension phone. Helen is mentioned as being retired.

FINAL EPISODE

When the *Jerry* pilot is bought by NBC, Jerry and George are given a free trip to Paris by NBC. Elaine and Kramer are invited to join them, but the NBC jet experiences engine trouble and lands in Massachusetts for repairs. While sightseeing, the four witness a carjacking but do nothing to stop it and are arrested for violating the Good Samaritan law. During their trial, a parade of hostile witnesses (people the four encountered throughout the series) condemn them. "The New York Four," as they are called, are sent to prison. The series' overall catchphrase is "Yadda, yadda, yadda" (said by most everyone).

THE PILOT

On July 5, 1989, NBC presented a pilot film called *The Seinfeld Chronicles*, which was reworked to become the 1990 series *Seinfeld*. Jerry, George, and

Kramer (called Kessler) are basically the same as in the series, but Elaine does not appear. Instead, the female foil is Claire (Lee Garlington), a waitress at the gang's hangout, Pete's Cafe.

7th Heaven
(WB, 1996–2006; CW, 2006–2007)

Cast: Stephen Collins (Eric Camden), Catherine Hicks (Annie Camden), Jessica Biel (Mary Camden), Barry Watson (Matt Camden), Beverley Mitchell (Lucy Camden), David Gallagher (Simon Camden), Mackenzie Rosman (Ruthie Camden).

Basis: Life with the Camden family: parents Eric and Annie and their children Matt, Mary, Lucy, Simon, and Ruthie, residents of Glen Oak, a small California community.

ERIC AND ANNIE CAMDEN

Eric—the son of a retired army colonel, John Camden (Peter Graves), and his wife, Ruth (Barbara Rush)—is a Protestant and minister of the Glen Oak Community Church. He was in his teens when he found his true calling in life (a summer camp counselor at the time and helping people). He attended Binghamton Elementary School, Kennedy High School (in a band called the Flower and Vegetable Show), and Crawford College. He is the author of an unpublished novel (*Lover, Can You Hear Me?*) and hosts a help line call-in talk show on the Crawford College radio station (KRHC, 106.9 FM). Deborah Raffin plays Eric's younger sister, Julie Camden-Hastings.

Midway through the series, Eric developed a heart condition and required double-bypass heart surgery. While recovering (and having doubts about returning to the ministry), the church board hired Chandler Hampton (Jeremy London), an associate pastor, to temporarily replace him.

Anne, maiden name Anne Jackson and called "Annie," first met Eric at Crawford College (where she was majoring in psychology). They dated and married shortly after; Annie dropped out when she became pregnant with their first child (Matt). She became a full-time mother over the next 20 years. She later returned to Crawford to acquire her psychology degree and found a job as a morals teacher in an unnamed private school. Roasted chicken with potatoes was the first meal Annie prepared for Eric.

Annie can be seen as a jack-of-all-trades (cooking, cleaning, and repairing leaky pipes) and has a steadfast rule: never leave the house without lipstick (as Ruthie says, "No lipstick, that's bad"). Eric and Annie are strict parents (e.g., they do not believe in video games and will not allow any of their children to

Barry Watson, David Gallagher, Happy the dog, Jessica Biel, Catherine Hicks, Stephen Collins, Beverley Mitchell, and Mackenzie Rosman. *Warner Bros./ Photofest © Warner Bros.*

play or own one). Mary and Lucy feel, for example, that when it comes to their dating lives, their father has nothing but time, and "no one can embarrass us like our mother." On February 8, 1999, Annie gives birth to twins Sam and David (Lorenzo and Nikolas Brino).

The family lives in a large house at 527 Evergreen Place, 555-0157 is their phone number, and Happy is the family dog. All the children were born at Glen Oak Hospital. When Annie was pregnant with Mary, she took up plumbing, and when she was pregnant with Lucy, she took up electricity; Eric calls these times "pregnancy projects." Also, when Annie was pregnant with Mary, Matt sang the theme song to *The Mary Tyler Moore Show* ("Love Is All Around"), which was Annie's favorite TV show, and started a tradition. With the birth of each child, "Love Is All Around" was sung by the family. Graham Jarvis played Annie's widowed father, Charles Jackson; Beverly Garland was his fiancée, Ginger.

MATTHEW "MATT" CAMDEN

Matt is the eldest child (16 when the series begins) and attends Kennedy High School. He becomes valedictorian of his graduating class and enrolls in a precollege program in Washington, D.C., in then First Lady Hillary Clinton's Summer Work Program. His dream of entering politics is somewhat shattered by his experiences, and he turns his attention to the medical profession (enrolls as a student at Crawford College). It is at this time that he becomes an orderly, first at the Free Clinic, then in the food services department at Glen Oak Hospital. He is next a premed student, then a doctor in 2006. His actual first job was during high school when he worked at the Dairy Shack.

While Matt seemed to have his life in order, it changed dramatically when he met Sarah Glass (Sarah Danielle Madison), a fellow medical student who was Jewish. Sarah had been raised to marry within her religion, and Matt, being Protestant, was not acceptable to Sarah's parents. Despite the objections of his parents, Matt converted to Judaism and married Sarah. They moved to Manhattan, where they began an internship at New York Hospital (at which time Barry Watson left the series, although he returned on occasion as a "guest star"). Richard Lewis and Laraine Newman played Sarah's parents, the Reverend Richard Glass and Rosina Glass.

MARY CAMDEN

Mary, the second-born child (14 when the series begins), was also the most troublesome child. She is attending Kennedy High School and wears jersey 3 as captain of the Wildcats, the girls' varsity basketball team. Mary is very athletic and has a recurring dream that she will become a professional player for the Los Angeles Lakers. While Mary tries to be her best at everything, she overexerts herself during a game and seriously injures her knee, making her incapable of playing basketball. With her hopes shattered, Mary's personality and attitude change. She remained with the team (hoping for a miracle to cure her) but became bitter that she had to sit on the sidelines. It was at this time that Mary became the victim of sexual assault when her coach (whom Mary believed was trying to help her overcome her knee injury) tried to seduce her.

After graduating from Kennedy High, Mary appeared not to have a future direction. She first worked as a waitress at Pete's Pizza, then at Eddie's Pool Hall, before she believed she found her calling as a firefighter. She failed to focus and flunked the endurance test. It came as a blow to Mary, and she hit rock bottom. She squandered what little money she had, maxed out credit cards, took and quit jobs, drove while intoxicated, and fell in with the wrong crowd. Unwilling to see Mary ruin her life, Eric and Annie sent her to Buffalo, New York, to live with Eric's father, a strict, disciplined, retired army officer called "the Colonel," on November 13, 2000, in hopes of straightening her out. Mary began work at the Community Center for the Homeless and enrolled in college (at which time Jessica Biel left the series). On January 29, 2001, a reformed Mary returned to Glen Oak to surprise her father on his birthday. She had acquired a job as a flight attendant for Jet Blue Airlines (she now lives in Fort Lauderdale, Florida, the airline's home base) and appeared on an occasional basis. Mary mentioned that her favorite dinner was pot roast and that her favorite pie was apple; she later marries a man named Carlos.

LUCILLE "LUCY" CAMDEN

Lucille, called Lucy, is the third-born child (12 years old) and very bright, sassy, and carefree. She receives an allowance of $5 a week and loves Rocky Road ice cream. As a child, she attended what she called "Camp All by Myself," as she was the only camper assigned to her own bunk. Lucy is mechanically inclined (she has her own toolbox and can fix cars) and attended Walter Reed Junior High School, Kennedy High School, and Crawford College (where she is studying theology to become a minister). At Kennedy High, she was voted Homecoming Queen and used her carpentry skills as a volunteer for Habitat for Humanity (building homes for deserving people). Romance entered Lucy's life when she met Kevin Kinkirk (George Stults), a police officer; they married in April 2003. They set up housekeeping in a converted room over her parents' garage; Lucy became a minister in 2005, and she and Kevin had a child they named Savannah.

SIMON CAMDEN

Simon (10 years old when the series begins) attended Walter Reed Junior High School, then Kennedy High School. He is good in math and was called "the Bank of Simon," as his parents allowed him to do their tax returns. His first job was delivering papers for the *Gazette*, then a waiter at Pete's Pizza, before he acquired an after-school job as a janitor with his girlfriend, Cecilia (Ashlee Simpson), whose father owned a janitorial service.

Simon was smart and basically a good kid, but his life changed dramatically when he was involved in a fatal car accident that claimed the life of a young man. While the accident was not Simon's fault, Simon was riddled with guilt and could no longer live in Glen Oak and chose to attend college out of state (at which time [2003] David Gallagher left the series and his relationship with Cecilia ended). He returned in 2005 and became romantically involved with Rosie (Sarah Thompson), and they later married (in the last WB episode, May 8, 2006).

RUTH "RUTHIE" CAMDEN

Ruthie, five years old when the series begins, is the youngest of the children (before the birth of twins Sam and David) and considers herself "a pint-sized snoop. Everything that happens in this house is my business." She shares a bedroom with Lucy, and her side of the room reflects her love of Hello, Kitty posters and dolls ("Hello, Kitty is very important to me," she says). At one point, she wanted to become an astronaut and live on the moon "because the Earth bores me." She has two favorite dolls (Amy and Zin Zin; Amy is lactose intolerant; Zin Zin is allergic to strawberries) and a security blanket she calls "Blankey." She also has an imaginary friend named "Hooey."

Ruthie attends the Eleanor Roosevelt School (a private institution that has its own stables, and she has a horse named Ed). She later attends the Walter Reed School (where she is a straight "A" student) and earns money babysitting. *Xena: Warrior Princess* and the mythical *Snappy the Stegosaurus* are her favorite TV shows. She enjoys riding her bike, writing stories, and drinking orange soda. She mentions lasagna as her favorite dinner.

Ruthie won her second-grade art pageant with a totem pole of clay noses she called "A Camden Nose." Each Christmas, Ruthie performs in the Glen Oak church's holiday pageant and always gets nervous—"I get dinosaurs in my stomach." Ruthie helps her mother care for the twins and held a job delivering newspapers for the *Gazette*. As a young girl, Ruthie's favorite activity was getting her brother, Simon, into trouble.

FINAL CW EPISODE (MAY 13, 2007)

It is mentioned that Mary was now a schoolteacher in New York City. Eric, who had suffered from heart issues, decides to give up the ministry and take a motor tour of America with his family. The last seconds of the episode show Annie christening their motor home "7th Heaven."

Ruthie was now a junior in high school (and works at the concession stand of the local movie house); Lucy, who appears to be taking over for her father (she is now the associate pastor of the Glen Oak church), is pregnant with her second child; she and Kevin have two dogs: Samson and Delilah.

Sex and the City
(HBO, 1998–2004)

Cast: Sarah Jessica Parker (Carrie Bradshaw), Kim Cattrall (Samantha Jones), Kristin Davis (Charlotte York), Cynthia Nixon (Miranda Hobbes), Chris Noth (Mr. Big).

Basis: An intimate look at the lives of four beautiful women who live and work in New York City: Carrie, Samantha, Miranda, and Charlotte. Central focus is on the women's sex lives and their attempts to deal with being women in the twenty-first century.

CAROLINE "CARRIE" MARIE BRADSHAW

Background: From the 2012 CW series *The Carrie Diaries*, which details Carrie's life before *Sex and the City*. Carrie (Anna Sophia Rob) is 17 years old (born on June 15, 1966) and living in Castlebury, Connecticut. She attends Castlebury High School and lives with her father, Tom, a recent widower (his wife, Carrie's mother, died of cancer), and her sister Dorrit. Carrie dreams of becoming a writer begin to materialize when she moves to Manhattan and acquires a job at *Interview* magazine while also attending classes at New York University.

Occupation: Columnist (of "Sex and the City," about living and loving in Manhattan) for the *New York Star*. Carrie later becomes a fashion reporter for *Vogue* magazine.

Reputation: Known for writing the juiciest columns in Manhattan (her billboards read "Carrie Bradshaw Knows Good Sex").

Books: Sex and the City, MenHatten, and *A Single Life* (based on her columns; published by Clearwater Press). After her first book is published, she celebrates at the restaurant Gray's Papaya.

Measurements: 34-24-35. She stands 5 feet, 3 inches tall and wears a size 7½ shoe.

Model: Carrie appeared in a layout for *New York* magazine called "Single and Fabulous."

Fault: Never follows the advice she gives to her readers, thus creating many of her problems with men.

Obsession: Shoes (Miranda estimates that she has at least 100 pairs of shoes, most
   of which cost $400 or more). Carrie is extravagant not only here but also on
   the expensive designer clothes she buys (at one point, she became addicted
   to floral patterns, and her wardrobe reflected flowers).
Addiction: Shopping. Carrie has a moderate income yet spends way beyond her
   means. She maxes out credit cards, is unable to secure bank loans (due to
   her poor savings record), and has a bad credit rating.
Favorite Department Stores: Saks Fifth Avenue, Bloomingdale's, Barneys, and
   Bergdorf-Goodman.
Signature Accessory: A gold name necklace.
Favorite Drink: A Cosmopolitan.
Habit: Smoking (Marlboro Lights cigarettes).
Address: A brownstone at 245 East 73rd Street on Manhattan's Upper East Side
   (between Park and Madison avenues).
Catchphrase: "I couldn't help but wonder . . ."
Confession: Carrie lost her virginity when she was in the eleventh grade (on the
   ping pong table in Seth Bateman's Game Room in Connecticut); in Man-
   hattan in 1988, when Carrie was 22, she had a one-night stand that resulted
   in her having an abortion.
Show Quirk: Will show her figure in sexy lingerie but will not appear nude.
Computer Screen Name: Shoegal.
Favorite Cookie: Double Stuff Oreos.
Favorite Candy: Whoppers (which she enjoys at the movies).
Favorite Baseball Team: The New York Yankees.

Note: Carrie Bradshaw is actually the alias for Candace Bushnell, the author
of the actual *Sex and the City* columns (for the *New York Observer*) that were
made into a book (on which the series is based). The Carrie Bradshaw character
became so real that the paper the *Guardian* named Carrie Bradshaw an icon,
stating, "She did as much to shift the culture around certain women's issues as
real-life female groundbreakers."

SAMANTHA JONES
Background: The daughter of middle-class parents, she earned money by selling
   Dilly Bars at Dairy Queen. She mentions having two siblings (as she says, her
   mother "was saddled with three kids and a drunk husband"). In the *Carrie
   Diaries* prequel series, Samantha (played by Lindsay Gort) mentioned being
   "born in the Everglades" (in Florida) and eating alligator for breakfast. In the
   Sex and the City series, Samantha reveals that she moved to New York City,
   where she actually grew up and enjoyed partying at Studio 54. She also had
   two abortions, one while she was attending college.

Kim Cattrall, Cynthia Nixon, Sarah Jessica Parker, and Kristin Davis. *HBO/ Photofest © HBO*

Occupation: Owner of her own public relations firm. She earned extra money by posing nude for a photographic session.

Address: Apartment 45 in a building on the Upper East Side of Manhattan. She later moves to a more expensive residence in the meatpacking district of Manhattan.

Favorite Drink: Cosmopolitan.

Measurements: 36-27-37. She stands 5 feet, 7 inches tall and wears a size 9½ shoe and a size 8 dress.

Favorite Baseball Team: The New York Yankees.

Trait: Being seductive and having a good time. She believes in sex on the first date and hates to be called "the older woman" in a relationship (according to Carrie, "Samantha has been 35 for so long she can't remember how old she really is").

Character: Samantha knows she is beautiful and has "the look." Her wardrobe is anything that can make her look sexy—from deeply plunging, cleavage-revealing necklines to provocative skirts and dresses. She wears fake nipples to accentuate her breasts (she claims to have gotten jobs from men because of her breasts). She demands the best in what she does and whomever she chooses to date. Samantha is promiscuous and admits that she has lost her ability to climax (she also says she's a "try-sexual—I'll try anything once"). Samantha knows what she wants and radiates confidence in virtually every-thing she does. She often leaves her lingerie behind in a man's apartment, and the idea of being with another woman excites her. She began a brief les-bian affair with Maria (Sonia Braga), an artist, but it ended when Samantha missed men and Maria felt that Samantha had intimacy issues.

Favorite Baseball Team: The New York Yankees.

Trauma: Samantha is diagnosed with breast cancer during the final season. Chemo-therapy caused hair loss, but Samantha continued to retain her look through wigs, makeup, and hats.

MIRANDA HOBBES

Place of Birth: Philadelphia.

Occupation: Attorney with a prestigious Manhattan law firm (she is later a partner).

Education: Harvard Law School (Class of 1990); she drinks her coffee from a Harvard mug.

Address: A stylish Upper West Side Manhattan apartment.

Character: Elegant and feminine but the classic overachiever (a 16-hour day is normal to her). She is not afraid to say what she thinks. Whether in the courtroom or in the office, Miranda knows how to dress for success. Her conservative tailored suits, coupled with her stylish look, make Miranda the perfect fashion statement—but that is at work; at home it's T-shirts, jeans, and sweats.

Trait: Self-assured, tough, and down to earth (she feels that being aggressive is the only way to succeed in the business world).

Favorite Cake: Devil's food.

Favorite Cookie: Oreo.

Favorite Baseball Team: The New York Yankees.

Favorite TV Show: The mythical *Jules and Mimi* (a sexually charged British series).

Favorite Drink: Cosmopolitan.

Measurements: 32-23-36. She stands 5 feet, 11 inches tall. In high school, Miranda mentions that she wore a 36A bra to impress boys.

Dating: Miranda dated what she considered "boring businessmen" until she met Steve Brady (David Eigenberg), owner of a bar called Scout (named after his dog) by whom she became pregnant. They have a son they name Brady Hobbes, and during her pregnancy, Miranda developed a craving for fried chicken. In the final season, Miranda and Brady move to a townhouse in Brooklyn.

Experiment: Miranda pretended to be a lesbian to discover what it would be like to be with another woman. She believes she participated in a three-way but was drunk and can only remember that she "woke up in someone else's bra."

Pet Cat: Fatty.

CHARLOTTE YORK

Parents: Dr. Stephen Foster York and Sandra Whitehead York. Charlotte is a descendant of Samuel Huntington, one of the signers of the Declaration of Independence, and her mother has the nickname "Muffin."

Education: Smith College (a member of the College Republicans and the Kappa Kappa Gamma sorority; she lived on campus in the Haven-Wesley House dorm and majored in art history). She mentions being a teen model, prom queen, varsity cheerleader, and captain of the track-and-field team.

Occupation: Operates an art gallery in Manhattan. A continuity error in the final season claims that Charlotte's occupation is an editor for *Fashions* magazine.

Nickname: Because of her old-fashioned beliefs and naïveté, Charlotte is called "Park Avenue Pollyanna" by Carrie in her narrations.

Trait: According to Miranda, Charlotte is incapable of telling a believable lie, and her passion is "hot men in tights."

Measurements: 32-25-35. She stands 5 feet, 6 inches tall.

Dream: A marriage and family. She has been dating since she was 15 years old and now admits that at 35 years of age, "I'm tired of dating." She did, however, marry Trey MacDougal (Kyle MacLachlan), but they divorced over their inability to agree on having children. She then married her divorce lawyer, Harry Goldenblatt (Evan Handler), and learned, at age 36, that she was unable to conceive naturally and underwent hormone therapy. Before the therapy works, she and Harry adopt a baby girl from China (Lily); Charlotte later gives birth to a girl they name Rose.

Hobby: Collecting decorating magazines and fabric samples for her dream home—a country cottage.

Pet Dog: Elizabeth Taylor (after her favorite actress; the dog was originally named Princess Dandyridge Brandywine).

Favorite Drink: Cosmopolitan.

Favorite Baseball Team: The New York Yankees.

Obsession: Shoes (which must be as elegant as the clothes she wears).

Wardrobe: Basically pastel with accessories that highlight her feminine side. She feels sexiest in her black evening gown (which she wears to the ballet and charity events).

MR. BIG

Mr. Big, named for his status of becoming the next major tycoon (after Donald Trump), is actually John James Preston (played by Chris Noth), Carrie's on-and-off romantic interest. They met after accidentally bumping into each other on the street. Like a gimmick used on the TV series *Charles in Charge* (who had no last name), every opportunity to mention Big's full name (or Charles's last name) is interrupted before it can be said. When they each begin to continually bump into each other (as was done on the series *Bewitched* for Samantha and Darrin), they agree to bump into each other on purpose, and thus begins their relationship (which underwent numerous ups and downs over the course of the series and even in the two feature films *Sex and the City* and *Sex and the City 2*). Big calls Carrie "Kid."

Sisters

(NBC, 1991–1996)

Cast: Patricia Kalember (Georgie Reed); Swoosie Kurtz (Alex Reed); Sela Ward (Teddy Reed); Julianne Phillips (Frankie Reed); Heather McAdams (Cat); Jo Anderson, then Sheila Kelley (Charlotte Bennett Hayes).

Basis: The relationship between four close sisters (Georgie, Alex, Teddy, and Frankie) who are also best friends and how each tries to be there for the other despite the difficult circumstances each sister faces.

OVERALL SERIES INFORMATION

Georgiana (called Georgie), Alexandra (Alex), Theodora (Teddy), and Francesca (Frankie) are the daughters of Tom (now deceased) and Bea Reed (Elizabeth Hoffman); each has a male nickname because Tom had hoped for boys. The sisters attended West High School in Winnetka, Illinois, and a mythical TV movie called *A Sister's Love—Four Sisters for Each Other Forever* was made based on their lives.

ALEX REED HALSEY BARKER

Position: The eldest of the sisters (39 when the series begins).

Husband: Wade Halsey (David Dukes), a plastic surgeon who cross-dressed and later divorced Alex when he fell in love with a younger woman.

Daughter: Reed (Kathy Wagner, then Ashley Judd, then Noelle Parker). Alex was in labor with her for 24 hours. Reed was rebellious, and after dropping out of a Catholic high school, Alex sent her to a private boarding school in Paris. Reed's immoral conduct caused her expulsion, after which Alex enrolled her in the Plumdale Private School in Chicago. This quickly ended, and Reed joined a cult (the Nature of Science), changing her name to Ineka. After leaving the cult, Reed eloped with filmmaker Kirby Philby (Paul Rudd) and moved to Los Angeles, where his film *Pigs to the Slaughter* won acceptance at the American Academy of Film. They had a daughter (Halsey) but divorced shortly thereafter. When Reed lost custody of Halsey (being an unfit mother; Kirby gained full custody), she found work running a high-priced call girl ring. She was caught, arrested, and sentenced to community service (which actually reformed her).

Measurements: 34-24-35. She stands 5 feet, 4 inches tall.

Character: Alex is organized and loves yard sales; she is considered the miser of the family (although she is also said to be a shopaholic). She has a small lightning bolt tattoo on her right breast and sleeps with a shotgun under her bed for protection.

Occupation: After Wade divorced her, Alex became the host of the TV program *Alex Live*, an interview series on Channel 3.

Second Husband: Alvin "Big Al" Barker (Robert Klein), one of Alex's show sponsors (a discount appliance store) who billed himself as "The Prince of Price Town"; he called her "Little Al." He later ran for and won the position of mayor; he was also Jewish and embraced his religion by using his real last name of Barkowitz.

Car License Plate: 89F 890.

Medical Issue: Alex was diagnosed with breast cancer (which became a recurring story line beginning with 1993 episodes).

Flashbacks: Teenage Alex (Alexondra Lee, then Sharon Martin); young Alex (Sharon Gayr). Mother, Bea Reed (Mary Ann Calder); father, Dr. Thomas Reed (John McCann, then Peter White); young Wade (Mark Patrick Gleason).

TEDDY REED MARGOLIS FALCONER SORENSON

Position: The second-born sister (age 35 when the series begins).

Ex-Husband: Mitchell "Mitch" Margolis (Ed Marinaro).

Daughter: Catherine (called Cat). Cat is 15 years old when the series begins, and she and Teddy are living with Georgie. Cat is very close to her mother and longs for a stable home. She likes clothes that are "stylin'," but around the house she parades about in her bra and panties (a habit Georgie is trying to break, as she has two sons). After attending college, Cat chooses to become a Chicago police officer and becomes close to her partner, Billy Griffin (Eric Close), in season 6.

Measurements: 37-25-37. She stands 5 feet, 7 inches tall and wears a size 8 dress.

Trait: Teddy is a recovering alcoholic and is regarded as "the unstable sister." She has a carefree attitude about life and will go anywhere when the mood strikes her. She takes whatever jobs she can find and is a budding architect.

Occupation: Waitress at a soda shop called Sweet 16; telephone solicitor at 555-MOAN, a line for lonely men (she used the name Ramona; the cost was $5 for three minutes); salesgirl at Wonderful You Cosmetics; fashion consultant at the Chandler-Klein Department Store; designer of a clothing line called "Teddy Ware"; and, finally, the chief financial officer for the IDH Corporation in New York City. Teddy mentions that in her youth, she posed nude for pictures that were displayed at the Douglas Gallery in Chicago.

Trait: Each of the sisters agrees that Teddy has "the perfect breasts."

Second and Third Husbands: James Falconer (George Clooney) and Dr. Gabriel Sorenson (Stephen Collins). Before the final season, Cat was raped while attending college; police detective James Falconer was assigned the case; he and Teddy met at an Alcoholics Anonymous meeting, fell in love, and married. He was later killed in a car bombing meant to stop him from testifying against a criminal in court. Gabriel Sorenson was Teddy's neurosurgeon, whom she married in final-season episodes. He was married three times before (had a daughter named Melissa), and as the series ended, Teddy became pregnant with a daughter.

Flashbacks: Teenage Teddy (Jill Novick, then Devon Pierce).

GEORGIE REED WHITSIG

Position: The third-born sister (32 when the series begins).

Husband: John Whitsig (Garrett M. Brown). John was a certified public accountant who quit his job to become a singer (his dream is to release a record album called *The Sound of Whitsig*; it was mentioned that he actually had a hit song called "Thank You, Babe, for Leavin' Me"). He later returned to work as an accountant when their son Evan was diagnosed with leukemia.

Children: Trevor (Ryan Francis) and Evan (Dustin Berkovitz).

Occupation: Broker for Maple Leaf Realties.

Measurements: 34-24-34. She stands 5 feet, 8 inches tall.

Education: Chicago University (has a PhD in anthropology; she gave up her dream of becoming an anthropologist when she became pregnant). She later returns to college to become a therapist.

Favorite Breakfast: Blueberry pancakes.

Member: The Maple Leaf Rags bowling team (where she is called "Striker Whitsig").

Trait: Excellent cook and housekeeper and truly enjoys the holidays, especially Christmas (although she complains that the only holiday video they have is the Christmas episode from the series *Eight Is Enough*).

Address: A house with the street number 844.

Telephone Number: 555-7842.

Car License Plate Number: PC2 726.

Pet Dog: Watson.

Flashbacks: Young Georgie (Riff Regan); young John (Mike Simmrin).

FRANKIE REED MARGOLIS

Position: The youngest sister (29 years old when the series begins).

Marital Status: Single until Teddy divorces Mitch and Frankie falls in love with him (they married in 1993). Frankie has had a crush on Mitch since she was 12 years old. Mitch owns a fresh-fish store called Mitch's Catch of the Day. When Frankie was sent to the store to buy sea bass for her mother, she first saw Mitch, and it was love at first sight (for her). Mitch has a pet lobster called Louie.

Occupation: Market analyst for the firm of Frye, Birnbaum and Coates (where Teddy also worked for a short time); later the owner of a restaurant called Sweet 16 (where Cat also worked as a waitress).

Character: Totally self-sufficient and totally dedicated to work. Teddy calls her "Stinkabell." Although it appeared that life was progressing well for Frankie, especially after her marriage to Mitch, it begins to take a downward spiral when she learns she cannot have children (infertile). It is at this time that she asks Georgie to become her surrogate mother. Georgie gives birth to her child, Thomas George, but Frankie's total devotion to her career causes her and Mitch to divorce (at which time she bought Sweet 16). She later moves to Japan to find work (to explain Frankie's absence when Julianne Phillips left the series).

Flashbacks: Young Frankie (Rhianna Janette, then Tasia Schutt); Frankie, age 12 (Annie Barker); teenage Mitch (Josh Lozoff).

DR. CHARLOTTE "CHARLEY" BENNETT HAYES

Charley, the previously unknown fifth sister, resulted from an affair that Tom, a doctor, had with his nurse; it can be seen that she too carried a male's nickname. Tom's affair led Bea to become an alcoholic. Charley was slowly phased into the series beginning with the fourth season. Charley was raised in several foster homes, and her initial reaction to meeting her sisters was one of dislike (and resentment) more than anything else. She eventually accepted Georgia,

Alex, Frankie, and Teddy as her sisters. Charley was a doctor with the free health clinic and eventually married Dr. Wesley "Wes" Hayes (Michael Whaley), the free clinic director.

Spin City
(ABC, 1996–2002)

Cast: Michael J. Fox (Michael Flaherty), Charlie Sheen (Charlie Crawford), Barry Bostwick (Randall Winston), Heather Locklear (Caitlin Moore), Richard Kind (Paul Lassiter), Alan Ruck (Stewart Bondek), Michael Boatman (Carter Heywood).

Basis: Political satire that profiles a mythical mayor of New York City (Randall Winston) and his staff (Michael, Charlie, Caitlin, Paul, and Stewart).

MICHAEL "MIKE" FLAHERTY

Michael is the deputy mayor of New York City. He is a graduate of Fordham University in the Bronx and in his unnamed high school had the nickname "Newt" ("like the small lizard"). He is hyper, controlling, and highly competitive and has a fear of commitment (he feels being intimate with a woman will lead to something he doesn't want—marriage). He does date, but everything must revolve around him, and thus he is known as "the king of failed relationships."

Michael, a Capricorn, lives in an apartment that overlooks Central Park and enjoys playing the guitar. He feels his biggest challenge is to make the mayor look good despite all the incidents that seem to put Randall in a bad light (e.g., when Randall was asked to throw out the first ball at a Little League game, he did so but did it "throwing like a girl"; he also visited hospitalized children and gave a child in the diabetic ward a Hershey's candy bar).

Michael began his political career as an intern to a congressman named Owen Kingston. He is often overworked and has little time for any leisure activities. He fantasizes about people (whom only he and the viewing audience see), and he manipulates people and the press to make him and Randall look good. At times when things do not go his way, "he rants like an idiot in search of a village." After working with Randall for four years, Michael secures a job as an environmental lobbyist in Washington, D.C. (at which time Michael J. Fox left the series). When he returned for a visit, it is seen that he was now married to Allison (Olivia d'Abo).

CHARLES "CHARLIE" CRAWFORD

Charlie, a ladies' man, replaced Michael as the deputy to Mayor Winston in 2000. He had been raised by a father (Roy) with few morals (e.g., Charlie had his first taste of beer at Callahan's Tavern before he was 10 years old and hung out at pool halls with Roy since he was seven). He believes, "I do all the work of the mayor without the glory, pay, or prestige." He has been voted one of the 11 sexiest men in Manhattan. Like Michael, he suffers from a fear of commitment and is reluctant to date a woman with kids ("I'm not good with kids"). He doesn't smoke but carries a pack of cigarettes "in case a girl asks me for a smoke" and claims, "I've been dating 23-year-old girls for 20 years."

Charlie had a gambling problem, wears Italian silk shirts (called "blouses" by Caitlin), and is an excellent cook (stuffed salmon being his signature meal). He lives in Apartment 7D in Manhattan, and his reckless ways resulted in his being expelled from the following colleges: Michigan State, Arizona State, Alabama, Syracuse, and Northeastern. In another episode, it is stated that Charlie never graduated because he missed his final exam in Spanish and had to take the exam years later at New York University to acquire his degree with a "C" average. At Western High School, he played third base for the school's baseball team, the Lions.

Charlie and Caitlin have an on-and-off romantic relationship (hindered by Charlie's roving eye). Caitlin also frowns on having dinner at restaurants with Charlie because he hits on waitresses, makes rude noises, and is a bad conversationalist.

RANDALL WINSTON

Randall is a man of wealth who, after serving as the Manhattan borough president for six years, was elected mayor of New York City. Randall's grandfather made a fortune by bootlegging whiskey during the 1920s, and it was that money that put him through college. Randall rarely takes his job seriously, and to him "eight hours is like three work days." He is oblivious to other people's feelings or suffering and believes that his most redeeming quality is "my trustfulness." Randall also has a habit of using the nonsense word "further-the-less" as a real word in conversations, and if faced with an important meeting or keeping his massage appointment at the same time, he opts to get his massage. Randall does know how to play a crowd after a speech and come out looking good; however, if there is a pretty girl in the crowd and she looks at him, he goes to pieces. His favorite sport is racquetball (and he hates to lose).

Randall, a Capricorn, was born in Fairfield, Connecticut, and raised by parents who showed him little love (especially his mother, who overshadowed everything he did). At Yale University, Randall showed an interest in film and made a movie that Yale's *Daily News* dubbed "an incoherent mess." *Wheel of Fortune* and *All My Children* are his favorite TV shows (he has a knack for guessing puzzles on *Wheel* before all the letters are revealed). Randall collects driftwood sculptures, has his own action figure (the "Mayor Winston Action Figure"), and enjoys meals with his staff at the Landmark Tavern (he claims to despise street vendor food—"It repulses me").

Randall receives a death threat in the mail every Tuesday and keeps large amounts of cash in his office in a fake bank called "Don Quixote." He is divorced from Helen (who received a million-dollar divorce settlement) and had a brief romance with Judge Claire Simmons (Farrah Fawcett), whom he called "Claire Bear." He has a polo pony named "Little Miss Muffy," and the Keebler Room is his favorite cigar bar. Blue is his favorite color; he "reads" great literary books on tape and was on his unnamed high school football team. He attempted to become an actor after college (appearing in *West Side Story* and *The Sound of Music*) and hosts a weekly radio program he calls *The Mayor Winston Weekly Radio Show*. Randall drives a 1966 Mustang and has a rather weird recurring dream: being on a yacht and being fed strawberries by a young Angie Dickinson (TV's *Police Woman*). He also has a strict rule about attending social events: "No models, no mayor." Alyssa Milano played his daughter, Meg.

CAITLIN MOORE

Caitlin is a stunning blonde (with blue eyes) who works as Randall's campaign manager. She was born in Vermont and majored in political science in college (she was also president of the Young Democratic Society); another episode mentions Caitlin as being born in Massachusetts and attending Harvard University (where she majored in psychology and did fashion modeling). She is divorced from Trevor Wolfe and uses her maiden name. Like Randall, Caitlin had show business tendencies (fancying herself a singer) and appeared on the then-real TV series *Star Search* (but lost, proving to be an awful singer). She was a guest host on *Live with Regis and Kathie Lee* (where she spilled hot coffee on herself and "cursed 50 or 60 times" on live TV; Kathie Lee Gifford is her favorite TV host). Caitlin proved to be a wise investor, as she is a founding shareholder in Microsoft.

Caitlin measures 37-27-36 and wears a size 8 dress and a size 7 shoe. She stands 5 feet, 5 inches tall and enjoys attending the theater, jazz music, and riding her bicycle in Central Park. She is also consumed by what other people think of her (she is currently suing the *New York Times* for publishing a picture of her in the middle of a blink). Every two months, Jane, Caitlin's mother, runs an ad in the *New York Post* to find her a husband (as Caitlin is the last single girl in the family). Caitlin reads *Fashion Lady* magazine, lives in an apartment (5C) in Manhattan, and mentioned that her father deserted the family when she was six years old (her mother worked two jobs to support the family). Before having a relationship with Charlie, she and Michael Flaherty were an item. Caitlin is terrible at lying and always fashionably dressed, and when she becomes nervous, she compulsively cleans her hands. Sean Whalen appeared as her cousin Steve.

PAUL THOMAS LASSITER

Paul is Randall's press secretary. He is cheap, never shows up on time for work, is a moocher, and steals office supplies (e.g., he has taken 10,000 pens and sold them as City Hall souvenirs). He is abrasive, freaks out over everything, takes advantage of other people, and is his own greatest asset. He reads the newspaper only for its comic section and is capable of playing the banjo.

Paul rises at 4 a.m. each day, does his daily yoga exercises, eats Rice-A-Roni out of the box, and enjoys meatball sandwiches for lunch. To make sure no one takes his morning donut at work, he places his name on the bottom of one. He appears to be absentminded (revises old memos, takes naps in the janitor's closet, places a cardboard cutout of himself at his desk to represent his being there, and leaves work early). Paul collects antique dolls and Denny's Restaurant menus. In college, he was recording secretary of the audiovisual club and drives a car with the license plate QAG 286. He was the spokesman for the New York State Department of Education and was married to a woman named Claudia (who left him to become a nun). Paul is a "fake Jew" (pretends to be one; even had a bar mitzvah), keeps his money safe in a no-interest checking account, and scours the City Hall parking lot each morning looking for dropped change. He appeared as a contestant on the TV game shows *Who Wants to Be a Millionaire?* (where he won $1 million and invested it in a politically themed restaurant called Wonk) and *Blind Date*. Paul's yearly tradition is asking Randall for a raise, but he never gets it (Randall calls the pay hike refusals "the bagel" "because he gets nothing"). Paul is seen smoking a cigar in some episodes.

STEWART BONDEK

Stewart, a rather unsavory character, is Randall's political aide (Paul calls him "a cruel vindictive bastard"). He delights in belittling people (especially women), thinks he is a ladies' man, and has unconventional sex with girls he picks up at bus stations. He has a beauty pageant paperweight on his desk called "Boob Meister" (purchased at a sex shop called the Knocker Locker), and women with large breasts excite him (he calls "well-stacked" girls "sweater meat").

Stewart's nights are often spent watching Internet porn, and he claims to be an activist—"If there was a petition to close a strip club within 10 blocks of a school, I would be right there to see that the school is closed." Stewart's amusement comes from playing practical jokes on people, and he passes the time by making prank phone calls. He reads the personal ads for laughs and calls the most pathetic ones "to give them a ray of hope." He doesn't take messages, attend meetings, or ever offer to volunteer for anything. Believing he is God's gift to women and hitting on girls were apparently his qualifications for the job (as he gets paid for doing nothing). He mentions being a fan of the New York Knicks basketball team.

CARTER HEYWOOD

Carter, the mayor's minority representative, is African American, gay, and overly obsessed with his pet dog Rags (so much so that he takes him to his stylist to have his teeth whitened). Carter is a stylish dresser (especially fond of leather coats) but is often the subject of Stewart's off-color jokes or remarks. Carter is working for the underdog and believes in volunteer work, "and the harder the job, the more rewarding the pleasure" (although he will find the easiest tasks to perform when he does volunteer). Carter shares an apartment (3A) with Stewart in Manhattan and is looking for a man "who is smart, well-traveled yet stylish." His favorite TV show is the PBS series *Antiques Roadshow*, and his favorite part of the newspaper is the fashion section. He is a gourmet cook, and when he needs to be someplace where he doesn't want to be known, he uses the alias "Dexter St. John." He is seen smoking both a pipe and cigars.

Star Trek Voyager
(UPN, 1995–2001)

Cast: Kate Mulgrew (Kathryn Janeway), Jeri Ryan (Seven of Nine), Roxann Dawson (B'Elanna Torres), Tim Russ (Tuvok), Ethan Phillips (Neelix), Robert Picardo (the Doctor).

Basis: Star Trek spin-off that charts the progress of the U.S. Starfleet spaceship *Voyager NCC-7465* as it seeks a way back to the Federation after becoming lost in the dangerous Delta Quadrant following the pursuit of an enemy Maquis warship.

KATHRYN JANEWAY

Position: Captain of *Voyager*.

Parents: Edward and Gretchen Janeway.

Place of Birth: Indiana on May 20 (possibly in late 2330 or early 2340).

Background: Studied ballet (at the age of six, she performed in "The Dying Swan") and six years later became interested in playing tennis. Kathryn wanted to be more than just a farm girl. She yearned to explore new worlds and made that her life's goal.

Education: Starfleet Academy (graduated top of her class).

Assignments: Science officer aboard the USS *Al-Batani*; captain of both the USS *Billings* and *Voyager*. She was promoted to Admiral when, after being lost in the Delta Quadrant for seven years, she incorporated an alien Borg Transwarp Conduit to return to Earth.

Character: Tough and not afraid to take chances. Kathryn is well versed in science, math, American Sign Language, and chromo-linguistics. She loves

music but regrets never learning to play an instrument. She had an Irish
setter named Molly.

Hero: Amelia Earhart (possibly giving her the motivation to pursue her dream).

Dislike: Being called "sir" or "ma'am" (she prefers "captain").

Relaxation: Enjoys the Holodeck room on *Voyager* (where she is able to experience role-playing in gothic novels, skiing, and sailing).

Favorite Book: Dante's Inferno.

Garrett Wang, Robert Picardo, Robert Beltran, Robert Duncan McNeill, Jeri Ryan, Ethan Phillips, Roxann Dawson, and Kate Mulgrew. *UPN/Photofest © UPN*

SEVEN OF NINE

Position: Voyager crew member with knowledge of foreign species but with no specific rank or assignment.

Background: Seven of Nine is actually Annika Hansen, an Earth girl who was born in the Trendara Colony on star date 25479. She is the daughter of Magnus and Erin Hansen, exobiologists who were studying the Borg race when, aboard their ship, the *Raven*, they were assimilated by the Borg, a collective of a billion minds thinking as one. Annika, a young girl at the time, received the Borg designation Seven of Nine. Twenty years later, she was rescued by the crew of *Voyager* (disconnected from the Borg collective mind; the upper spinal column in her neurotransceiver was neutralized, and she was able to break free); extreme medical treatments returned her to her human form. Eighty-two percent of her Borg implants were safely removed; the remaining implants are needed for her to sustain life. Her human metabolism and immune system have also been restored through the Borg nanoprobes in her bloodstream (her body contains 3.6 million nanoprobes, and each has a specific purpose, and the misuse of one could spell disaster). While Seven of Nine appears human (and extremely sexy) in appearance, she does retain evidence of her Borg assimilation: an ocular implant over her left eye and assimilation tubes on her left arm. As a Borg, Seven of Nine insisted on absolute perfection and was responsible for destroying countless millions. She requires weekly maintenance checks and must rejuvenate in her alcove (which requires 30 megawatts of electricity to power). When she disobeys Kathryn, she is sent to Cargo Bay 2 as punishment. As a child, Annika was afraid of the dark, and her father called her "Muffin."

TUVOK

Position: Security chief.

Place of Birth: The planet Vulcan in the year 2264.

Background: Tuvok followed in his parents' footsteps and joined Starfleet Academy in 2289. He graduated at the age of 29 in 2293 and was assigned to duty on the USS *Excelsior*. He married a fellow Vulcan, T'Pel, in 2304 and became the father of Asil and Sek, at which time he resigned from Starfleet Academy to raise his children and explore his race's regime of nonemotion. While doing so, he became a Starfleet instructor, cadet trainer, and an archery instructor at the Vulcan Institute for Defensive Arts. In 2343, he returned to active service and was first assigned to the USS *Wyoming*, then to Captain Janeway on her ship, the USS *Billings*. In 2371, when Kathryn was given command of *Voyager*, Tuvok became her security chief. Three years later, he was promoted to lieutenant commander.

Character: A skilled botanist with a fondness for growing orchids. He is a master of the game of Kaiton and practices Keethara meditation.

B'ELANNA TORRES
Position: Chief engineer.
Parents: A human father (John Torres) and a Klingon mother (Miral).
Place of Birth: The planet Kessik IV in the twenty-fourth century (possibly the 2350s). She grew up with her mother; her father abandoned them when B'Elanna was a child, and B'Elanna believes it was her Klingon heritage that drove him away.
Character: Tough, independent, and knowledgeable. Despite the inner conflicts her human and Klingon heritage present, B'Elanna joined Starfleet Academy and acquired her training as a Starfleet engineer. Prior to her duties aboard *Voyager*, B'Elanna fought to save the Maquis race by joining a rebellion against the Cardassians in the early 2370s. Aboard *Voyager*, B'Elanna and crewmate Tom Paris fell in love and were married by Kathryn; in 2378, they became the parents of a daughter (Klingon in appearance) they named Miral.

CHAKOTAY
Position: First officer.
Background: Chakotay, a Native American (born in 2329), is the son of Kolopak and has a Mayan background (his ancestry can be traced back to the Rubber Tree People of Central America). When Chakotay was 15, his father traced his people's ancestral home to the Central American jungles. At this time, Chakotay allied himself with the Starfleet crews that patrolled the border and developed an interest in space travel.
Education: Starfleet Academy (2344–2348). He became an instructor in Starfleet's Advanced Tactical Training Program but resigned in 2370 to join the Maquis rebellion and fight the invading Cardassians when they threatened their way of life. Thirteen years later, he returned to Starfleet and was assigned first officer on *Voyager*.
Character: Cherishes his Mayan background and uses a spirit summoned from his medicine bag for guidance. He also has a tattoo over his left eye as a symbol of his heritage.

THE DOCTOR
Position: Chief medical officer.
Background: The Doctor, as he is called, is an EMH (emergency medical hologram) with the designation AK-1. He has been programmed to perform all types of medical procedures and is a combination of light force fields

powered by an atomic computer. The Doctor was activated by Dr. Lewis Zimmerman of Starfleet at the Jupiter Holo-Programming Center. He has the knowledge of 3,000 cultures and more than 5,000 medical procedures. His office is located in Sick Bay on Deck 5. He responds with "Please state the nature of the medical emergency" when called and is able to move about the ship by use of his mobile emitter. He enjoys music, especially opera, and has taken on qualities far beyond those for which he was programmed (achieved through his interactions with the various alien races he treats).

NEELIX

Position: Morale officer.

Background: Neelix, a Talaxian, was born on Rinax, a moon of the planet Talas in the Delta Quadrant. He also serves as a goodwill ambassador and calls the galley his home (as he is an excellent cook). He left the command of Captain Janeway in 2378 to live with a fellow Talaxian (Dexa) and her son (Brax) on a Delta Quadrant asteroid (Talax was destroyed by an invading army, and Neelix is one of the few survivors).

Step by Step
(ABC, 1991–1997; CBS, 1997–1998)

Cast: Suzanne Somers (Carol Foster), Patrick Duffy (Frank Lambert), Staci Keanan (Dana Foster), Angela Watson (Karen Foster), Christopher Castile (Mark Foster), Christine Lakin (Alicia Lambert), Brandon Call (J. T. Lambert), Josh Bryne (Brendon Lambert), Sasha Mitchell (Cody Lambert), Emily Mae Young (Lily Lambert).

Basis: Carol Foster, a widow with three children (Dana, Karen, and Mark), marries Frank Lambert, a divorced father with three children (Alicia, J. T., and Brendon), and the program explores the life of a blended family.

CAROL FOSTER

Place of Birth: Port Washington, Wisconsin.

Mother: Ivy Baker (Peggy Rea).

Sister: Penny Baker (Patrika Darbo).

Education: Port Washington High School (a cheerleader for the Wildcats football team); East Wisconsin University (studied cosmetology).

Address: 201 Winslow Street (in Port Washington).

Business: Carol's Beauty Boutique (which she operates from her home).

Character: Very pretty, very sexy, and an excessively neat housekeeper. She alphabetizes soup cans, irons Karen's and Dana's lingerie, has a no-temper policy, and uses beauty parlor stories to discipline the children.

Measurements: 38-28-38. She stands 5 feet, 5 inches tall and wears a size 8 dress.

Contest: In 1971, Carol was first runner-up in the Miss Small Curd Cottage Cheese Beauty Pageant (Carol claims, "I lost to a girl with bigger curds").

Dislikes: Being called a nag by Frank (Carol doesn't believe she nags; she claims it is her way of getting what she wants from her mostly uncooperative family).

FRANK LAMBERT

Father: Bill Lambert (Richard Roat).

Marriage: Frank and Carol were married at the Wedding Shack in Jamaica and set up housekeeping in Carol's home. Frank's prior wife left him to become a lounge singer in Las Vegas. He and his children are, as Carol says, "slobs" (actually just untidy).

Occupation: Owner of Lambert Construction.

Membership: The Mallard Lodge, the Sheboygan Super Bears bowling team, and president of the Milwaukee Tile and Grout Association. He coaches a Little League baseball team called the Cubs.

Dislike: Being called a liar by Carol (Frank doesn't consider stretching the truth to be lies). He feels that his construction site stories provide the means by which to teach the children a lesson—not Carol's beauty parlor "fairy tales."

Car: A GMC pickup (plate 129 815; later 527 P9); he uses Royal Carnauba Wax (at $15 a can at Auto World) to polish it.

DANA FOSTER

Relationship: Carol's 16-year-old daughter (born at 10:47 p.m. on January 15, 1976).

Education: Port Washington High School (a straight "A" student and member of the Honors Society; a writer for the school newspaper, the *Wildcatter*); East Wisconsin University (nicknamed "Cheese Whiz U"), where she is studying to become a lawyer. It was in college that Dana received her first and only "D" grade: "for using too many big words with no meaning" on a term paper.

Character: Very pretty but also very sensitive to the fact that she has small breasts (as Alicia puts it, "You're smart, and it's a good thing because you have no boobs").

Childhood: Carol called Dana "Princess Bubble Bath" when it was time for her bath. Carol keeps a "Dana Book," a photographic record of Dana's life—from her first tooth, first step, and even first kiss (Carol "just happened" to be in a tree with an infrared camera and zoom lens). She is closest to her mother.

Occupation: Student, although she held after-school jobs as the assistant manager of the 50s Café and volunteer work at the Tri County Mission.

Car License Plate: TNA 5H1.

KAREN FOSTER

Relationship: Carol's 14-year-old daughter.

Place of Birth: Port Washington on June 9, 1978.

Education: Lincoln Elementary School; Port Washington High School (a cheerleader for the Wildcats football team).

Character: Karen knows she is gorgeous ("I'm what the guys call a babe") and is often mistaken for a model ("I just look like one, but I'm not"). She is very concerned about her appearance, especially her makeup ("A mirror is my best friend"), and Carol believes her obsession started the day she gave Karen a Brooke Shields fashion doll. Alicia can't comprehend Karen's behavior and believes Karen "is a wuss because everything frightens her."

Favorite Magazines: Cosmopolitan and *Chic.*

Favorite Lipstick: Cha Cha.

Occupation: Student; teen fashion model at Peterson's Department Store.

Trauma: Missing a sale at the mall; even if she is five minutes late, she feels there are other girls buying the things meant for her.

Childhood: Karen had a washcloth with a mouse on it that she called "Mouthy" (Carol called it "Mousy," but Karen was unable to pronounce it that way).

Dating Advice: Comes from a tape cassette called "Teenage Dating Tips."

ALICIA LAMBERT

Relationship: Frank's middle child.

Nickname: "Al."

Education: Miss Daisy's Ducky Room Preschool; Port Washington Junior High and Port Washington High School.

Character: While Dana and Karen are always impeccably dressed, Alicia is somewhat of a tomboy and dresses to please herself—not other people. She always fears the worst in a situation (her rather pessimistic view changed as the series progressed).

Pet Pig: Bullet (dropped early in the series).

Pride and Joy: A rattlesnake's head preserved in a jar.

Sports: Loves baseball and is a catcher for the Beavers Little League team.

Trait: A smart aleck (Dana knows she needs an attitude adjustment and calls her "you little criminal"). Frank considers her "the son he never had," as she shows potential to enter the construction field, unlike his flaky son J.T.

Membership: Dave's Video Store (rents movies based on books to do her book reports for school).

Band: Plays drums in the all-girl Chicks with Attitudes (their first gig was at Greco's Bowl-A-Rama).

Occupation: Student. She held her first job as a waitress at Mr. Chips, at the cookie store in the mall, then as a waitress at the 50s Café under the name Peggy Sue.

Regret: Alicia never felt she was as gorgeous as Karen or Dana, but her down-to-earth looks landed her a magazine ad for Stop Jeans.

Career Ambition: Becoming an actress. She starred in the Community Playhouse production of *Death of a Salesman.*

JOHN THOMAS "J. T." LAMBERT

Relationship: Frank's eldest child.

Education: Port Washington High School (not the brightest of students; he is a member of the track team).

Character: A walking disaster. He has no flair for construction (or even working) and feels more comfortable working as Carol's shampoo boy in her beauty salon.

Dana's Term of Endearment: She sees J. T. as "a pea-brained idiot."

J. T.'s Vision: Fancies himself a teenage ladies' man.

Occupation: Student. Besides being a shampoo boy, J. T. worked as the waiter Cubby at the 50s Café and with his cousin Cody hosted the cable access TV program *J. T. and Cody's World* (wherein they gave opinions on life, its problems, and how to solve them).

After-School Hangout: The Burger Palace.

Favorite Food: A burrito.

CODY LAMBERT

Relationship: Frank's nephew. He believes he is "the coolest guy on the planet" ("No chick can resist my personal magnetism"; Dana believes he is "a brain-dead idiot").

Occupation: Construction demolition expert. He and J. T. also hosted the access cable channel TV show *J. T. and Cody's World.*

Home: A van he calls "Lucille" in the driveway of Carol and Frank's home.

Character: Somewhat dim-witted and always in a good mood; to occupy his time, he began an exercise club for "major babes" (women over 70) called "Body by Cody." Cody was suddenly dropped from the series without explanation until the episode of June 19, 1998, when he returned to tell the family he left on a spiritual quest to find the ultimate hamburger (which he did at a McDonald's in Tibet).

Nickname: "The Codeman" (as called by J. T.). He calls Dana a "hot babe" ("If she were a prehistoric creature, she'd be a Babertooth Tiger"); he calls Karen "Care Bear."

Education: The University of Wisconsin (a member of the Delta Beta fraternity).

House Plant: Gordon.

Favorite Magazine: Biker's Quarterly.

Hero: Ed, the attendant at the Texaco gas station.

MARK, BRENDON, AND LILY

Very little information is given. Mark, Carol's youngest child, attended Canyon Elementary School, then Port Washington High. He is the brains of the family and has a working model of the human intestine in his bedroom. He also has Charlene, his sexy female-voiced computer.

Brendon, Frank's youngest child, is shy and loves Double Stuff Oreos and spaghetti and meatballs. In the 1995 season finale, Carol gives birth to a daughter whom she and Frank name Lily Foster-Lambert. When the series returned for a new season, Brendon was dropped (like he was never there), and Lily advanced to the age of five (Emily Mae Young), giving the family six children, not seven; Lily's favorite plush toy is Mr. Buttons, a rabbit.

The Steve Harvey Show
(WB, 1996–2002)

Cast: Steve Harvey (Steve Hightower), Cedric the Entertainer (Cedric Robinson), Wendy Raquel Robinson (Regina Greer), Terri J. Vaughn (Lovita Jenkins).

Basis: A former musician (Steve Hightower) takes on a new life and responsibilities when he becomes a music teacher at a public high school on Chicago's West Side.

STEVEN "STEVE" HIGHTOWER

Place of Birth: Detroit, Michigan.

Address: Apartment 1412 (building not identified).

Education: Booker T. Washington High School (called "Booker T").

Occupation: Music teacher at Booker T. (his classes are held in room 104). He plays the piano and sax and was previously in a group called the High Tops (creative differences led to the band's breakup). They played funk music and achieved one gold record. Steve also managed an all-girl group called Jailbait under his company, Steve Hightower Management.

Trait: Uses his past glory as a musician to attract women and is still hoping for another big break in the music industry; he and Cedric perform as the Soul Teachers.

Awards: A Grammy; honored by Detroit's Funk Café as "The King of Funk Music." At Booker T., he is famous "for squashing the 1996 mysterious meat riot in the cafeteria."

Shoe Size: 12.

Quirk: Likes his grilled cheese sandwiches "with the edges burned"; pretends to be somebody he is not to meet women (e.g., he joined the group Sexually Addicted "to meet funky women").

Romantic Interest: Regina Grier (see below).

Car: A Ford Taurus.

Notable Students: Romeo Santana (Merlin Santana), the ladies' man, and Stanley Kuznocki (William Lee Scott), called "Bullethead," Romeo's somewhat dense friend.

CEDRIC JACKIE ROBINSON

Relationship: Steve's best friend.

Occupation: Health teacher and coach of the Cheetahs basketball team at Booker T.

Address: Shares an apartment with Steve and later an apartment across the hall when he and Lovita marry (see below).

Business: Runs an inner-city company for youths called the Cookie Man.

Almost Award: Nominated eight times for "Teacher of the Year" (but lost).

Keepsake: A "little black book" that contains his childhood memories.

Nickname for Steve: "Dawg"; Steve calls him "Ced."

Performer: Joins with Steve (as the Soul Teachers) to entertain at charity functions.

Idea: Opening a culturally friendly hardware store called the Homey Depot (he failed at "Bro Black—black golf balls for black golfers").

Relatives: Cedric's Grandma Puddin (Cedric the Entertainer), the oldest member of the Robinson family. He mentions his mother, who is grossly overweight, and who calls on him to get her out of the bathtub when she gets stuck.

LOVITA ALIZAY JENKINS

Place of Birth: Alabama.

Occupation: Administrative assistant to Regina Greer, the principal of Booker T.

Character: Very sweet and pretty but complex. She calls Regina "Boss Lady," believes in séances and voodoo, and feels she has the ability to contact spirits.

Boyfriend: Cedric Robinson, the school's athletic director (later her husband). Lovita has a dream to move to Florida and open a store called Ceddie and Lovita's House of Honda Parts and Hair (as she is a talented hairstylist).

Nicknames: Calls Cedric "Ceddie" and "Ceddie Bear."

Car: "The Ceddie Mobile" (as called by Lovita).

Cooking "Ability": None ("because my mother never taught me"; her mother used the kitchen to operate a beauty shop). When Lovita first cooked, she fried catfish in Afro Sheen hair gel and nearly killed her father; Cedric, however, says, "Nobody dials takeout like my baby."

Playwright: Lovita took a course at the Intercity Arts Center and wrote a play called *Madame Sister President* (about a girl from the ghetto who goes from fashion designer to U.S. president).

Fashion School: Miss Claudine's School of Style and Hair Weaving.

Cosmetics Purchases: Rite Aid.

REGINA GREER

Place of Birth: Detroit.

Education: Booker T. Washington High School; Chicago University.

Occupation: Teacher, then principal of Booker T. Washington High School.

Record: Holds the title "Undefeated Scrabble Champion of Booker T. High."

Character: Very attractive but demanding and seeking a man who can accept her as his superior. She believes that she has stunning good looks and a dancer's legs, "and that will get me any man I want."

That Man: Steve Hightower (they attended school together; at that time, Regina was overweight and called "Piggy" by Steve). They reunite when Steve joins the teaching staff, and love eventually develops between them. She most often calls Steve "Hightower."

Address: Apartment 204 (building not identified).

Trait: Although slim now, she still loves to eat; has a minifridge in her night-stand; starts each day off with a raspberry scone; and offers office visitors a Chunky-brand candy square.

Favorite Ice Cream: Chunky Monkey.

Favorite Breakfast Cereal: Lucky Charms.

Car: Mentioned as being a Miata.

Essence Magazine Award: "I'm Every Woman Power Professional."

Amusement Park Thrill: The roller coaster.

Pet Pig: As a child, she had one named Bentley.

Activity: Teaches dance classes at the "Regina Greer Dance Ensemble of Chicago."

Suddenly Susan

(NBC, 1996–2000)

Cast: Brooke Shields (Susan Keane), Kathy Griffin (Vicky Groener), Judd Nelson (Jack Richmond), Nestor Carbonell (Luis Rivera), Andrea Benderwald (Maddie Piper), David Strickland (Todd Stiles).

Basis: Events in the life of a beautiful, single newspaper columnist (Susan Keane) as she navigates life in San Francisco.

SUSAN KEANE

Parents: Bill (Kurt Fuller, then Ray Baker) and Liz (Caroline McWilliams, then Swoosie Kurtz) Keane.

Place of Birth: San Francisco on May 29, 1965. She weighed 10 pounds, 4 ounces at birth; her mother was in labor for 23 hours.

Address: 3135 Washington Street (an apartment she can't afford; she is still paying off student loans and needs a new oven: "A repairman died in the old oven while trying to fix it").

Telephone Number: 555–4858.

Measurements: 34-27-36. She stands 5 feet, 11 inches tall; has brown hair and green eyes; and wears a size 2 dress and a size 11 shoe.

Education: Hillcrest High School (where "I was a pie-loving kid who was overweight"; she also wrote for the school newspaper); State College (majoring in journalism).

Occupation: Newspaper columnist for the San Francisco *Gate.*

Column: "Suddenly Susan" ("It's about life and what happens to me"). Her columns "have to be 1,800 words and funny."

Favorite Dinner: Lemon peel chicken.

Favorite Drink: Tequila.

Favorite Restaurant: Chan's.

Favorite Bar: Bucky's Tavern (later O'Malley's Bar, then McMurphy's Bar).

Favorite TV Show: Reruns of *Charlie's Angels.*

Life's Outlook: Bright and cheery; she believes other people see her as adorable (as Jack says, "Yeah, like a giant Olsen twin" [referring to Mary-Kate and Ashley Olsen]).

Pet Dog: Duchess.

Political Campaign Slogan: "I'm Keen on Keane" (when she ran but lost for a seat on the San Francisco Board of Supervisors).

Hates: Having her picture taken ("I always look like I'm just reentering Earth"; as Vickie says, "Susan's pretty in person, nasty on film"). This changed when she was photographed in a sexy pose and her picture was used to promote the magazine when it was sold and reopened as *The Gate—Now Open.*

Childhood Incident: At the age of 10, Susan went on a hunger strike when Sizzler discontinued the hot rib sandwich.

Curse: Susan feels that if she lies, bad things will happen.

Relatives: Grandmother, Helen "Nana" Keane (Barbara Barrie).

VICTORIA "VICKIE" GROENER

Occupation: Food critic for the *Gate.* She also writes about the hip scene (calls herself the "Empress of Hip") and held a job where she wore a padded bra to become a hostess at Juggs, a bar that features busty girls.

Address: 101 Valley Drive.

Phone Number: 555-2634.

Favorite TV Show: Felicity.

Favorite Food: Sweet and sour shrimp.

Character: Often nasty and insults people but feels good about herself for being the way she is ("I'm not as gorgeous as Susan, but I'm cute and spunky"). She never has a positive outlook on life ("because girls like Susan get all the breaks"), and she has to struggle for what she wants. She dresses in what she calls "trashy clothes" in the hope that she will be sexually harassed. She loves to show cleavage (although she often wishes "I had more to show").

Sports: A member of the Vixens, an all-girl basketball team (their outfits are red; Vickie wore jersey 1, while Susan wore jersey 31).

Enjoyment: Seeing other people miserable.

About Men: Vickie believes she is a "man magnet" but says, "I'm a tramp at heart." When she gets depressed over a man, she says, "I need pizza, booze, and male strippers to get me over it."

Parking Space: Wherever she wants, as she has a fake handicap parking permit.

JACK RICHARDSON

Occupation: Editor and publisher of the *Gate*. Jack later sells the magazine to Ian Graham (Eric Idle), who moves the editorial offices from a swank uptown building to a less desirable location in Chinatown. Ian felt the magazine "was a rag sheet" but liked the name, circulation, and staff and changed its focus to men and their issues.

Address: An apartment at 268 Preston Place.

Phone Number: 555-9980.

Hobby: Rock climbing (he has a rock-climbing wall behind his office desk).

Favorite TV Shows: The Bionic Woman, Police Woman, and *Wonder Woman.*

Favorite Movie: The Day the Earth Stood Still.

Relatives: Brother, Kip (Anthony Starke).

OTHER REGULARS

Madelyn "Maddie" Piper is a columnist for the *Gate* who was also a classmate of Susan's from Hillcrest High School. They didn't get along then (as Maddie always teased her and played practical jokes on her; Susan refers to this time as "Silence of the Lambs with a hall pass." Susan fantasized about getting back at her—"Like messing with her car or putting her in a wood chopper"). Maddie is a snob and is disliked by all the staff except Susan, who is trying to befriend her. Vickie believes Maddie should have been one of the Spice Girls—"Bitchy Spice"—and calls her "Little Blondie Pants" and "Mad-a-la a ding-ding."

Todd Stiles is the magazine's music critic. He enjoys attending baseball games for only one reason—to fulfill a dream and catch a foul ball. Before attending each game, he performs "the Foul Ball Dance." Kids call him "Todd the God" because he pays for their video game play at the local arcade. He is tormented by fans of the Grateful Dead (for having a steady job, short hair, and no tattoos) for once giving a bad review to one of their performances.

Luis Rivera is the magazine's photographer. He was born in Cuba (where he learned his craft) and considers himself a ladies' man. He is an excellent photographer but doesn't always impress people (e.g., Maddie calls him "a macho idiot"; she also thinks Todd is "just a plain idiot"). Luis and Todd take pottery classes together at Color My World and pooled their resources ($17,000) to begin a business called Lemon Legs, producing yellow bell-bottom pants for women.

Third Rock from the Sun
(NBC, 1996–2001)

Cast: John Lithgow (Dick Solomon), Kristen Johnston (Sally Solomon), French Stewart (Harry Solomon), Joseph Gordon-Levitt (Tommy Solomon), Jane Curtin (Mary Albright), Wayne Knight (Don Leslie Orville).

Basis: Extraterrestrials (Dick, Sally, Harry, and Tommy) experience a new life as part of a mission to explore the planet Earth.

OVERALL SERIES INFORMATION
On orders from the Big Giant Head, the leader of a planet called the Home Planet, four scientists are assigned to study life on Earth. The aliens travel across 3 billion galaxies to reach their destination and land in Rutherford, Ohio, where they take up residence at 417 Pensdale Drive.

DICK SOLOMON
Cover: Quantum physics professor at Pendleton University. His classes are held in Room 239, and his office is in room 109 in the Hunt Hall Building.

Character: Pompous, self-absorbed, and naive when it comes to Earth life (he takes everything literally and often makes a fool of himself). When he is lonely or depressed, he goes to the planetarium for comfort.

Favorite Breakfast Cereals: Lucky Charms and Cheerios.

Work Lunch Box: A U.S. Postal Service logo box.

Marital Status: Unclear: In some episodes, he is single and never married; in others, he is married; and yet in others, he is a widower ("My wife burned up on reentry").

Favorite Bar: Balaska's Bar.

Favorite Ice Cream Eatery: Mr. Frostie Smooth.

Car: A red Rambler with the plate DLW 4S7.

French Stewart, Joseph Gordon-Levitt, John Lithgow, and Kristen Johnston.
NBC/Photofest © NBC

Daily Reports: Dick sends daily status updates to the Big Giant Head in lim-
    erick form.
Job: For extra money, Dick became "a counter boy" at the Rusty Burger.
Earth Experience: Heat, electricity, and cooked meals make him feel weak.
Girlfriend: Dr. Mary Albright, an anthropology professor at Pendleton; later
    dean of the Arts and Sciences Department (has office 108). Mary believes

she teaches "half-baked morons at a second-rate university." As a kid, she had a dream to become a torch singer named Marlena Albright, and as a young adult, she posed nude for black-and-white photos in an art class. She has a dog named Pepper and wrote the book *Where's Mommy: Dissecting the Typical American Family* based on observing Dick.

Final Episode: Dick and his family are transported back to the Home Planet.

SALLY SOLOMON

Position: The security officer (she was a lieutenant in the Home Planet military).

Relationship: Unclear: First said to be Dick, Harry, and Tommy's sister; then Dick's wife (Harry and Tommy are their children); then single.

Character Choice: Sally was actually a male on the Home Planet. One of the aliens had to become "the woman" to study the human female, and Sally says, "I lost."

Issues: Sally has a difficult time being a female ("I can't adjust to mood swings"), and her male self often manifests itself in her actions (making her appear abnormal at times). As a woman, she measures 36-25-34 and stands 6 feet tall. She calls her breasts "the girls, Cindy and Monique" and believes she has a body that needs to be seen (she volunteered to pose nude for *Playboy* magazine's "Coeds of the Midwest" issue, "but I was rejected for being too old").

Education: A degree in interstellar exploration from the Home Planet University.

Ability: Digest glass.

Housekeeper: Untidy, has difficulty using appliances, and has a fondness for Lemon Pledge furniture polish.

Quirks: Hates "chick flicks" and has a "pet" tomato plant (Jeremy).

Jobs: Sally's Actual Salon, a Real Business (closed by the IRS for not paying taxes); a fact-checker (company not named); the weather girl (Sally Storm) on WRTF-TV; and consultant at Bower and Stein, Inc., a human resources company.

Boyfriend: Police officer Don Leslie Orville. He loves bowling (on a team called the Three Amigos), takes sick days, "to catch up on my soaps," and puts money into expired parking meters to avoid the ticket paperwork. Sally's reassignment back to the Home Planet ended the relationship.

HARRY SOLOMON

Position: Transmitter (relays messages to the Big Giant Head). Said to be Dick's brother, then son.

Favorite Activity: Watching TV. He gets severe headaches if he misses *Good Morning, Rutherford* and *Good Afternoon, Rutherford*.

Trait: Dim-witted and easily fooled.

Dream: To have the largest soda can collection listing in the *Guinness Book of World Records.*

Jobs: Bartender at McSorley's Bar; radio talk show host (on WBDL); and Hargo, the alien, at the LePine County Fair.

Home Planet Pet: A lower life form named Pickles.

TOMMY SOLOMON

Position: The information officer. He is the oldest of the four aliens but was chosen to play the youngest to study Earth culture. Said to be Dick's brother, then son.

Earth Education: Rutherford High School (editor of the school newspaper, the *Zephyr*); Pendleton University; the Picnee School for the Gifted.

Band: The Whiskey Kings (plays guitar).

Job: Counter person at Fetzels Homemade Pretzels.

Note: Although often talked about, the Big Giant Head appeared only once (played by William Shatner). He came to Earth to visit the Solomons and posed as Stone Phillips. He wore an "I Love New Jersey" baseball cap but was overwhelmed by Earth alcohol, which made him intoxicated and complicated life for the Solomons.

Touched by an Angel
(CBS, 1994–2003)

Cast: Roma Downey (Monica), Della Reese (Tess).

Basis: An angel (Monica) sent by God and guided by her mentor (Tess) helps deserving people overcome their problems.

MONICA

Age: Unknown.

History: Monica began her heavenly life in the Angelic Choir; she was moved to Special Appearances, then Search and Rescue, to save souls. When she saved a doomed airliner, she was promoted to case worker, granted powers, and assigned to Tess, "an Angel as old as God," to learn the ropes of being an angel.

Contradiction: It is later seen that Monica cannot sing, and her greatest wish "is to sing like an angel." Hundreds of years ago, after completing an errand of mercy, Monica stumbled on the Heavenly (not Angelic) Choir and just joined it. When it was found she could not sing, "I was kicked out, and I wasn't even a member. I'm the worst singer you ever heard."

Favorite Song: "Panas Angelicas."

John Dye, Roma Downey, and Della Reese. *CBS/Photofest © CBS*

Ability: Talks directly to God but receives assignments from Tess.

Nickname: Tess calls Monica "Miss Wings" and "My Baby."

Human Characteristics: Once being a human, Monica is prone to catching "Earth viruses" like anger when someone annoys her.

Addiction: Coffee ("I can't explain why," she says). She also became intoxicated for the first time when she had Irish cream coffee.

Favorite Earth Food: Olives.

Fear: Water (until she learned to conquer it).

Trait: Breaking the rules. Angels are not permitted to interfere in human destiny. But "when my instincts kick in," Monica has to do things her way despite what the higher powers believe.

Reveal: When Monica does reveal herself to humans, she appears in a glowing light and says, "I'm an angel sent by God."

Transportation: Monica and Tess travel in Tess's pride and joy, her red 1972 Cadillac El Dorado (license plate 758 R2G).

Evil Twin: Monique (Roma Downey), a demon who takes on Monica's appearance to cause confusion and destruction to the people Monica helps.

Assistant: Valerie Bertinelli joined the cast in 2001 (with the episode "The Face of God") as Gloria, an accident-prone but intelligent angel assigned to Tess to teach her the ways of the twenty-first century.

Final Episode: Monica is promoted to supervisor and begins a journey of helping people on her own. Tess presents her with the red Cadillac as a parting gift.

Unhappily Ever After
(WB, 1995–1999)

Cast: Geoff Pierson (Jack Malloy), Stephanie Hodge (Jennie Malloy), Nikki Cox (Tiffany Malloy), Kevin Connolly (Ryan Malloy), Justin Berfield (Ross Malloy), Bobcat Goldthwait (voice of Mr. Floppy).

Basis: A husband (Jack), separated from his wife (Jennie) and living in the basement of their home, struggles to provide for his children: Ryan ("The Accident"), Tiffany ("The Girl"), and Ross ("The Mistake")—with the help of Mr. Floppy, a puppet that speaks only to him.

JACK MALLOY
Occupation: Salesman at Joe's Used Cars.
Address: 30220 Oak Avenue, Van Nuys, California.
Salary: $40,000 a year.
Marital Status: Separated and living in a small apartment (13) when the series begins. Before Jennie allows Jack to live at home, Ross gives him Mr. Floppy, his plush rabbit. Mr. Floppy then comes to life for Jack and becomes his guiding light.
Character: Loves basketball and "young busty babes" and fears the fact that he is getting older. He and Mr. Floppy watch Spanish TV "for the girls in bikinis and high heels," and each talks constantly about supermodels and women's breasts.
Trait: Jack is a terrible father. He sees Ryan and Ross as losers but is overly protective of Tiffany, whom he considers the high point of his pathetic life (and, as Jack says, "If it weren't for Tiffany, the WB would have canceled us long ago"). Nikki Cox, as Tiffany, was the sexiest and most beautiful teenage girl on TV at the time (hence all the annoying "hoots and whistles" from the studio audience). Mr. Floppy is the offspring of Yogi Bear. But when Yogi

became a big cartoon star and couldn't take care of a kid, "he tossed me into the toy bin." Mr. Floppy is a "ladies' puppet" and has had many affairs (especially with a Barbie doll takeoff called Berbie "in the toy box"). Mr. Floppy longs for (but can't get) Luscious Locks Loni, the doll of his dreams. He also has a crush on actress Drew Barrymore and often addresses the camera urging her to come on the show (she never did). Mr. Floppy also claims he gave the Muppet Grover (from *Sesame Street*) his start (Grover, suffering from stuttering, was cured when Mr. Floppy stuck his finger into an electric light socket). Mr. Floppy also makes Jack his favorite snack, onion dip.

JENNIFER "JENNIE" MALLOY

Character: Just as Jack is a terrible father (except to Tiffany), Jennie is an irresponsible mother. As a child, she played with dolls, helped her mother around the house, and was good in school. But after 16 years of marriage and three kids, she had enough and chose to separate from Jack. She pays more attention to her three dogs (Annie, Emily, and Jasper) than she does to her family. She has an unseen cat (Kitty) and a beloved glass-top coffee table (Sheila). As a kid, Jennie had a dog (Buttons) and a cat (Snuffles).

Jennie's Fate: In 1997, while tanning at Guy Macaroni's House of Tanning, Jennie fell asleep on the table and "was turned into beef jerky remnants." She returned as a ghost to help guide her family, but the story line did not work, the concept was dropped (Jack called it "the writer's mistake"), and Jennie was returned to her normal self. The following year, Jennie was written out via dialogue wherein she was said to have run off with her lesbian lover (although Jack insists she was abducted by aliens).

Internet Name: Vickie Vixen.

Regret: Never had the opportunity to play Juliet in her high school production of *Romeo and Juliet* (she lost the role to classmate, now actress, Charlene Tilton).

Quirk: Separates her dinner into three separate dishes ("so I can have three distinct flavors").

Car License Plate: 2M FE 967.

Relatives: Mother, Maureen Slattery (Joyce Van Patten).

TIFFANY MALLOY

Place of Birth: Van Nuys, California, on May 16, 1979.

Character: Considered the only child of Jack and Jennie Malloy, as Jack only cares for her. She knows that she is beautiful and wears tight jeans, miniskirts, and low cut, cleavage-revealing blouses. She is proud of the fact that she is voluptuous and has built her whole life around her physical attributes. Weighing herself makes her happy.

The Unthinkable: In 1995, Tiffany went into a panic when she got a pimple ("Oh help me, help me, I'm deformed," she cried).

Measurements (1999): 36-23-35. She stands 5 feet, 7 inches tall.

Education: Priddy High School (although Howe High School can be seen in cafeteria scenes; she played Juliet in a production of *Romeo and Juliet*); Northridge Junior College. Although she is a straight "A" student, she feels she has been disgraced when she scored a "B" on a book report on *The Scarlet Letter* ("Now I have a 'B' for bad"). She is also a National Merit Scholar and writes for her school newspaper, the *North Ridgeon.*

Goal: "I want to marry an old geezer who's loaded and has only a month to live" (her motto is "I will never trade my purity except for financial security").

Hope: To one day own a Corvette: "I look this gorgeous and have to have a flashy car to put me in."

Character: Other than being beautiful, Tiffany has little talent. In grade school, she acted in a production of *Swan Lake* ("but I drowned in the paper water"). She tried twirling a baton ("but I couldn't catch it") and attempted to play the accordion but never did (Tiffany looked down at her breasts, then the camera, and shook her head "no"). Tiffany was a member of her high school volleyball team (she wore jersey 17 but joined only because the red uniforms made her look sexy). It can be seen that if a boy breaks Tiffany's heart, Jack goes for the rifle in the den.

Occupation: Student. Tiffany did work as a counter girl at the Granny Goddess Ice Cream Parlor and as a waitress at Cali-Burger Dreamin' (where the owner named a burger after her—"The Tiffalicious Tiffany Burger—the Most Beautiful Burger Named after the Most Beautiful Girl"). She was also the spokesgirl for Ultra Bank ("Hello, I'm Tiffany Malloy, the face of tomorrow. Whatever you've got, I can sell").

Volunteer Work: Collects money for the homeless ("so they can buy cheap wine").

Image Change: When Tiffany felt she needed to be bad and change her "goody-goody image," she got an iron-on Popeye tattoo, called herself "Toughany," and stole a lipstick (Bad Girl Scarlet). When her conscience bothered her, she returned the lipstick and dropped the image.

Greatest Fear: The kitchen closet (Ryan locked her in when she was young, and she feared the closet monster; she has been haunted by the incident ever since).

Final Episode: Tiffany is accepted into Harvard University.

RYAN MALLOY

Character: Naive and totally disorganized and believes he is a loser when it comes to the opposite sex ("Girls find me completely repulsive").

Education: Priddy High School (a poor student whose average grade is an "F," which Ryan believes stands for "phenomenal"). He works in the school cafeteria.

Favorite TV Show: Only the Lonely Late Night Theater.

Moneymaking Scheme: Selling sexy images of Tiffany over the Internet on a website called "Cyber Sex Tiffany" (www.tiffanymalloy.com).

Game Show: Appeared with Tiffany on *Smart and Stupid Siblings* (his ignorance actually won them the game).

Superhero: During a thunderstorm, Ryan hid in a metal garbage can, was struck by lightning, and believed he acquired super powers as Lightning Boy.

The Writer's Mistake?: Ryan started out annoying and progressed to just unbelievable. To get Ryan out of his hair, Jack would tell him to go bother someone on another WB show (via the WB Time Machine) when he was not in a scene.

ROSS MALLOY

Ross considers himself a member of the family, although he is totally neglected by that family. When Jennie left, Ross took over the role of mother (cooking, cleaning, and even being referred to as "Mom"). He is called "a sad little man" by Tiffany, and Jack feels ignoring and degrading him will toughen him up. He is also the only character who, at the beginning of an episode, is told by Jack whether he will be needed. Ross has a pet turtle (Skippy), has been dressed as cheese to "catch the giant rat in the basement," and has a strange fantasy for a grammar school kid—"To be hugged by my math teacher, 38 Triple D Miss Bushnick." He also believes he has "the secret to attract chicks"—leaving his dirty bike in the driveway and washing it shirtless.

Veronica's Closet
(NBC, 1997–2000)

Cast: Kirstie Alley (Veronica Chase).
Basis: A former model (Veronica Chase) begins a new life as the owner of Veronica's Closet, a chain of lingerie stores.

VERONICA CHASE
Place of Birth: Kansas City, Kansas.
Education: Royal Oaks Elementary School; Kansas City High School.
Childhood: Mostly normal, an average student, but developed earlier than her girlfriends. Veronica mentions wearing her first bra when she was in sixth grade, and although teased by the boys, she never let it bother her. In her sophomore year in high school, she mentions wearing a 38C bra and became not only the envy of all the girls but also an attraction to the boys (this time, however, relishing all the attention she was getting).
Career: After graduating from high school, Veronica acquired a job as a waitress at Dairy Queen. Although she did not flaunt her figure, a customer (a photographer) saw what Veronica didn't—great assets that should be shared with the world. Veronica was persuaded to model a macramé swimsuit, and her career took off. She next modeled bikinis, then lingerie, and critics praised her as gorgeous and extremely sexy.
Change: Apparently, the lingerie companies Frederick's of Hollywood or Victoria's Secret did not exist, as Veronica constantly complained that finding sexy lingerie was a problem. She designed her own intimate apparel, invested her money, started Veronica's Closet, and became a multimillionaire when the brand took off. She also earns money as an author of romance novels (thus earning her the title "The Queen of Romance").
Magazine Covers: Glamour, Mademoiselle, Time, Life, Harper's Bazaar, Redbook.

Veronica's Closet Address: 609 Seventh Avenue in Manhattan.

Nicknames: "Princess" (by her father); "Ronnie" (by her friends).

Doll: The Sherman Toy Company produced "The Veronica Doll," a role model doll for girls that resembles a Barbie doll (but less busty and a bit heavier).

Reluctance: Never posing nude (she turned down $1 million to appear in *Playboy* and *Penthouse* magazines).

Home Address: 703 Park Avenue.

Pet Dog: Buddy.

Trait: Easily exasperated when the simplest things go wrong; can relax only in a hot bubble bath.

Favorite Bar: Finselli's.

Ex-Husband: Bryce Anderson (Christopher McDonald). After 14 years of marriage, his infidelity, which was flaunted by the newspapers, was hurting her reputation and business, and divorcing him was the only way to salvage her livelihood.

Assistants: Olive Massery (Kathy Najimy), her outspoken best friend and senior merchandising head; Josh (Wallace Langham), Veronica's gay assistant (he could never understand why his attempts to seduce women always failed until Veronica pointed out the reason why—"you're gay"; he makes Veronica's schedules and keeps her from going off the deep end with her favorite pastries); Perry Rollins (Dan Cortese) is the company's public relations director; Leo (Daryl "Chill" Mitchell) is the wet-behind-the-ears marketing executive; Pat Chase (Robert Prosky) is Veronica's father, who enjoys being her chauffeur.

Final Season: June Bilson (Lorri Bagley) becomes Veronica's business partner. It appears that Veronica's original partner, Alec Bilson (Ron Silver), met June, a somewhat ditzy waitress at Finselli's Bar, and married her three days later. On their honeymoon off the island of Jakarta, Alec perished in a freak volcano accident. June inherited a 51 percent share of the company and now drives Veronica insane with her antics. June claims she wore a bra in the second grade—"and that's how you get to the third grade." Veronica would like to take June's "little head and squeeze it until I smell helium."

V.I.P.
(Syndicated, 1998–2002)

Cast: Pamela Anderson (Vallery Irons), Molly Culver (Tasha Dexter), Natalie Raitano (Nikki Franco), Leah Lail (Kay Simmons), Shaun Baker (Quick Williams).

Basis: Vallery Irons, a beautiful young woman with no specific skills, runs V.I.P. (Vallery Irons Protection), a Los Angeles–based protection company. She is assisted by Tasha, Nikki, Kay, and Quick.

OVERALL SERIES INFORMATION
Prior to V.I.P., Vallery worked as the owner of a Tail of the Pup food franchise in Hollywood. When an assassin tries to kill the star (Brad Cliff) at a movie premiere she is attending, Vallery is mistaken for a bodyguard by the press when she uses her penny-filled purse to knock out the assassin. Tasha, Nikki, and Quick, owners of the debt-ridden Colt Arrow Services Bodyguard Agency, believe having Vallery on their team will bring in needed clients. Although dismayed when Vallery confesses to them that she is not a bodyguard, Tasha feels employing Vallery as a figurehead will solve all their problems. The company becomes Vallery Irons Protection, and although she is not to become involved in cases, Vallery does as she pleases, bringing her inexperience to complicate matters.

VALLERY IRONS
Place of Birth: Vancouver, British Columbia, Canada, on July 1, 1973.
Parents: Jed (Lee Majors) and Carol Irons (Loni Anderson). Jed was a CIA agent who abandoned his family to protect them when a mission went wrong and he was framed for killing agents (Vallery believed he was a house painter). The last memory Vallery had of her father was his buying her a *Star Wars* kite. Carol works at STX Consolidated, a Canadian-based computer company.
Invisible Childhood Friend: Dirk.
Education: Eastern Vancouver High School (class of 1990; straight "A" student, gymnast, and captain of the girls' volleyball team). She currently attends classes in hypnotism at the University of California, Los Angeles.
Measurements: Her bra size varies by episodes (38D, 36DD, and 34D). She stands 5 feet, 6 inches tall and weighs 120 pounds. She has blonde hair, green eyes, and a mole on her left shoulder. She buys her lingerie at Sheer Elegance.
Wardrobe: Low-cut, cleavage-revealing (and see-through) blouses and very tight jeans and doesn't appear to have any shame as she flaunts what she has for all to see. She has a wardrobe of 8,762 outfits, and the lingerie company Cleo's Passion produced sexy lingerie and active wear called "the Vallery Irons Undercover Collection."
Address: 10867 Whittier Boulevard, then 299 Ocean Avenue.
Social Security Number: 904-38-2832.
Home Phone Number: 310-555-1836.
Bank: The Commerce Bank of Beverly Hills.
Occupation: Chief executive officer of V.I.P.

V.I.P. Address: 9100 Sunset Boulevard, Beverly Hills, California 90210-0176 (also said to be located on the ninth floor at 3500 Hollywood Boulevard).

V.I.P. Phone Number: 310-555-9276 (then 310-555-1846, 555-0199, and 555-1-VIP).

Vallery's Federal Identification Number: 904-382812.

Company Fees: $25,000 a day plus a $100,000 retainer.

Character: Vallery is called "The Bodyguard to the Stars." Her knowledge of criminals stems from watching reruns of *Law and Order.* She hyperventilates when she gets scared and enjoys going to 7-Eleven "to see what the latest Slurpee flavor is." She is better at fashion and makeup than she is at protecting (as she always needs rescuing). Her haphazard crime-fighting skills have led criminals to believe that her incompetence is her secret weapon.

Favorite Fashion Magazines: Vogue and *Open Toe.*

Favorite Bar: Foam.

Favorite TV Show: Donny & Marie (with Donny and Marie Osmond).

TV Appearances: A commercial for "Oliver King's Rare Treasures"; contestant on the FTS network survivor show *Danger Island* (hoping to win $2 million).

Robotic Dog: Bowser.

Car: A red Viper (then a Jaguar) with the plate VIP VAL. She drives recklessly, never gets a ticket, and hates car chases ("You gotta watch out for speed bumps and baby squirrels").

V.I.P. Computer Password: Val Gal.

Best Friend: Maxine Della Cruz (Angelle Brooks). Maxine, a fashion designer, calls Vallery "Val Gal," while Vallery calls her "Max." They have their nails done at the Transcend Salon and are addicted to what Val calls cybershopping (TV home shopping clubs). They enjoy watching old movies on TV while munching on popcorn and potato chips. Max, an inventor of sorts, created "The Max Case," an attaché case "that holds a girl's curlers, makeup, and fax machine."

Objective: To end the reign of Joan Archer (Pamela Anderson), an ex-undercover cop she calls "the Evil Me" who was drummed out of the police department and now uses Vallery's identity to commit crimes.

TASHA DEXTER

Character: The most ruthless of the girls. She has a violent temper and a short attention span—"And I got an itchy trigger finger if the baddies take too long to answer my questions." Tasha gets uptight around Vallery "because no matter what case we're on, Vallery needs protection"; she also says, "I do all the dangerous work, and Val gets all the credit."

Background: Tasha claims she was a double agent for the CIA ("I was a spy for the Soviet Union before I switched sides"), then a KGB operative (spent one year in a KGB prison), a member of the Israeli army, and an agent for MI-5 (British military intelligence). She was a fashion model before becoming a spy and has also been married and divorced four times.

Character: Quick to use violence and treats each case as if it were a military maneuver. She is a martial arts expert and "will sleep with the enemy" to get information but gets really angry "if I did it for nothing and it doesn't pay off in results."

Car: A blue Mustang with the plate VIP TSH. She is also a licensed helicopter pilot.

Favorite Movie: Born Free.

Favorite Meal to Cook: Veggie lasagna.

Address: 312 Rhodes Avenue.

Telephone Number: 310-555-9816.

NICOLETTE "NIKKI" FRANCO

Place of Birth: Los Angeles in 1966.

Education: St. Theresa's High School for Girls.

Family: A member of the notorious Franco crime family (the Mafia), although her parents kept her away from the crime end of the family.

Character: Being the granddaughter of Mafia boss Don Franco (David Groh), Nikki did inherit a love for guns and violence (she claims bullets and guns are the only way to deal with the enemy; she is a fan of *Dirty Harry* movies and pictures herself as a female version of Clint Eastwood's character— "only more forceful and deadly").

Guns: A pair of .357 Magnums.

Favorite Weapon: A grenade launcher (which she carries as "emergency equipment" in the back of her car).

Expertise: Bombs and explosives (she has an "electronic sniffer," a bomb detector shaped like a dog she calls Rex). Nikki loves firing ranges, and "when I get depressed, I like to blow something up."

Fascination: High-speed racing (she drove the XJ-219, an experimental electric car).

Car: A Ford Mustang, then a Dodge with the license plate VIP NIK.

Nickname: Called "Queen of Explosives" and "Car Crazy" by Vallery.

Address: 11 Prescott Lane.

Telephone Number: 555-3353.

KATHERINE "KAY" EUGENIA SIMMONS

Place of Birth: Kentucky in 1965.

Trait: Extraordinary intellect. At the age of seven, she attended Neo Tech, "a school for brainy kids." She won the seventh-grade science fair "with my Black Plague in a shoebox diorama." She was teased for being smart (which would make her cry, and she acquired the nickname "Cry Baby Kay").

Education: Lexington College (editor of her college yearbook for three years, "including one year after I graduated").

Favorite TV Series: Star Trek.

Affiliation: Member of the Champions of Freedom, a conservative group.

Address: 817 Oakdale.

Phone Number: 818-KL5-9415.

Skill: A computer genius whose abilities make her the perfect office associate, but she would like to become active in the field—"I can be mean and vicious as long as I don't hurt anyone." When Kay is permitted to assist Tasha and Nikki, she gets a nervous stomach, "and I need to take my Mylanta."

Character: Very sweet and trusting. She shows ample cleavage (like Vallery), while Tasha and Nikki are just the opposite (as they rarely show any).

Minivan License Plate: VIP KAY.

Computer Password: Muffin Girl ("I like muffins").

Achilles' Heel: Her curiosity.

Dislike: "My middle name. I'd rather it be Danger. Anything is better than Eugenia."

QUICK WILLIAMS

Quick is a former boxer who was first called "the Iron Bull," then "the Boxer with the Mighty Quick Hands." He was forced to quit the ring when he refused to take a dive and was framed on drug charges.

Quick lives at 3420 Alto Cello Drive in Los Angeles (323-555-7704 is his phone number). He took tap dancing lessons as a kid and served a hitch in the army after high school (stationed at Fort Irving but sentenced to a psychiatric ward for running naked across the base). Quick is quick with his fists and skilled in the martial arts. Although he works with four beautiful women, Quick does not always take the beatings—Tasha and Nikki get equal treatment (Vallery and Kay are too feminine for the rough end of the business).

Walker, Texas Ranger
(CBS, 1993–2001)

Cast: Chuck Norris (Cordell Walker), Clarence Gilyard Jr. (Jimmy Trevette), Sheree J. Wilson (Alexandra Cahill).

Basis: A dedicated Texas Ranger's (Cordell Walker) unorthodox battle against crime.

CORDELL WALKER

Parents: John Firewalker, a full-blooded Cherokee Indian, and Elizabeth, a Caucasian woman (they met at a rodeo).

Upbringing: Cordell was 10 years old when John and Elizabeth were killed by three intoxicated thugs at a Texas county fair (a deadly fight ensued after Elizabeth was insulted "for marrying a Redskin"). Cordell was taken in by his Uncle Roy and raised on the Cherokee Reservation. Here he was given the Indian name "Warshaw" ("Lone Eagle") and brought up in both the ways of the Indian and the white man.

Upbringing Change: A later episode explains that Cordell's parents were killed in a car accident and Cordell was sent to the Cherokee Reservation in Oklahoma (not Texas) to be raised; still later, after the death of his parents, Cordell was raised in the Santa Rosa Orphanage in Texas.

Address: A ranch (belonging to his parents and where he now lives with his Uncle Roy) on South Road 8 in Springfield, Texas.

Telephone Number: 555-4928.

Occupation: Texas Ranger with the Texas Department of Safety (a division of the Texas Rangers).

Military Service: Captain during the Vietnam War (where he was called "the Nighthawk" for his deadly maneuvers against the enemy in the dark). He joined the Rangers after the war ended.

Abilities: Martial arts expert (especially in kickboxing; he was the 1978 Kickboxing Champion); skilled in hand-to-hand combat. He runs a drug-free program for children called "Kick Drugs Out of America" (where he also teaches children to use karate).

Car: Dodge 4×4 (license plate DV4 708, then 495 3XA and AUQ 075).

Ranger Car Code: 8175.

Favorite Dinner: Turkey.

Horses: Amigo, Cookie, and Ranger.

Resemblance: Although not mentioned as being related to Walker, Chuck Norris also plays (in flashbacks) Hayes Cooper, a former Old West Texas Ranger.

Favorite Bar: C. D.'s Bar and Grill.

JAMES "JIMMY" TREVETTE

Occupation: Texas Ranger (Walker's partner); he was originally a Texas police officer. He was assigned to stop a riot and was attacked by several protestors. From out of the shadows, a Texas Ranger appeared and saved him. Jimmy saw the Ranger's badge and knew that becoming a Texas Ranger was his true calling (it was not until Jimmy became a Ranger and was teamed with Walker that he learned that Walker was that mysterious Ranger who saved his life). It is next said that after college in Pennsylvania, Jimmy found his way to Texas and joined the Highway Patrol; he was then assigned to the Narcotics Division of the Texas Police Department. Another scenario places Jimmy in Texas after graduating from college but down on his luck and saved by a former Texas Ranger (C. D.) who helped him get his life back together and opened the doorway for his becoming a Texas Ranger.

Place of Birth: Baltimore "on the wrong side of the tracks." He grew up on the streets but avoided a life of crime. He saw firsthand how crime can affect a community and wanted to become a law enforcer to stop it.

Education: Penn State University. He was first said to be a member of the wrestling team. Jimmy later mentions he was on the school's football team and showed potential for becoming a pro. A shoulder injury ended his chances.

Address: 90 Old Balboa Road.

Car License Plate: 595 NYD (also seen as FY4 161, 278 566, and 853 4FP).

Member: The Browns basketball team.

Favorite TV Show: The Lone Ranger.

Character: Not as impulsive or as skilled as Walker when it comes to the martial arts. Like Walker, he will use a gun if necessary.

ALEXANDRA "ALEX" CAHILL

Place of Birth: May 14, 1958, in Texas.

Occupation: Assistant district attorney of Fort Worth, Texas.

Romantic Interest: Cordell Walker (who calls her "Alex"); they married in May 2000 and became the parents of a girl they named Angela in the final episode.

Activities: Alex teaches law enforcement classes at the Irving Campus of Mid-Texas University, conducts a women's support group (Victims of Crime) on the south shore of Stuart Lake (that she calls "Camp Cahill"), and oversees a center called H.O.P.E. (Help Our People).

Address: While Alex does live in Fort Worth (2456 Davidson Place), she also owns a ranch on RFD 63 (that appears to be close to Walker's ranch).

Horse: Amber.

Favorite Movie: Spartacus.

Favorite Month of the Year: May.

Character: Alex is stubborn and will fight for what she believes in.

OTHER CHARACTERS

C. D. Parker (Noble Willingham) is a retired Texas Ranger turned owner of C. D.'s Bar and Grill (virtually always called "C. D.'s" in dialogue). He was a Ranger for 15 years and was forced to retire on a medical discharge when he was shot in the knee in 1988. He drives a 1964 Cadillac that he calls "Old Goldie" with the license plate 519 FUL. He has a boat (*Winky Dink*) and writes an advice column for the *Gazette* under the pen name "Trail Buddy."

Sydney Cook (Nia Peeples) and Francis Gage (Judson Mills) are Texas Rangers who assist Walker and Trevette in later episodes (little information, however, is given about them). Sydney and Gage are well versed in the martial arts. Sydney caught the bouquet at Alex's wedding and often goes undercover on assignments with Gage while Walker and Trevette direct operations. Gage is never called by his first name ("I use my last name because of my first name"). His car license plate reads 364 H24; Sydney's car license plate is 777 J9H. Both she and Gage do volunteer work for kids at the Christian Community Center.

The West Wing
(NBC, 1999–2006)

Cast: Martin Sheen (Josiah Bartlet), Stockard Channing (Abigail Bartlet), Allison Janney (C. J. Cregg), Bradley Whitford (Josh Lyman), John Spencer (Leo McGarry), Alan Alda (Arnold Vinick), Janel Moloney (Donna Moss), Richard Schiff (Toby Ziegler), Rob Lowe (Sam Seaborn), Dule Hill (Charlie Young).

Basis: Political drama that explores the life of Josiah Bartlet, the president of the United States (1998–2006); his family; and the White House personnel who surround him. The program uses off years for presidential elections, here being 1998, 2002, and 2006.

JOSIAH EDWARD "JED" BARTLET

Position: President of the United States. In 1998, Bartlet, a Democrat, ran for the highest office with the slogan "Bartlet for America" (he won the Electoral College vote, 303 to 235; former senator John Hoynes [Tim Matheson] is his vice president).

Prior Service: New Hampshire governor for two terms; member of the New Hampshire State Board of Education; three term member in the U.S. House of Representatives.

Place of Birth: Manchester, New Hampshire.

Father: Dr. Bartlet (now deceased; seen in a flashback [Lawrence O'Donnell]). He also has an unseen brother, Jonathan Bartlet.

Wife: Abigail Barrington-Bartlet (a thoracic surgeon); see below.

Children: Elizabeth Bartlet Westin (Annabeth Gish), Eleanor Emily "Ellie" Bartlet (Nina Siemaszko), and Zoey Patricia Bartlet (Elisabeth Moss).

Ancestry: A direct descendant of Josiah Bartlett, a signer of the Declaration of Independence. It is not explained why Josiah's last name is spelled with one "t" when his ancestor has two "t's." He is also related to Paul Revere and has a carving knife that Revere once used.

Religion: Catholic (by his mother's choosing; his father wanted him to be raised as a Protestant).

Education: Phillips Exeter Academy (scored 1,590 on his SAT exams; his father was the school's headmaster); University of Notre Dame (earned a BA in American studies with a minor in theology); the London School of Economics (master's degree and a PhD in economics); honorary doctorate in humane letters from Dartmouth College.

Languages: English, French, German, and Latin.

Award: Nobel Prize in Economics.

Book: Theory and Practice on Macroeconomics in Developing Countries.

Affliction: Multiple sclerosis.

Accomplishments: Appoints the first Hispanic Supreme Court justice; the first female chief justice; instituted Social Security reform and a strong foreign policy. He was unable to balance the budget.

ABIGAIL "ABBEY" BARTLET

Position: Josiah's wife and the First Lady.

Occupation: Physician (married to Josiah for 30 years). While attending Notre Dame, Josiah thought of becoming a priest until he met Abbey and found romance.

Education: Harvard Medical School. She is on the staff of Boston Mercy Hospital and New York Presbyterian Hospital and is a professor of thoracic surgery at Harvard Medical School.

Loss of License: Abbey's efforts to conceal Josiah's illness from the public fail when she breaks American Medical Association rules by secretly treating him. She gives up practicing medicine while Josiah is in office but works at a Washington clinic to perform nonlicensed medical procedures (like taking blood, giving vaccinations, and administering X-rays).

CLAUDIA JEAN "C. J." CREGG

Position: White House press secretary; White House chief of staff.

Place of Birth: Dayton, Ohio.

Religion: Catholic.

Father: Tallmadge Cregg (Donald Moffat), formerly a math teacher at West Dayton High School (suffering from Alzheimer's disease); his first wife is deceased; his second wife, Molly Lapham Cregg (Verna Bloom), is a former high school math teacher.

Siblings: Said to have two older brothers, one of whom is married with a teenage daughter named Hogan (Evan Rachel Bloom).

Education: West Dayton High School (member of the basketball team); Williams College (National Merit Scholar; master's degree in political science).

Occupation: Agent with the public relations firm of Triton Day in California turned Josiah's 1998 presidential campaign manager. When Matthew "Matt" Santos is elected president in 2008, C. J. becomes his special counselor. Matt is married to Helen (Teri Polo), and Miranda (Ashlyn Sanchez) and Peter (Joshua Cabera) are their children.

Husband: Danny Concannon (Timothy Busfield). Danny, a graduate of the University of Notre Dame, is a Pulitzer Prize–winning journalist who covers the White House for such publications as the *Washington Post*, the *New York Times*, and *Time* magazine.

Trademark: A goldfish (Gail) that lives in a bowl on C. J.'s desk (her fishbowl decoration changes to match the episode theme, such as a Christmas tree and a turkey for Thanksgiving).

JOSHUA "JOSH" LYMAN

Position: White House deputy chief of staff; Josiah's political adviser.

Place of Birth: Westport, Connecticut.

Parents: Noah Lyman, a lawyer (died in 1998 on the night of the Illinois primary); his mother (unnamed) lives in Florida.

Sibling: Joanie (his older sister; died in a house fire when he was young).

Education: Harvard University (worked at the *Harvard Crimson*, the university's daily newspaper); Yale Law School.

Religion: Jewish.

Favorite Sports Team: New York Mets.

Occupation: Democratic legislative director of the House of Representatives; Democratic floor director in the Senate; member of the "Bartlet for America" campaign and the Matt Santos presidential campaign (when Matt wins, Josh becomes the White House chief of staff).

LEO THOMAS McGARRY

Position: Secretary of labor before coming to work for President Bartlet.

Place of Birth: Chicago, Illinois, in 1948. Leo, a recovering alcoholic, is addicted to Valium; his father, also an alcoholic, committed suicide.

Ancestry: Irish and Scottish.

Wife: Jenny McGarry (Sara Botsford).

Daughter: Mallory O'Brien (Allison Smith).

Sisters: Elizabeth McGarry (not seen); Josephine McGarry (Deborah Hedwall), the Atlanta School District superintendent.

Military Service: U.S. Air Force (served in Vietnam with the 335th Tactical Fighter Wing Unit).

Occupation: Senior adviser to the president on daily White House operations.

Education: Michigan State University.

WILLIAM "WILL" BAILEY

Position: White House communications officer, then congressman.

Place of Birth: Belgium.

Father: General Thomas Bailey, NATO Supreme Allied Commander.

Stepsister: Elsie (Danica McKellar).

Military Service: Air Force Reservist (served with JAG).

Education: Unclear: Carnegie Mellon University (by the shirt he wears) or Cambridge University in England (president of the Union Society).

Occupation: White House communications director; congressman representing the Fourth District in Oregon.

ARNOLD VINICK

Position: California Republican senator; presidential nominee in 1998.

Trait: Fiscal conservative and social moderate (for immigration reform and parental consent laws and limited government involvement in people's lives; is opposed to gay marriage and partial-birth abortion). He is supported by Independents and Libertarians, but his weakness on foreign policy, gun control, and border security cost him the election to Bartlet in 1998.

Parents: Richard, a public school teacher, and Patricia, a community activist.

Place of Birth: Brooklyn, at New York Methodist Hospital. Four years later, his family moves to Santa Paula, California, where Arnold later volunteered at the local library.

Wife: Catherine (now deceased after 30 years of marriage). Her passing caused Arnold, a Catholic, to stop attending mass.

Hobby: Collecting rare first-edition books (based on Catherine's presenting him with a seventeenth-century copy of the King James Version of the Bible).

Final Episode: Arnold, nearing the age of 70, runs for president but loses. He joins the Santos administration as his secretary of state.

DONNA MOSS

Donna was born in Minnesota but raised in Wisconsin when her family relocated. She attended the University of Wisconsin, Madison, for two years and in 1998 became the senior assistant to Josh Lyman, the political director for the "Bartlet for America" campaign. In 1999 (to 2005), she was the senior assistant to the deputy White House chief of staff for strategic planning. She was then an aide in the failed "Bob Russell for America" presidential campaign (2005–2006); the press secretary for the Santos presidential campaign ("Santos for a Brighter America" in 2006), and finally the chief of staff to Matt Santos's wife, Helen Santos, the First Lady, when he defeated Arnold Vinick for the presidency.

TOBIAS "TOBY" ZACHARY ZIEGLER

Toby, the White House communications director (under Bartlet), was born on December 23, 1954 in Brooklyn (raised in Brighton Bach). He attended New York University, is divorced from Andrea Wyatt (Maryland congresswoman), and is the father of fraternal twins Molly and Huckleberry. He is a Democrat and a fan of the New York Yankees. He mentioned having a brother, David, who is an astronaut. Toby previously worked on political campaigns as a consultant for the Bronx borough president, the Manhattan City Council, the New York governor's race, the U.S. House of Representatives, the U.S. Senate, and the "Bartlet for America" campaign. A flash-forward sequence reveals Toby's fate: retired from politics to become a professor at Columbia University in New York City.

SAMUEL "SAM" NORMAN SEABORN

Sam is the deputy communications director (under President Bartlet) and the deputy White House chief of staff (under President Santos). He was born in Laguna Beach, California, and is a Democrat but an idealist and somewhat naive as to the political climate. He is a graduate of Princeton University (where he was the recording secretary of the Gilbert and Sullivan Society; he now uses "Princeton" as his Secret Service code name). He later attended Duke Law School (editor of the *Duke Law Review*). He first worked for the New York law firm of Dewey & Ballantine, then the more prestigious Gage-Whitney-Pace (he left to begin his political career as a speechwriter for Josiah Bartlet during his presidential campaign). Sam also ran for (but lost) a seat in Congress, representing his hometown (the 47th District in Orange County, California).

CHARLES "CHARLIE" YOUNG

Charlie was first Bartlet's presidential aide, then his deputy special assistant to the chief of staff. He is a graduate of Georgetown University (later a jurist doctor at the Georgetown University Law Center). Charlie's job is to see that the Oval Office runs smoothly. Charlie was born in Washington, D.C., then attended Theodore Roosevelt High School and later Georgetown University. He has a younger sister (Deena), but his mother, a police officer in Washington, was killed in the line of duty; his father abandoned the family when he was young.

Will and Grace
(NBC, 1998–2006)

Cast: Eric McCormack (Will Truman), Debra Messing (Grace Adler), Megan Mullally (Karen Walker), Sean Hayes (Jack McFarland).
Basis: The relationship between four close friends (Will, Grace, Karen, and Jack) is explored.

WILLIAM "WILL" TRUMAN

Place of Birth: Bridgeport, Connecticut, in 1966.
Parents: George (Sydney Pollack) and Marilyn Truman (Blythe Danner).
Brothers: Paul Truman (Jon Tenney) and Sam Truman (John Slattery, then Steven Weber).
Address: 155 Riverdale Drive, Apartment 9C, in Manhattan.
Childhood Memories: A dog named Daisy; his love for his Easy Bake Oven (which he claims is the reason that he is now a great cook).
Sexual Preference: Gay.
Roommate: Grace Adler, a straight woman (she learned Will was gay "when he put his hand on my boob and said, 'Is that a cashmere sweater'"; in later episodes, she learned he was gay when he told her at Christmas; later said to be on Thanksgiving Day).

First Meeting: At a college party at Columbia University. Will had not yet come out of the closet and began dating Grace (it was through his gay friend, Jack McFarland, that Will was able to confront his sexuality). When Will confessed he was gay to Grace, she avoided speaking to him. A year later while in a grocery store, Grace apologized, and they become inseparable friends. It is when Grace breaks up with her fiancé (Danny) that she moves in with Will.

Character Trait: A gourmet cook, good with money, controlling, and uncompromising. About Grace, he says, "Even if I was straight, I wouldn't marry Grace" (as Grace has to be "the star" of her relationship with a boyfriend and "better than he is"). As a kid, Will wanted a cowboy birthday cake, a *Josie and the Pussycats* TV lunchbox, and a red fire truck, but his parents gave him things they thought he would like better (like a water wiggle slide instead of the fire truck).

Education: Columbia University; New York University School of Law. At one point, Will hoped to become a playwright (wrote the play *Bye, Bye Sexual*, which told of his coming out of the closet). When his English professor told him it was bad, he switched his major to law. He was also in an improv group called the Zaniacs (with Grace at Columbia).

Occupation: Lawyer, first with the firm of Doucette & Stein (Gregory Hines plays Doucette, and Gene Wilder is Stein); he later becomes a partner when Margo (Lily Tomlin) takes over the firm. He was also an attorney to the mysterious Malcolm (Alec Baldwin) and the Coalition of Justice (providing legal help to people unable to afford it).

Hobbies: Embroidery (makes his own kitchen aprons from McCall patterns; enters the Statewide Needlepoint Competition).

Treasured Item: "Squatsy," a garden gnome he bought for his parents when he was a child.

Favorite Coffeehouse: Kitty's Coffee Shop.

Favorite Eatery: Pablo's Cantina.

Favorite Gay Bars: Adam's Bar, the Tight End, and Crisco Disco.

Relief from Stress: The sweater department of Bergdorf's Department Store.

Husband: Will marries his boyfriend, Vince D'Angelo (Bobby Cannavale), in season six, and they become parents when they adopt a baby boy (Ben).

GRACE ELIZABETH ADLER

Place of Birth: Schenectady, New York, in 1967.

Parents: Roberta, called Bobbie, a singer (Debbie Reynolds), and Martin (Alan Arkin) Adler.

Sisters: Janet Adler (Geena Davis) and Joyce Adler (Sara Rue).

Education: Hawthorne High School; Columbia University (where she met Will; they were in the improv group the Zaniacs together); the Fashion Institute.

Occupation: Interior designer (runs Grace Adler, Interior Designs, from the Buck Building in Manhattan). A typo in her Yellow Pages phone book reads "The Breast Designer" instead of "The Best Designer."

Hope: To win the decorators' Sublime Divine Award for her work.

Religion: Jewish.

Childhood: Had a pet dog named Toki; attended Sunday school for 10 years; had her biggest disappointment when she learned that hamsters cannot fly.

Blood Type: A-B negative.

Distinguishing Mark: A scar on her thigh ("from a cousin who was sleepwalking and thought I was a salami").

Figure Issues: Grace stands 5 feet, 8 inches tall; has auburn hair; and wears a size 6 dress and a size 9½ shoe. She is self-conscious about having small breasts (she mentions wearing a 32A bra, and Karen's constant reminder "that you have no boobs" makes her shudder when people refer to her breasts as "boobies"). As a child, her mother was so desperate for Grace to have a figure that she padded her school gym uniform. Grace even wore a water bra "for extra perkiness" but embarrassed herself when it sprung a leak.

Address: 155 Riverdale Drive, Apartment 9C (which she shares with Will, who is gay; see above); she later moves across the hall to Apartment 9A (figuring that "it is healthier for the both of us"), then back again with Will. In between the moves, she lived in Apartment 2K in Brooklyn.

Favorite Flower: The Lily.

Favorite Candy: Hershey's Chocolate Dove Bar; Twizzler's strawberry licorice.

Clothes Shopping: Designer markdowns at the Paramus, New Jersey, Mall.

Greatest Fear: Getting older ("really old"; she tends to cry over this).

Worst Day of Her Life: Occurred at Bloomingdale's "when a young girl bumped into me and said, 'Excuse me, ma'am.'"

Reputation: "The ability to turn men gay" (as several of her boyfriends became either gay or bisexual).

Quirks: When she gets upset, she must have a slice of white bread; it's cheesecake when she is mad. Grace switches on the TV manually, then sits on the couch; she will watch whatever is on "because I'm here [on the couch] and the remote is over there [on top of the TV]." She loves to attend concerts but gets carried away by singing along (at Joni Mitchell's performance, Joni asked Grace to leave; at Melissa Manchester's concert, Melissa called for security to escort Grace out).

Favorite Cable Channel: Lifetime (although she mentions a different channel show, *The Pet Psychic*, as being her favorite).

Dislikes: Flavored coffee and clowns ("Because they think they're so funny").

Sexual Orientation: Straight (she does mention making love to another woman, "but it wasn't my thing").

Belief: People mistake her for actress Julia Roberts or Rita Haworth because of her auburn hair. Her dry cleaner calls her "Nice Lady."

Megan Mullally, Sean Hayes, Debra Messing, and Eric McCormack. *NBC/ Photofest © NBC*

Husband: Grace married Dr. Leo Markus (Harry Connick Jr.) on November 21, 2002, but the marriage ends shortly after when Leo cheats on her with a Red Cross nurse while working with Doctors Without Borders in Cambodia. A chance meeting on a flight to London reunites them, and after a one-night affair, Grace becomes pregnant, and the two remarry. They have a daughter, Laila, and move to Brooklyn.

KAREN WALKER
Year of Birth: 1959.

Mother: Lois Whitley (Suzanne Pleshette); her father is deceased (died when Karen was seven years old).

Sister: Gin Whitley (Bernadette Peters), a dancer.

Childhood: To support themselves after her husband's passing, Lois and Karen moved from town to town and lived off scams (Gin is not mentioned). Karen, called "Kiki" by Lois, had an unstable upbringing. When Karen became a teenager, she and Lois had a falling-out, and Karen ran away from home when she could no longer con people (Lois now works as a waitress at Paddy's Pub in Yonkers, New York).

Education: Sarah Lawrence College under her maiden name of Karen Whitley.

Occupation: Personal assistant to Grace Adler. Prior to this, Karen called herself Karen Delaney and played a maid in an X-rated adult fetish film (called both *Next to Godliness*, then *Dirty Little Pig Boy*); guest starred on the TV series *Mama's Family* (but her role as a bank teller was edited out) and in two episodes of *Dynasty*. She also worked as Jack's assistant on his OutTV program.

Marriages: Karen has been married four times: "Hubby number 1" (last name of St. Crox); a second husband with the surname of Popeil; the grossly overweight Stanley "Stan" Walker (never seen), the owner of Stanley Walker, Inc.; and Lyle Finster (John Cleese), who became rich by selling rattraps to breweries (the marriage ended after 20 minutes when Karen learned that Lyle cared more for work than her).

Figure: Karen is 5 feet, 4 inches tall and wears a size 10 dress and a size 6 shoe. She has a high, shrill voice and is most proud of her physical beauty. She refers to her breasts as "a killer rack" but says "I was flat-chested" in high school. But by the age of 16 (after taking what she calls "horse pills"), she prided herself on wearing a 36D bra. She now wears a 38D bra and believes that by showing ample cleavage (or even her breasts), she can accomplish a goal.

Sexual Orientation: Bisexual (by her comments that she is attracted to beautiful women and kisses them; Grace is one such woman she has kissed. She mentions making love to another woman, "but she wasn't as pretty as I was"). She is most proud "when people admire my large bosom."

Quirk: Most enjoys Halloween because of the sexy "boobs up and out" costumes she can wear; is neurotic (takes "a blue pill," labeled "Beautiful Feeling," every 15 minutes and claims that if there are not pills for her numerous imagined aliments, "they will make it for me"). She likes to "pig out," as she says, but does so under the name Anastasia Beaver-Haven (who will do something that Karen would never do, like eating at Taco Time). She also relates sad incidents from movies as her own life experiences.

Fear: Elevators.

Address: With Stanley, a house in the country and a Manhattan penthouse suite.

Beauty Salon: Yolanda's Salon (where she has her weekly facial).

Inability: Karen cannot work a computer or a fax machine but knows people and can get what Grace needs. She also "gets back from lunch in time for dinner."

Racehorse: Owns one (through Stanley) called Lamar.

Relaxation: Appears to be relaxed by drinking (as she carries a flask with her at all times).

Life Changer: Stanley's infidelity (with Lorraine [Minnie Driver], the daughter of Karen's husband Lyle [see above]) results in Karen separating from Stan (she moves into the Palace Hotel). Shortly after, when Stan dies from a heart attack, Karen becomes the head of Walker, Inc., and sends her stepchildren (Olivia, known as "the Girl" and Mason, known as "the Fat One") to live with Stan's first wife. It is later revealed that Stan faked his death to avoid paying back the millions he borrowed, thus leaving Karen broke.

Archenemy: Beverly Leslie (Leslie Jordan), a rich gay whom Karen talks Jack into marrying to ensure her financial future (he can support Jack, and Jack can support Karen for her supporting him when he was in need). In a strange twist of fate, Leslie, who is short and weighs just 100 pounds, is blown off a building balcony and to his death by a gust of wind, leaving Jack to inherit $100 million.

Maid: Rosario Inez Consuelo Yolanda Salazar (Shelley Morrison). She was born in El Salvador and attended the University of Texas, where she acquired a degree in clinical psychology. Karen met Rosario in 1985 at a club (where Rosario was a cigarette lady) and hired her. In another episode, Karen claims she "bought" Rosario from her parents, and being an illegal immigrant, Karen forced her to marry Jack McFarland so she could get her green card (the marriage broke up when Rosario fell for Karen's gardener). It is also said that while in El Salvador, Rosario performed with the then-unknown Jennifer Lopez at the Shalom Retirement Center (where they also starred in a production of *Tea for Two*).

JOHN PHILIP "JACK" McFARLAND

Year of Birth: 1969 (also mentioned as 1970).

Parents: Judith McFarland (Veronica Cartwright); his birth father is unknown. Judith had sex at a pool party with a man wearing a Richard Nixon mask and never saw him again. Judith raised Jack as a single mother and later married Daniel McFarland (Beau Bridges).

Address: An apartment in Manhattan's West Village.

Sexual Orientation: Gay. "I'm here and I'm queer. Get used to it" is the oath Jack "took in front of God and my mother."

Occupation: Actor and playwright. He currently has a one-man play at the Duplex Theater in Manhattan called *Just Jack* (wherein he sings, dances, and acts; he updated it to *Just Jack, 2000* and *Just Jack, 2001: A Space Odyssey*). He also played Chuck Rafferty, a straight but alcoholic, womanizing cop on an unnamed TV series.

Other Accomplishments: Wrote a Caribbean fantasy play called *Love Among the Coconuts* (later called *Untitled Jack in Three Parts*) and an unpublished novel called *To Weep and to Willow*. He starred in a TV commercial for "Senior Mattresses" and an unnamed training film about sexual harassment for the Canterville Plate Glass Company (he also conducts such classes in the rectory of St. Mary's Church). He produced the movie *The Mystery of Karen Walker*.

Jobs: Caterer for Starlight Enterprises; salesman in the men's clothing department at both the Banana Republic and Barney's; usher for two performances of the Broadway show *Les Misérables*; man's hand bar soap distributor at Le Spa; and failed student at the Acrylic Nail School. He was a backup dancer to singers Jennifer Lopez and Janet Jackson and attended nursing school (voted "Most Popular Student"). While giving his farewell speech, he realized his dream was to become an actor and gave up nursing to pursue that goal. He also tried to make money by marketing his invention, "the Subway Tush" (a train seating cushion he promoted with a hand puppet called "Buttford, the Pantyhose Subway Tush"). In 2004, he became an employee of OutTV, a gay-run and gay-oriented television station in Manhattan.

Hope: To star in a gay Hollywood movie and have a line of gay action figure toys.

Favorite Magazine: Guy's World.

Religion: Catholic (an altar boy at St. Margaret's Church).

Pets: Gus (parrot); Klaus Von Puppy (dog).

Turnoff: Making love to a woman (makes him nervous, although he claims to know all about women because he had a "Growing Up Skipper Doll" as a child).

Fear: Smart men.

Nickname: Called "Poodle" by Karen.

Idol: Cher.

Dream House: Jeannie's bottle from the series *I Dream of Jeannie.*

Favorite TV Series: Buffy the Vampire Slayer (for the lesbian character of Willow, whom he finds intriguing).

Hobby: Collecting celebrity hair clippings (he has hair from each of the stars of *The Golden Girls* as well as Broadway icons Patti LuPone and Bernadette Peters).

Belief: That God is a woman and that every TV series and movie robot is gay (he watched *Star Wars* numerous times in an effort to prove that CP-30 was gay).

The X-Files
(Fox, 1993–2002)

Cast: David Duchovny (Fox Mulder), Gillian Anderson (Dana Scully).
Basis: FBI special agents Fox Mulder and Dana Scully investigate the X-Files, unsolved cases involving paranormal phenomena.

FOX WILLIAM MULDER
Parents: Bill and Teena Mulder.
Place of Birth: Maryland on October 13, 1961 (on a Friday). He has green eyes and brown hair and stands 6 feet tall. He lived at 2790 Vine Street and has a younger sister named Samantha (born in 1965). In 1973, when Samantha (Megan Leitch) was eight years old, she mysteriously disappeared (Fox claimed she was kidnapped by aliens; he was paralyzed by a bright light and unable to help her and does recall hearing the aliens say that Samantha would be cared for). The incident haunted Fox, and it led him to believe that the supernatural exists (UFOs, witchcraft, aliens—anything that cannot be explained in normal terms).
Childhood Desire: Wanting a peg leg (so people would not expect a lot from him).
Education: Oxford University (a bachelor of arts degree in psychology).
Occupation: Agent with the X-Files Division of the FBI (joined after college). He first worked with the Investigative Support Unit, then the Violent Crimes Unit at Quantico (earned a reputation for defying authority to do things his way). At one point, Fox also worked for the FBI's Behavioral Sciences Unit profiling serial killers. In 1990, he stumbled on the X-Files while working in the bureau's Behavioral Sciences Unit. He was teamed with Dana Scully, a skeptic who was assigned to analyze and disprove Mulder's findings of cases being associated with the unnatural.

David Duchovny and Gillian Anderson. *Fox Broadcasting/Photofest © Fox Broadcasting*

X-Files Office: The basement of the J. Edgar Hoover FBI Building in Washington, D.C.

Address: 2630 Hegal Place, Apartment 42, in Alexandria, Virginia.

Phone Number: 555-9355.

FBI ID Classification: 22791.

Trait: Fox has a photographic memory, is color blind, and earned the nickname "Spooky" for his beliefs and ability to process information and come to a logical conclusion.

Favorite TV Shows: Star Trek and *The Magician.*

Favorite Snack: Pistachio nuts and sunflower seeds.

Favorite Sports Teams: New York Knicks (basketball), Washington Redskins (football).

Favorite TV Channel: The Playboy Channel.

Favorite Music: Classic rock.

Favorite Board Game: Stratego (which he played with Samantha as a child).

Habit: Bouncing a ball when he becomes bored.

Dislike: Insects (was frightened by a praying mantis when he was a child).

Phobia: Fire (acquired as a child after his friend's home caught fire).

Exercise: Runs and swims.

Computer Password: Trust No 1.

Childhood Ambition: To become an astronaut (his hero was Colonel Marcus Belt, a NASA astronaut).

Fox's Fate: In 2001, Fox is designated as a general assignment agent; a year later, he resigns from the FBI to become a civilian. In 2008, he returns to active duty to become a consultant on a case. In 2016 (the Fox series reboot *The X-Files*), Fox returns to his former position with the reestablished X-Files Unit and is again teamed with Agent Dana Scully.

DANA KATHERINE SCULLY

Parents: William and Margaret Scully. William was a rear admiral with the U.S. Navy.

Date of Birth: February 23, 1964, in Maryland.

Siblings: William Jr., Melissa, and Charles.

Education: The Miramar Naval Air Base School; University of Maryland (medical diploma; her senior thesis was titled "Einstein's Twin Paradox: A New Interpretation"); the University of California (physics degree).

Religion: Catholic (she can be seen wearing a cross around her neck).

Favorite Childhood Movie: The Exorcist.

First Exposure to Evil: At the age of 13, Dana learned that pure evil exists when her Sunday school teacher, who called her "Scout," was murdered.

Occupation: FBI agent. She was recruited by the FBI after graduation and began her career teaching forensic science at the FBI Academy in Virginia. Two years later, she was teamed with Fox Mulder to investigate unusual cases as part of the X-Files.

Character: Dana has red hair and blue eyes and stands 5 feet, 3 inches tall. She is a skeptic and must prove there is a logical explanation for everything she and Fox encounter; she goes out of her way to debunk the unexplained phenomena she encounters (much to Fox's objections, as he believes what he sees).

Pet Dog: Queequeq.

Nickname: Called "Starbuck" by her father (who was a fan of the Herman Melville's *Moby-Dick* and named her after the first mate on Captain Ahab's ship, the *Pequod*). Dana, in turn, would call her father "Captain Ahab."

Distinguishing Feature: A tattoo on her back (a snake biting its tail).

Coffee: Cream with no sugar (she also enjoys an occasional glass of wine).

Favorite Foods: Fried chicken, pizza and lobster, and plain yogurt with honey added.

Favorite TV Channel: The Discovery Channel.

Favorite Movie Genre: Horror films.

Favorite Music: Classical.

Address: Apartment 35 in an unnamed building in Georgetown.

Cell Phone Number: 555-3654.

Romance: Fox and Dana became close over the series run, and in 2001, Dana gives birth to a son they name William. In 2008, they split up but were reunited in 2016 (when Fox aired the reboot *X-Files* series) as agents with the X-Files Unit of the FBI. Dana was also a doctor of internal medicine at Our Lady of Sorrows Hospital (since 2008).

Flashbacks: Young Dana (Tegan Moss, then Joey Shea); teenage Dana (Zoe Anderson [Gillian's real-life sister]).

Index

About the Author

Vincent Terrace is the TV historian for BPOLIN Productions, a film and production company. He is the author of more than 40 books on television and old-time radio, including *Narrated TV Program Openings since 1949* (Scarecrow Press, 2013) and four prior volumes in this series: *Television Series of the 1950s*, *Television Series of the 1960s*, *Television Series of the 1970s*, and *Television Series of the 1980s*, all published by Rowman & Littlefield.